FATHER LINCOLN

FATHER LINCOLN

The Untold Story of Abraham Lincoln and His Boys—
Robert, Eddy, Willie, and Tad

ALAN MANNING

Guilford, Connecticut

An imprint of Rowman & Littlefield

Distributed by NATIONAL BOOK NETWORK

British Library Cataloguing in Publication Information Available

Library of Congress Cataloging-in-Publication Data available

ISBN 978-1-4930-1823-9
ISBN 978-1-4930-1824-6 (e-book)

♾™ The paper used in this publication meets the minimum requirements of American National Standard for Information Sciences—Permanence of Paper for Printed Library Materials, ANSI/NISO Z39.48-1992.

I would like to dedicate this book to my inspirations and the loves of my life: my wife Karen and my four daughters, Sarah, Kate, Elizabeth, and Mary Grace. And to those who helped shape my character: my mother, Krystle Manning; my father, Albert V. Manning; my grandfather, Albert Manning; and my uncle, Forrest Brown.

CONTENTS

INTRODUCTION

ON THE AFTERNOON OF MAY 30, 1922, WHILE MOST AMERICANS WERE home for the Memorial Day holiday, more than three thousand invited guests and thirty thousand spectators gathered in Washington, DC, for the dedication of the recently completed Abraham Lincoln Memorial. The invited guests, each of whom had received an engraved invitation according them special seating on or near the memorial structure, included President Warren G. Harding and members of his cabinet, congressmen, governors, justices of the Supreme Court, military officers, diplomats, civic leaders, various distinguished citizens, and a handful of Civil War veterans from both the Union and Confederate armies, most of whom were now in their seventies and eighties. The ordinary spectators, who stood spread out across the vast grounds of the memorial and the reflecting pool leading to the Washington Monument, more closely represented the century-and-a-half-old nation: young and old, men and women, black and white, farmers, factory workers, clerks, housewives, and immigrants. Also present in the crowd were hundreds of former slaves and descendants of slaves.

Fifty-seven years had passed and three generations of Americans had been born since John Wilkes Booth, an angry Confederate sympathizer, assassinated Abraham Lincoln just days after General Robert E. Lee surrendered to General Ulysses S. Grant at Appomattox Court House, Virginia, effectively ending the nation's bloodiest war. During that time, America had transformed itself into an industrial power, asserted economic and political influence abroad, fought in a world war, and struggled with domestic upheavals over equal rights for blacks and labor rights for an increasingly urbanized workforce. America at the time of the dedication of the Lincoln Memorial was not the America of Lincoln's time. Yet on that day, the past and the present came together to honor the nation's sixteenth president.

One of the invited guests present on that beautiful spring day was seventy-eight-year-old Robert Todd Lincoln, the eldest and only surviving son of Abraham Lincoln. Except for having a beard, the gray and bespectacled Robert bore no physical resemblance to his famous father. With a rounded face featuring a wide nose and a short and stocky frame, which was by then slightly stooped with age, Robert more closely resembled his plump and fleshy mother than his six-foot-four father with his gangly arms and chiseled cheekbones. In further contrast to his father, whose dress was often awkward and careless, Robert was scrupulously fashion conscious. On this special day he wore a top hat, a crisply pressed white shirt, and a perfectly tailored black suit with a gold watch chain hanging prominently from his vest.

Assisted by two young marines, one on each side, Robert slowly climbed the fifty-eight granite steps leading to the east colonnade on the main level of the memorial, where the speakers and other special guests were seated in dark wooden Thonet cafe chairs. When Robert finally reached the top at about 2:30 p.m., the crowd burst into applause as he took his seat beside Mary Harlan Lincoln, his wife of more than fifty years and the daughter of a former United States senator from Iowa. Behind Robert, set back within the central chamber of the memorial and facing outward to the crowd, was the nineteen-foot-high statue of the seated Lincoln, painstakingly carved from the finest Georgia white marble. The statue aptly represented the larger-than-life figure that Lincoln had become in the eyes of most Americans.

Following the invocation and the presentation of colors, Dr. Robert R. Moton, who had succeeded Booker T. Washington as leader of the Tuskegee Institute, delivered the principal dedication address. The only black man on the speaker's platform, Moton focused his speech on Lincoln's impact on black Americans, fully crediting Lincoln with emancipation of the slaves and holding Lincoln up to a standard of immortality. With his voice being broadcast over amplification speakers placed around the memorial grounds—representing the latest in oratorical technology—Moton said of Lincoln that "[h]e freed a nation as well as a race. . . . Sixty years ago he stood in lonely grandeur above a torn and bleeding Nation, a towering figure of patient righteousness. Today his spirit animates the breasts of millions of his countrymen who unite with us to pay tribute to his lofty character and his immortal deed."

Poet Edwin Markham followed Moton with his own graceful tribute to Lincoln, entitled "Lincoln, The Man of the People," which included these lines:

> When the Norn Mother saw the Whirlwind Hour
> Greatening and darkening as it hurried on,
> She left the Heaven of Heroes and came down
> To make a man to meet the mortal need . . .
> And laid upon him a sense of the Mystic Powers
> Moving—all husht—behind the mortal veil,
> Here was a man to hold against the world,
> A man to match the mountains and the sea.

Former President William Howard Taft, who was by then the chief justice of the United States Supreme Court, spoke next. Taft accurately described the heights to which Americans had elevated Lincoln: "We feel a closer touch with him than with living men. The influence he still wields, one may say with all reverence, has a Christ-like character. It has spread to the four quarters of the globe. The oppressed and lowly of all peoples, as liberty and free government spread, pronounce his name with awe, and cherish his assured personal sympathy as a source of hope."

Ironically, it was President Harding, widely known for his bombastic and often wandering oratory, who added some historical perspective to Lincoln's role in emancipation by acknowledging that Lincoln initially saw preservation of the Union as more important than abolishing slavery:

> *The simple truth is that Lincoln, recognizing an established order, would have compromised with the slavery that existed, if he could have halted its extension. . . . Hating human slavery as he did . . . he was the last man in the Republic to resort to arms to effect its abolition. . . . He believed . . . firmly in the perpetuity of the Union of the States. . . . His was a leadership for a great crisis, made loftier because*

of the inherent righteousness of his cause and the sublimity of his own faith. Washington inspired belief in the Republic in its heroic beginning, Lincoln proved its quality in the heroic preservation.

Throughout much of the dedication ceremony, Robert remained quiet and reflective, lost in a world of distant memories. He did not deliver a speech, and perhaps that was fitting. As the speakers made clear, this was a day to remember Abraham Lincoln in all of his public greatness. To those present, it was a day to recall the Great Emancipator, the Savior of the Union, an American martyr, one of the greatest American presidents whose name and face and accomplishments were intimately familiar not only to all Americans, but also to much of the world. That man, however, was not the man that Robert knew best. To be sure, Robert knew Lincoln the president and was fully aware of the successful efforts by so many people to elevate Lincoln to greatness after his assassination in 1865—efforts that occasionally left a trail of myths and embellishments that became ingrained as fact in the American memory. Robert had quietly participated in efforts to ensure his father's proper place in history, though he scrupulously tried to keep the memories fair and accurate. But the man that Robert knew best was not Lincoln the president, it was Lincoln the father. On that spring day in 1922, however, just as the thousands of men and women who came to honor a larger-than-life figure were not interested in the personal story of Lincoln's relationship with his four children, the intensely private Robert was not interested in sharing that story with the gathered mass of admiring Americans.

Yet the story of Lincoln the father is worth telling. It is worth telling not only because it reveals a very human side of Lincoln largely ignored by his biographers, but because it illuminates a challenge that many fathers face: balancing a successful career with fulfilling the various roles that society assigns to fathers—roles that most fathers actually desire to play in their children's lives. That challenge was no less present in Lincoln's time than it is today. In fact, nineteenth-century fathers, far from being the detached and unemotional patriarchs often portrayed in books and movies, actually craved emotional attachment with their children and desired to be intimately involved in their upbringing, even though that desire often competed with their own ambitions and career demands.

Lincoln had to balance his ambition and demanding career with his fatherhood responsibilities. Robert presented Lincoln with the greatest challenge in achieving that balance. He was a child and adolescent when Lincoln was achieving great success as a trial lawyer and political leader, and with Lincoln's increasing success and notoriety came frequent absences from home. Historians have typically concluded that Robert's relationship with his father was always distant and strained largely as a result of the ambitious Lincoln spending little time with Robert when he was a boy. That conclusion is incorrect. The perceived emotional distance between Lincoln and Robert that is so often reported by biographers and historians has been based on incomplete research as well as comments and events taken out of context. It is true that Lincoln was often away from home on business during Robert's youth, sometimes for weeks at a time. Yet the complete record reveals a father who loved his son and who actively participated in the boy's upbringing despite these absences. Even after Robert left for college, Lincoln increasingly sought to maintain a close relationship with him. Faced with the prospect that his son was likely out of the house for good, Lincoln, who was by then the president of the United States, frequently made time for the young man, and Robert happily accepted his father's overtures.

In discussing his father in the years following Lincoln's assassination, Robert often minimized the amount of time that they spent together, suggesting that they did not really know each other well. As a result, most biographers have concluded that Robert's own statements were evidence of a strained relationship between father and son. It is now clear, though, that Robert minimized their relationship simply in order to fend off prying reporters so that a level of privacy could be maintained within the family. The record is full of interactions and conversations between Lincoln and Robert that demonstrate their closeness. Also, certain events that some biographers have characterized as slights or neglect that Robert felt at the hands of his father are more accurately explained by the fundamental differences in their personalities. Robert tended to share the formal and refined personality and mannerisms of the Todd family from whom his mother descended, and whose behavioral traits contrasted mightily with Lincoln's homespun persona. While Lincoln occasionally did things that may have embarrassed Robert, such occurrences are common parent-child experiences that are hardly indicative of a difficult relationship.

Lincoln also had a close relationship with his two younger sons who survived into childhood, Willie and Tad. During their formative years Lincoln was home in Springfield a bit more than he had been with Robert. Willie and Tad then later lived in the White House and thus were able to see their father throughout the day almost every day, often to the chagrin of important visitors who sought the president's undivided attention.

But the story of Lincoln the father is much deeper and more complex than merely calculating the amount of time that he spent with his children. Like most fathers, Lincoln had many roles to fulfill in his relationships with his children: educator, provider, disciplinarian, religious guide, moral example, counselor, and playmate. Lincoln played all of these roles and more. In doing so, he followed both his natural instincts and lessons learned from experience, often building upon what was good about his own childhood while trying not to repeat the mistakes of his father—and Lincoln believed that his own father had made plenty of mistakes. Indeed, during his adult years, Lincoln consciously distanced himself from his father as much as he could, and in doing so he treated him rather harshly. Moreover, just as Lincoln's career inevitably affected his relationships with his children, his relationships with his children affected his career. Lincoln found that it was neither easy nor always desirable to completely separate work and home.

For the modern historian far removed in time and place from the events of Lincoln's life, the most satisfying aspect of examining Lincoln the father is that there is no temptation to create a larger than life figure, elevate him to immortality, or minimize, ignore, or even amplify his shortcomings. For the modern father, the most satisfying aspect of examining Lincoln the father is coming to the inescapable conclusion that Abraham Lincoln was, as a father, quite ordinary. He was ordinary in the sense that he did things that most fathers do, felt things that most fathers feel, and made mistakes like most fathers make. And he was ordinary not only by nineteenth-century standards, but by modern standards as well. In Lincoln's life as a father, modern fathers can see themselves: their successes, their failures, their struggles, their hopes, their fears, their joys, and their sorrows.

Here we see not the imposing marble statue of a determined president sitting inside the Lincoln Memorial, gazing out across the reflecting pool toward the Washington Monument, but a man frolicking with his sons on the floor of the White House; we see not the thoughtful, burdened president delivering the Gettysburg Address to a war-torn nation, but a man quietly reading bedtime stories to his sleepy-eyed sons; and we see not the resolute commander-in-chief seeking out winning generals and forming war policy, but a man wrestling with his own grown son's desire to join the army and go off to war. Sadly, Lincoln twice experienced every parent's worst nightmare: the death of a child. Eddy, his second son, died before his fourth birthday, and Willie, regarded by some as Lincoln's favorite, died in the White House at eleven. While the death of a child is certainly an extraordinarily tragic event for any parent, Lincoln reacted to their deaths as any ordinary parent would: with a broken heart.

Lincoln, of course, did not parent alone. His wife, Mary Todd Lincoln, was intimately involved in raising the boys. The evidence is mixed as to whether theirs was a thoroughly happy marriage. Nevertheless, two things clearly emerge from the record. First, Mary could be a very difficult spouse at times. She had a short temper and was prone to jealousy, craved an extravagant lifestyle and high social acceptance, and spent money well beyond her and her husband's means. Second, Lincoln had a great fondness for her—indeed, he loved her, and she loved him. While some may fairly question whether she satisfied all of his emotional needs and whether her difficult personality wore on him, his surviving correspondence to her reveals a great affection. There has never been a credible allegation that he was unfaithful in their marriage or that he sought to end their marriage by divorce. In many ways, they were a typical married couple, with differences, disagreements, and occasional hurt feelings, but with an underlying bond of love that was perhaps strengthened by the presence of their children. Though Lincoln's relationships with his sons cannot be viewed in isolation from his marriage, his marriage was not a dominating factor in those relationships. To some extent, Lincoln saw his time with the boys as an escape from the pressures that Mary imposed on him. Mary also reinforced Lincoln's paternal role and encouraged him to spend as much time with them as possible. Mary, however, did not greatly influence Lincoln's relationship with his sons one way or the other. For better or for worse, his performance as a father was largely guided by his own instincts and experiences.

For more than a century and a half, countless historians have told the story of Lincoln the president. In doing so they have asked and answered, or at least attempted to answer, the question, "What kind of president was Abraham Lincoln?" Now, here is the complete story of Lincoln the father, which asks and answers the question, "What kind of father was Abraham Lincoln?"

CHAPTER 1

Thomas Lincoln and His Son

SOMEONE ONCE SAID THAT MOST MEN ARE TRYING TO EITHER MAKE UP for their father's mistakes or live up to their father's expectations. So it was with Abraham Lincoln. In Lincoln's case, Thomas Lincoln's mistakes as a father, rather than any meaningful expectations that he had for his son, burdened and influenced the future president as he later sought to fulfill his own paternal roles and obligations. If the largely illiterate and unambitious Thomas expected anything of his son, it was simply that he would continue to live on the rapidly developing western frontier and work the land. Thomas saw his young son's interest in reading and learning as both wholly unnecessary and an unwelcome infringement on the rugged work ethic required to achieve even minimal success as a subsistence farmer. One historian correctly observed that Lincoln's "ambitions exceeded his father's expectations." But it could also be said that Lincoln's ambitions as a lawyer and politician developed and thrived despite his father's lack of any meaningful expectations of him.

It was Thomas Lincoln's mistakes as a father—or at least his mistakes as Lincoln perceived them—that often weighed on Lincoln and later influenced the way that he raised his own sons. Lincoln clearly wanted to be a different kind of father to his boys than Thomas was to him, but with no other close role models to emulate, he often struggled to break free from Thomas's influence. On parental responsibilities related to education, discipline, work ethic, favoritism toward siblings, and spiritual guidance, Lincoln sometimes repeated mistakes that he himself thought

Thomas made with him and sometimes parented on the opposite extreme from Thomas, as if to maximize the contrast between them.

Early Lincoln biographers were not kind to Thomas. Caught up in efforts to elevate Lincoln to near godlike proportions, they promoted a "self-made man" image by contrasting his rise to power with Thomas's lack of career success. Relying on candidly harsh recollections of Lincoln's family and friends given shortly after his assassination, these writers portrayed Thomas as a ne'er-do-well drifter who was both chronically unlucky and a failed farmer and businessman. Princeton political science professor Woodrow Wilson, who himself would one day occupy the White House, wrote that Abraham Lincoln "came of the most unpromising stock on the continent, the 'poor white trash' of the South." By diminishing Thomas, biographers were better able to immortalize Lincoln by making his rise to power and prominence all the more remarkable in light of his humble beginnings.

Even John Hay and John Nicolay, who had served as Lincoln's secretaries, were tempted to pile onto Thomas. Two decades after Lincoln's assassination, they were writing what could be considered the closest thing to an official biography of the late president. Lincoln's eldest son, Robert, provided the men with virtually unlimited access to his father's papers. Their initial draft of the biography, which they shared with Robert, described Thomas as an "idle, roving, inefficient" man who lacked both "will" and "intelligence" and thus "accomplished little." In letters to Hay following his review of that draft, Robert sought to soften their assessment of Thomas. "It is beyond doubt that my departed grandfather Lincoln was not an enterprising man and it is likely that your graphic assaults on him *in passim* are not undeserved but I could not help feeling better if you 'let up' on him a little on a final revision. . . . It was a rough life, the Lord knows, and my grandfather had so much of the roughness from the very start, and nothing else, that I don't want to see him sat down on."

Perhaps taking a cue from Robert, modern historians and biographers have somewhat rehabilitated Thomas's reputation by evaluating him squarely within the context of the late eighteenth- and early nineteenth-century social and economic structure that prevailed on the western frontier. Viewed through the proper lens of his times, Thomas can be seen in a more sympathetic light as what Professor Kenneth Winkle described as "a respectable, landowning farmer who was broadly typical of the time and place in which he lived," a man of limited means and limited faculties, who probably did the best that he could with what he had. Yet Thomas's lack of education and dogged acceptance of physical labor as the only legitimate way of life, typical as those traits may have been at the time, collided with his son's burning desire to develop into a man of thoughts and words rather than blood and sweat. This collision and other tensions between Thomas and his son resulted in an emotional distance between the two men that was never remedied. Though Lincoln used stories of his humble roots for political gain by, for example, endorsing his image as a rail-splitter, behind closed doors he constantly sought to separate himself from his father and the only world his father ever knew.

Born in rural Virginia in 1776, Thomas, at the age of ten, watched in horror as Indians murdered his father on the family homestead in the backwoods of Kentucky. At the time of his death, Thomas's father owned several thousand acres of land in Kentucky, but the family was not wealthy. They were, like many frontier settlers, "land poor," meaning that they had substantial land holdings but had to work the land themselves to barely eke out a living as subsistence farmers. With five children ranging in age from six to fifteen, Thomas's mother, Bathsheba, struggled to keep the family together following her husband's death.

Under the laws of primogeniture that prevailed in Kentucky at the time, Thomas's oldest brother, Mordecai, inherited his father's entire estate upon reaching majority. But Mordecai, who was just fifteen at the time his father died, had to wait several years to realize his inheritance. In the meantime, the family needed help to survive. Shortly after her husband's death, Bathsheba moved the family to a neighboring county where, for the next five years, they lived with a cousin of her late husband. Despite some help from the family, Bathsheba still lived in what Lincoln later described as "very narrow circumstances." Nevertheless, she managed to keep the family under one roof until all of her children reached adulthood.

Without paternal guidance, and needing to help support the family, Thomas became, in Lincoln's words, "a wandering, laboring boy, and grew up literally without education." At the age of nineteen, Thomas enlisted for a short stint in the Fourth Regiment of the Kentucky militia. The following year, he worked as a common laborer for several weeks helping to build a mill and millrace in a neighboring county. Thomas later worked as a hired hand with an uncle in North Carolina and, according to family lore, once joined family friend Daniel Boone on a short venture into the Missouri territory.

In 1803, at the age of twenty-five, Thomas purchased a 238-acre farm at Mill Creek in Hardin County, Kentucky. To buy the farm, he used money he had saved from his labor as well as money given to him by Mordecai, who had recently sold some of their father's lands. Thomas soon began to enjoy the benefits and responsibilities of land ownership. He paid taxes, served on juries, and petitioned the local government for road improvements. Thomas not only farmed his land, but earned money from carpentry work and as a hired hand on a flatboat carrying goods to New Orleans, something that his son would later do himself to make ends meet. It was a subsistence life: just getting by with no thought of getting ahead.

In 1806, Thomas married Virginia native Nancy Hanks, who some historians believe was the illegitimate daughter of Lucy Hanks and an unknown father. The newlyweds soon moved to a fourteen-by-fourteen-foot cabin that Thomas built on a lot that he purchased in Elizabethtown, a small but thriving village eight miles south of his Mill Creek farm. Their first child, a daughter they named Sarah, was born there in 1807. If Thomas was indeed "a wandering, laboring boy" as his son later described him, he grew up to become a wandering, laboring man, constantly moving his family. Some of these moves were rooted in Thomas's desire for better land to farm, while others resulted from disputes over land titles that Thomas ultimately lost or simply failed to pursue aggressively. Land title disputes were a common problem in frontier Kentucky, where "the unskillful hands of the hunters and pioneers" drew the surveys, wrote the land patents, and kept the title records that ultimately "piled upon each other, overlapping and crossing in endless perplexity."

Less than two years after Sarah was born, Thomas purchased and moved his family to a three-hundred-acre farm at the South Fork of No-lin Creek, not far from their home in Elizabethtown. Three months after settling in, a son, the future president, was born on February 12, 1809. The one-room, ramshackle cabin in which Lincoln was born, typical of the "mean and little" homes that dotted the frontier, reflected both the simplicity of the life that Thomas had established and the impermanence with which he saw his roots. Western frontier settlers like Thomas experienced the same challenges that their forefathers had in settling regions farther east as they migrated from New England, as "climate and disease often cut life short, creating an unstable atmosphere in which families had difficulty surviving long enough to build for the future."

In 1811, when a dispute arose over the title to the South Fork farm, Thomas moved the family to Knob Creek, less than ten miles away, where they rented a farm that had some of the most fertile soil in the area. A second son, Thomas Jr., was born there in 1812 but died shortly after birth. In 1814, Thomas sold the Mill Creek farm (less 38 acres he had lost in a title dispute) and the next year purchased a 230-acre farm in Knob Creek, near their rented farm. Less than a year later, however, Thomas lost the entire Knob Creek farm in yet another title dispute. Having lost all or parts of three properties to title disputes in less than six years, Thomas decided to move his family from Kentucky into neighboring Indiana in search of more reliable land ownership. Abraham Lincoln was just seven years old when he made the rough hundred-mile journey north to the new homestead with the rest of his family. It was there that Lincoln would spend his formative years.

Two years before leaving Kentucky, six-year-old Lincoln attended a country subscription school for about three months, and he later briefly attended a school near the family farm in Indiana. The cumulative total of his formal education was less than one year. The balance of Lincoln's education came from helpful relatives and neighbors. While Lincoln undoubtedly had Thomas's permission to attend school for those brief terms, Thomas saw little benefit in education. Though one neighbor later recalled that Thomas "had suffered greatly for want of an education and . . . determined that Abraham should be well educated," in reality Thomas merely tolerated Lincoln's learning efforts. As Lincoln reached adulthood and his interest in learning continued unabated, Thomas reportedly told a family friend, "I suppose that Abe is still fooling hisself with eddication. I tried to stop it, but he has got that fool idea in his head, and it can't be got out. Now I hain't got no education, but I get along far better than if I had." Thomas also predicted of his young son that "if Abe don't fool away all of his time on his books, he may make something yet." Thomas's second wife, Sarah, whom he married less than two years after the death of his first wife when Lincoln was nine, tried to put the best face on Thomas's opposition to Lincoln's education. In an interview given shortly after Lincoln's assassination, she said that her late husband "was not eas-ily reconciled" to Lincoln's desire to attend school, but that he eventually gave in. "When Abe was reading," Sarah recalled, "we took particular care not to disturb him—would let him read on and on till Abe quit of his own accord." Another family member recalled, however, Thomas "having sometimes to slash him for neglecting his work by reading," while others said that Thomas sometimes hid or destroyed some of Lincoln's books to keep him from reading.

It is not difficult to imagine Thomas resisting Lincoln's efforts to learn. Having lived all of his life in the backwoods of the western fron-tier, and never setting foot in a city with a population larger than three thousand inhabitants, the prospect of an education bringing any mean-ingful benefits to his son was beyond Thomas's contemplation. Thomas, according to someone who knew him, "looked upon bone and muscle being sufficient to make the man and, that time spent in school as doubly wasted." Friends described Thomas as "not a lazy man—but a tinker—a piddler—always doing but doing nothing great—was happy—lived easy—and contented. Had but few wants and supplied these."

Supporting his family by working the land and earning extra money here and there by hiring himself out as a laborer defined Thomas's own paternal role and that which he sought for his son. In that way, Thomas was fairly typical of late seventeenth-century and early eighteenth-cen-tury frontier patriarchs, whose "authority grew out of the very nature of the agricultural world in which [they] lived." One relative described early on what it took Lincoln historians generations to realize: "Well, you see, he was like the other people in that country. None of them worked to get ahead. The[re] wasn't no market for nothing unless you took it across two or three states. The people just raised what they needed." Generally, frontier men of Thomas's generation viewed the family as an economic unit, with each member being required to contribute in order to ensure survival of the family with no consideration given to the economic or educational advancement of any one member.

Although Thomas's emphasis on agricultural subsistence and de-emphasis on education was typical of eighteenth- and early nineteenth-century frontier farmers, it was not typical of East Coast farmers of that era, especially those close to urban areas. When future president John Adams was an early teenager in the mid-1700s, he told his father, who was a farmer on the outskirts of Boston, that he did not like school and would be content to follow in his footsteps and work the land. After one laborious day of cutting thatch, Adams's father said, "Well, John, are you satisfied with being a farmer?"

"I like it very well, sir," Adams replied, though the work had been hard and muddy.

"Aya, but I don't like it so well: so you will go back to school today."

Thomas's ambivalence toward his son's education and his insistence that Lincoln carry his share of the hard labor needed to support the family resulted in a strained relationship between the father and son. Whatever latitude Thomas granted Lincoln to pursue his learning, Thomas expected the boy to both work the farm and hire himself out to others to earn extra money for the family. It was commonly understood that frontier parents would, in a sense, profit from the labor of their children. At the age of six, boys were typically expected to be "breeched" from their mothers and perform at least half a man's work until age twelve to sixteen, when they assumed a full man's workload. Lincoln wryly recalled that at a very young age he "had an axe put into his hands" and that thereafter "he was almost constantly handling that most useful instrument." Thomas once hired young Lincoln out to a neighbor to earn money to repay a debt that Thomas had incurred. Lincoln, however, preferred learning to working, and that preference was evident to all who knew him. "Lincoln was lazy—a very lazy man," noted Dennis Hanks, a cousin of Lincoln's mother. "He was always reading, scribbling, writing, ciphering, writing poetry, etc." Another family member wrote that "Lincoln was not industrious as a worker on the farm or at any kind of manual labor, he only showed industry in attainment of knowledge." A neighbor for whom Lincoln sometimes worked concurred with these assessments and recalled Lincoln's own view of his father's work ethic: "Abe was awful lazy. Was always reading and thinking—[I] used to get mad at him. . . . [He] didn't love work but dearly loved his pay. Lincoln said to me one day that his father taught him to work but never learned him to love it."

Lincoln's distaste for farming was matched by his distaste for the distinctly masculine job of hunting. For Thomas, field work necessary for a small subsistence farm was suitable for both women and children. Hunting, however, was the exclusive province of males. Thomas was "fond of hunting and a fine hunter" who "like most pioneers delighted in having a good hunt," one relative recalled. "Thomas Lincoln could with propriety be classed with the 'Hunters of Kentucky,'" wrote one admiring contemporary, who noted that "he seldom failed of success." Lincoln, however, did not take to hunting the way that his father did. Lincoln later wrote that, shortly after he moved to the Indiana farm, he "took an early start as a hunter, which was never much improved afterwards." Just before his ninth birthday, Lincoln shot a turkey, but "never since pulled a trigger on any larger game." Lincoln's aversion to hunting and his apparent lack of skill at it must have disappointed Thomas, who thrived when he had a rifle in his hand and boasted when he brought home a good kill for supper. The seasonality of crops and their inherently uncertain yield forced the family to rely on the abundant game for their food. According to cousin Dennis Hanks, "We always hunted. It made no difference what came for we more or less depended on it for a living—nay, for life." Moreover, good marksmanship was necessary for daily security as well as sustenance. "The deer, the turkeys, the bear, the wild cats, and occasionally a big panther afforded [Thomas] no small amusement and pleasure—and a great source of subsistence as the wild turkeys and deer were very abundant." But Lincoln declined to participate in this activity, which Thomas clearly saw as central to family life.

Lincoln would never push his own sons into physical labor or hunting, for the family's urban, middle-class lifestyle did not require it. Curiously, though, as will be seen, Lincoln had a mixed record in pushing education on his sons. His eldest son, Robert, attended prep school and Harvard with his father's support and encouragement, and Lincoln displayed a genuine interest in the specifics of Robert's studies. Lincoln also arranged for Willie to attend school in Springfield and later to have tutoring in the White House. On the other hand, Lincoln took a rather cavalier approach to Tad's education, which resulted in the boy falling substantially behind his peers in the ability to read and write. This ambivalence toward Tad's education was primarily due to Lincoln's belief that the boy had a learning disability that would have subjected him to ridicule by his peers, although Lincoln preferred to leave others with the impression that he simply did not want to push Tad into doing anything tedious in the way that Thomas had pushed him with physical work. Lincoln did attempt to teach a work ethic to his sons by bringing them to the office with him or letting them accompany him on official duties. But that was an altogether different experience than he had with Thomas. In order to see his father at work, Lincoln had to work side by side with Thomas as he toiled in the fields or undertook carpentry projects for which the son held little interest. Lincoln, however, would offer his own sons a glimpse of his career by letting them tag along and have a good time.

The strain between Lincoln and his father ran deeper than just differences over the value of an education and the rugged work ethic that children should undertake in order to contribute to the family's economic survival. The distance between them was also rooted in Thomas's methods of discipline, favoritism toward Lincoln's stepbrother, and commitment to organized religion, all matters that later influenced Lincoln's own relationships with his sons.

Thomas was a stern disciplinarian who physically punished his children when he thought they were out of line. When Lincoln did something wrong in Thomas's eyes, the father would "sometimes knock him a rod" or give him a "drilling." The young boy struggled to maintain his pride as he received his punishments. A relative who observed some of the beatings said that "Abe when whipped by his father never bawled but dropped a kind of silent unwelcome tear, as evidence of his sensations." While Lincoln later wavered on the degree to which he emphasized formal education for his own sons, he never wrestled with the degree of physical punishment to impose on them: there is no record of Lincoln ever spanking his own sons. In fact, he rarely imposed any meaningful degree of discipline on the boys, physical or otherwise, even when, by any objective measure, they were out of control or otherwise warranted punishment.

When Thomas remarried after the death of Lincoln's mother, he brought into the household his new bride's three children, a boy and two girls. The boy, John D. Johnston, was a year younger than Lincoln. Unlike his older stepbrother, Johnston showed little interest in learning, though he eventually became literate. Johnston followed in Thomas's footsteps as a laborer and subsistence farmer. Johnston was, in the words of one historian, "a pioneer who continually sought a better piece of land for his family farther westward," a description equally applicable to Thomas. Johnston's interest in Thomas's way of life stood in stark contrast to Lincoln's preference for books, and that interest must have been evident to Thomas. One relative observed that Thomas "never showed by his actions that he thought much of his son Abraham as a boy; he treated him rather unkind than otherwise. Always appeared to think much more of his stepson John D. Johnston than he did of his own son Abraham but after Abe was grown up and had made his mark in the world the old man appeared to be very proud of him." One historian argued, however, that whatever Thomas may have thought about Lincoln in later years, it is likely that Thomas's "preference for Johnston hurt Lincoln deeply." If true, Lincoln's reaction was typical of a child who senses that a parent favors another sibling over him or her. Yet as a father, Lincoln may have subconsciously repeated the favoritism that he endured under Thomas. As many observers noted, Lincoln's third son, Willie, was his "favorite," in part because the boy was most like him in terms of temperament and interests.

Thomas's inability to interest his son in religious activities was likely another source of distance between father and son. Thomas grew up at a time when, as Professor Anthony Rotundo pointed out, "a father was charged with the moral and spiritual growth of his children." Little reliable evidence exists pinpointing the time of Thomas's own religious conversion. Having grown up fatherless, and given the eighteenth-century cultural norm that fathers were responsible for religious education, Thomas's primary spiritual awakening likely occurred after he reached adulthood.

Wherever the roving Thomas lived as an adult, he attended church regularly and became active in the leadership of the congregation. At one point he was, according to one biographer, "one of the five or six most important men" in his local church. Though young Lincoln read the Bible and grasped the principles of Christianity, he did not, in the words of Dennis Hanks, hold "any views very strong." "I cannot tell you what his notions of the bible were," explained Lincoln's childhood friend Nathaniel Grigsby. "He talked about religion as other persons did but I do not know his view on religion—he never made any profession while in Indiana that I know of." Lincoln's own stepmother later recalled that "Abe had no particular religion—didn't think of that question at the time, if he ever did. He never talked about it." Perhaps realizing that children often shade the truth in order to please their parents, she went on to note candidly that Lincoln "read the bible some, but not as much as he said."

While Lincoln's religious beliefs deepened over time and crystallized upon the death of his second child, at no time in his life did he join an organized church. While no record exists of whether Thomas ever expressed disappointment to Lincoln over his refusal to join an organized church, it is quite likely that he did so. Throughout his adult life, Thomas was a member of various sects of Baptist churches whose influence typically reached well beyond Sunday services and touched the everyday lives of their members. "If there ever was a religion that functioned during the week-days as well as on Sundays," noted one Lincoln historian, "it was the type found among the pioneers." That Thomas would enthusiastically subscribe to this degree of religious involvement and not chastise his own son for failing to do so seems unlikely, and thus Lincoln's disinterest must have been a source of friction between the two. While it would be tempting to suggest that the absence of a role model in Thomas's youth was responsible for his own struggle to interest his son in organized religion, in reality, many religiously oriented parents of his time encountered the same struggle (as do modern parents). Lincoln, however, dealt with his responsibility to provide spiritual guidance to his children in a much different way than Thomas. Though he allowed the boys to attend church and often read the Bible in their presence, Lincoln never pushed religion on his own sons, even as the depth of his own faith strengthened in the face of continuing adversity.

Some of these spheres of conflict between Lincoln and his father were clearly rooted in changing notions of masculinity. Thomas came of age in a time of transition between an eighteenth-century family culture that depended on agrarian subsistence and an emerging nineteenth-century family culture that increasingly emphasized upward mobility and urbanization. In a sense, Thomas was caught in a twilight zone of patriarchy, when the very essence of what it meant to be a man was being transformed. Where Thomas "looked upon bone and muscle being sufficient to make the man," Lincoln's generation aimed to enter "the distinctly male worlds of politics and finance." Where Thomas came of age at a time when father-son relations were best described as "distant, didactic, and condescending," Lincoln matured at a time of increasingly "intense emotional involvement between generations of males." Where Thomas saw his role as being the patriarch of a family where all members were obligated to contribute to the economic survival of the whole, Lincoln saw himself as the head of a household and the sole economic provider. Thomas brought home food, while Lincoln brought home money. For Thomas, success was measured by the quality of a crop or the size of the prize bagged on a hunt; for Lincoln, success was measured by earning power, accumulation of material things, and recognized advancement in a profession.

In 1831, less than a year after helping his father relocate yet again, this time to Coles County, Illinois, Lincoln left home for good. He was twenty-two, over the age for which Thomas could claim any legal dominion over him. Thereafter, Lincoln tried to put as much distance between himself and his father as possible. Though they lived in the same state, Lincoln did not invite Thomas to his wedding, and Thomas never saw any of his own grandchildren and never even met Lincoln's wife. Although Lincoln would name his fourth son after his father (the first three boys were named after Lincoln's father-in-law, a family friend, and a brother-in-law), he did so only after Thomas died, depriving Thomas of the satisfaction of knowing that he had a namesake. Even then, Lincoln always called the boy "Tad" rather than Thomas. When Lincoln's stepbrother, John Johnston, informed him that Thomas was dying and requested that Lincoln come home to say farewell, Lincoln declined, directing Johnston to tell Thomas "that if we could meet now, it is doubtful whether it would not be more painful than pleasant." After Thomas died, Lincoln neither attended the funeral nor contributed to the purchase of a gravestone. Reflecting on Lincoln's relationship with his father, cousin Dennis Hanks said, "I never could tell whether Abe loved his father very well or not. I don't think he did." Lincoln did, however, use his humble origins for some political advantage. His presidential campaign biography, which he authorized, said that "it would be difficult to conceive of more unpromising circumstances than those under which he was ushered into life." Lincoln himself later wrote, "I happen temporarily to occupy this big White House. I am a living witness that any one of your children may look to come here as my father's child has." In a sense, the more undistinguished and obscure he could render Thomas, the more he could claim credit for being a self-made man.

Armed with the memories and lessons of his childhood, and with Thomas as the role model to either follow or ignore, Lincoln embarked on his own journey of fatherhood. He would first choose to establish himself in a career and next find a wife to bear his children. Only then would Lincoln begin to make up for the mistakes of his father and offer his own style of fatherhood.

CHAPTER 2

Putting Down Roots

As Lincoln began life on his own, he had not yet mapped out a career path. He knew, however, that he did not want to follow in his father's footsteps and eke out a living as a farmer and carpenter. Despite having the physical strength ideal for hard labor—he was six feet, two inches tall by the time he was sixteen—Lincoln deliberately sought work that required the use of his mind rather than his body. In this way, he joined many young frontier men of his generation who were increasingly leaving the farm in search of a more prosperous and stable life in both small towns and larger urban areas. Lincoln reportedly told his cousin John Hall that he "intended to cut himself adrift from his old world."

In March of 1831, after several months of roaming about Illinois working at odd jobs, Lincoln migrated to Springfield, a town of about seven hundred residents that was on the verge of more rapid growth. Springfield offered a variety of occupations for young men, ranging from manual labor and skilled crafts to entrepreneurial and professional careers unavailable and even unknown in the backwoods of Kentucky and Indiana. Unfortunately for Lincoln, with the increasing numbers of young men flowing into the growing town, many of whom were college educated, competition for the good jobs was fierce. Though Lincoln later became Springfield's most famous and beloved resident, his first attempt to settle there was a failure. Lacking the education and intellectual skills necessary to practice a profession, the capital needed to become an entrepreneur, and the social connections required to break into the higher echelons of the community, Lincoln abruptly left Springfield just as he had arrived there two months earlier: in his own words a "strange, friendless, uneducated, penniless, boy" who "did not know much."

Lincoln departed Springfield on a flatboat hauling goods down the Mississippi River to New Orleans, just as his father had done years earlier. While in Springfield, he met Denton Offutt, a local merchant. Offutt told Lincoln that he planned to open a general store in New Salem, Illinois, and offered Lincoln a job there when he returned from the South. New Salem was a tiny village located on a bluff above the Sangamon River, about twenty miles northwest of Springfield. Despite its relatively small permanent population of about one hundred residents, the village was a bustling commercial center that catered to the surrounding rural areas. Featuring a gristmill, sawmill, blacksmith shop, wheelwright, cooper, several general stores, a tavern, and even a doctor, New Salem presented young men with opportunities to explore various occupations in a setting far less competitive than larger towns like Springfield. Seeing himself as "a piece of driftwood," but intrigued by the opportunity presented by Offutt, Lincoln moved there in July of 1831. For Lincoln, New Salem offered not only brighter employment prospects, but an ideal geographic distance from his father. Thomas could not reasonably expect his son to frequently make the 150-mile trek over rough terrain for casual visits or to help with work, yet Lincoln was still close enough to reach the family in the event of an emergency.

Lincoln remained in New Salem until 1837. The six years that he spent there were crucial to his career path. During that time, Lincoln completed his journey from manual laborer to mental laborer. Along the way, he worked as a surveyor, postmaster, and storekeeper, the latter job being considered "an honorable occupation that naturally attracted any ambitious young man." His job as a postmaster allowed him to read all the newspapers that were sent to town for him to deliver to the local subscribers. In this way, Lincoln kept abreast of state and national political developments, matters in which he was developing a growing interest.

Not all of his career moves in New Salem were successful, however. Offutt's store failed not long after Lincoln arrived, leaving the ambitious young man unemployed. Lincoln and a friend eventually opened another general store, but that venture soon failed, too, this time leaving Lincoln both unemployed and deeply in debt. Starting in the late twentieth century, as college became more commonplace, many ambitious young men would begin their adult lives deeply in debt from student loans used to finance their education. Those debts followed them for years and acted as a drag on their economic advancement until fully repaid. For Lincoln, it was not college debt that burdened him as he developed his career, but debt from an entrepreneurial venture that he viewed as an opportunity to escape a life of hard labor experienced by his father. Though it took him years to pay off what he later wryly referred to as the "national debt," Lincoln eventually paid every cent that he owed, though not before suffering the humiliation of having some of his personal property seized by the sheriff to apply against amounts owed to one of his more impatient creditors.

At one point when he was broke and out of work, Lincoln volunteered for service in the Blackhawk War, the last organized and successful military campaign to eject Native Americans from Illinois. Lincoln later joked that during his uneventfully brief (eighty-day) stint in the military, "I had a good many bloody struggles with the musquitoes; and although I never fainted from loss of blood, I can truly say I was often hungry." Yet he was clearly proud of his service, which included being elected captain by the other men in his regiment who recognized leadership qualities in the future president. More than a quarter century later, Lincoln faced the prospect of his own son volunteering for a truly bloody conflict, where mosquitoes would be among the least of a soldier's worries.

Lincoln's entry into politics was the most significant product of his years in New Salem. His homespun personality fit in nicely with the other residents of the tiny village, and he "rapidly made acquaintances and friends." In early 1832, less than a year after moving to New Salem, friends and other citizens with whom Lincoln frequently interacted at Offutt's store and at the local taverns persuaded him to run for a seat in the Illinois General Assembly, the lower house of the state legislature. Unfortunately for Lincoln, he was little known outside of New Salem, and the legislative district stretched well beyond his hometown and even included Springfield. Running as a Whig, Lincoln finished eighth out of thirteen candidates vying for four seats. Undeterred by his loss, Lincoln ran again two years later. This time, with the help of farmers in the outlying areas whose votes he actively solicited, Lincoln was elected.

Before the first legislative session commenced, Lincoln began studying law using books he borrowed from lawyers in surrounding towns. The sessions in Vandalia, then the state capital, were brief, so Lincoln still needed employment back home. During the session breaks, he worked at various jobs back in New Salem, and in his spare time he continued to study law. When the legislature was in session, Lincoln networked with powerful colleagues, many of whom became increasingly impressed with his mastery of the law and his commitment to the Whig party. Voters reelected Lincoln in 1836, and shortly thereafter he persuaded two justices of the Illinois Supreme Court to license him to practice law throughout the state. The requirements of admission to the bar in Illinois at that time required only that a county judge attest to the applicant's good moral character and that the Illinois Supreme Court issue a license after the applicant passed a perfunctory exam. In a sense, Lincoln benefitted from the growing Jacksonian notion of opening up to ordinary citizens careers and professions that were once reserved only for the elite. Admission to the bar was no longer contingent upon family heritage or even education at an East Coast college. Now it was largely a matter of demonstrating a degree of "forensic bravura," something that came quite naturally to Lincoln, who liked to tell stories and make speeches.

During the first legislative session of his second term, Lincoln successfully led the fight to move the capital from Vandalia to Springfield, with a population that had more than doubled since Lincoln moved away. By Eastern standards Springfield was a small frontier town, but its rapid growth, busy commercial center, and well-planned layout that included a public square made it urban and cosmopolitan by Western frontier standards. One observer described Springfield this way: "The houses and villages on the line of the road were few and wide apart, and the sight of the wide rolling prairies bounded on all sides by the horizon had the appearance of the vast ocean." In the two decades following the legislature's designation of Springfield as the capital, its population soared from 1,500 to 9,000. By early 1861, when Lincoln left for Washington, it was the fourth largest city in Illinois. In an era in which there was a "dynamic and historically unprecedented expansion of cities" all across America, Springfield went right along for the ride.

In March of 1837, shortly after the legislative session ended, Lincoln returned to New Salem to say goodbye to his friends. To advance his career, he decided to move back to Springfield, soon to be the center of power in the state. New Salem had served Lincoln well, allowing him to more easily transition from his rural roots to urban life. Six years earlier, the "strange, friendless, uneducated, penniless, boy" had left Springfield in failure. Now he was returning to form a law partnership with John Todd Stuart, a fellow legislator, well-established lawyer, and leading Whig politician whom Lincoln had impressed with his command of the law and who offered to take him in as a junior partner.

The Stuart & Lincoln law firm was successful from the outset, with the two friends handling scores of cases in their first year. Because the official move of the capital to Springfield was not completed until 1839, Lincoln temporarily commuted to Vandalia when the legislature was in session. Moreover, to further boost the income of his law practice, Lincoln joined other lawyers and judges in the practice of "riding the circuit," the term used to describe how members of the bar traveled from city to city in Illinois trying cases in places that had no resident lawyers or judges. It was a way to build a practice and gain experience, especially for young lawyers who resided in cities where more established lawyers tended to control the best business.

The eighth judicial circuit in which Lincoln participated encompassed fourteen counties and required more than five hundred miles of travel over rough roads, across rivers and bogs, and through sweeps of prairie grass that often stood as high as a horse. The schedule called for two terms each calendar year, each lasting about ten weeks. The summer term generally ran from early April to mid-June, and the fall term ran from mid-August to the first week in November. These time frames tended to treat the beleaguered travelers to both the summer heat and the fall rains. Lincoln traveled mostly by horse and stayed in rustic inns, taverns, and rural farmhouses of the litigants, often sharing a bed with a fellow lawyer or sleeping on the floor. It was a distinctly masculine culture, where men battled men by day and then socialized with each other at night. It was also a culture that a lawyer could choose to enjoy or dread, depending on his own sense of propriety. Three-quarters of a century earlier, young lawyer and future president John Adams, who was raised in the Puritan tradition, wrote his future wife Abigail from the circuit in Massachusetts, describing the misery he was suffering:

> *I believe I could furnish a Cabinet of Letters upon these subjects which would be exceeded in Curiosity, by nothing, but by a set describing the Characters, Diversions, Meals, Wit, Drollery, Jokes, Smutt, and Stories of the Guests at a Tavern in Plymouth where I lodge, when at that Court—which could be equaled by nothing excepting a minute History of Close stools and Chamber Potts, and of the Operation of Pills, Potions and Powders, in the Preparation for the small Pox.*

While most lawyers tried to return home on weekends, Lincoln by choice only occasionally made the trip back to Springfield. He enjoyed the legal work that he was doing on the circuit, where he made many new contacts that could advance his political ambitions. In joining the circuit riders and commuting to Vandalia, Lincoln began his two-decade-long practice of spending substantial periods of time away from home to further his career both as a lawyer and a politician, a practice that would end only upon his election to the presidency.

By 1839 Lincoln was firmly established in his career with a modest annual income of about $1,000 plus his small legislative salary. Though still deeply in debt, Lincoln began thinking about finding a wife. He was thirty, and most men in Springfield were married by their mid-twenties. Though Lincoln increasingly gained confidence speaking in the courtroom and on the floor of the legislature, he was still awkward with women, and he knew it. "I have been spoken to by but one woman since I've been here," Lincoln complained (and probably exaggerated) shortly after arriving in Springfield, "and should not have been by her, if she could have avoided it."

Lincoln made two early attempts at finding a spouse, one of which ended in a broken heart and the other of which, like his first foray into

Springfield, ended in failure. In 1835, Lincoln courted Ann Rutledge, the twenty-two-year-old daughter of James Rutledge, one of the founders of New Salem. With blue eyes and auburn hair, she stood only five feet, three inches tall, more than a foot shorter than Lincoln. She was, according to those who knew her, a very pretty girl with "as pure and kind a heart as an angel—full of love—kindness—sympathy." When Lincoln first met Ann, she was already engaged to John McNamar, a farmer and businessman who had accumulated a degree of modest wealth in the New Salem area after moving there from New York. Soon after his engagement to Ann, McNamar left for New York, supposedly to arrange for his immediate family to move back to New Salem. But after McNamar left, he made no contact with Ann. Unsure of where she stood with her fiancé, Ann was reluctant to commit to Lincoln. The record is unclear as to whether Lincoln and Ann were ever formally engaged in any sort of conditional or unconditional manner. In any case, in the summer of 1835, Ann was stricken with typhoid and died. Lincoln was devastated and did not work for nearly a month.

In early 1836, Lincoln's married friend, Mrs. Bennett Abell, offered to bring her sister, Mary S. Owens, from Kentucky on the condition that Lincoln marry her. Lincoln had met the girl several years earlier when she visited her sister's home, and he was favorably impressed. But he knew little of the art of courting and romance. When Lincoln's mother died in Indiana in 1818, after an appropriate period of mourning Thomas traveled back to Kentucky in search of a new wife. There he found Sarah Bush Johnston, a widow whom he had known when she was a young girl. "Miss Johnston," Thomas said plainly and directly, "I have no wife and you no husband. I came a-purpose to marry you. I knowed you from a gal and you knowed me from a boy. I've no time to lose; and if you're willin' let it be done straight off." With that, the two were soon wed.

Remembering Thomas's example of marriage without courtship, Lincoln was open to Mrs. Abell's offer. "I had seen said sister some three years before," Lincoln later wrote, "thought her intelligent and agreeable, and saw no good objection to plodding life through hand in hand with her." When she finally arrived in New Salem, however, Lincoln was shocked at her deteriorated appearance. "She now appeared a fair match for Falstaff [the obese character in Shakespeare's *Merry Wives of Windsor* and *Henry IV*]," Lincoln later mused. "When I beheld her, I could not for my life avoid thinking of my mother; and this, not from withered features, for her skin was too full of fat to permit its contracting into wrinkles; but from her want of teeth, weather beaten appearance in general, and from a kind of notion that ran in my head, that nothing could have commenced at the size of infancy, and reached her present bulk in less than thirty-five or forty years." Yet Lincoln felt trapped, having promised Mrs. Abell that he would marry the girl. He first tried to slither out of his promise by writing Mary a letter laying out various reasons why she would be unhappy being married to him and offering to release her from any obligation that she felt to go to the altar with him. When that ruse failed, he reluctantly concluded that he "might as well bring it to a consummation without further delay" and offered a formal marriage proposal. "Shocking to relate, she answered, no," wrote the half-pleased and half-wounded Lincoln. On the one hand, he succeeded in getting "completely out of the scrape." On the other hand, he realized just how poorly Mary's rejection reflected on him: "I very unexpectedly found myself mortified almost beyond endurance. I was mortified, it seemed to me, in a hundred different ways. My vanity was deeply wounded by the reflection . . . that she whom I had taught myself to believe no body else would have had actually rejected me. . . . Others have been made fools of by the girls; but this can never be with truth be said of me. I most emphatically, in this instance, made a fool of myself. I have now come to the conclusion never again to think of marrying; and for this reason, I can never be satisfied with any one who would be block-headed enough to have me."

But Lincoln's aversion to marriage would be short lived. Two years after he moved to Springfield, friends introduced him to Mary Todd, the daughter of a prosperous banker and merchant from Lexington, Kentucky. Mary was in town for an extended stay with her socialite sister, Elizabeth, who was married to Ninian Edwards, the young Illinois attorney general and son of a former governor. Mary was eight years younger than Lincoln and stood in stark contrast to him both physically and in disposition. Mary was more than a foot shorter than Lincoln, and her slightly plump face and frame seemed exaggerated in comparison to his thin build and chiseled cheekbones. Her skin was soft and fair; his was rugged and worn, with "his face and forehead . . . wrinkled even in his youth." Her hair was always perfectly coiffed, his mostly unkempt. She was "cultured, graceful and dignified"; he lacked social graces. She could be "sarcastic, haughty, and aristocratic"; he was polite, humble, and self-deprecating. She had many suitors, including Lincoln's future rival for the presidency, fellow Springfield resident Stephen A. Douglas; Lincoln could barely find a woman to speak to him.

Yet they also shared much in common beyond their Kentucky roots. They both liked poetry and Shakespeare and often read their favorite poems and stories to each other. More importantly, however, Mary shared Lincoln's passion for the Whig party and its principles. Mary took a keen interest in politics, and she shared with Lincoln a deep reverence of fellow Whig and Kentuckian Henry Clay. She admired Lincoln's ambition, especially his interest in having a political career. Lincoln, she later wrote, had "a hope and bright prospects ahead for position—fame & power," and Mary once remarked as a young lady that she wanted to marry a future president. They began their courtship in early 1840 and became engaged later that year. During the course of their engagement, Lincoln traveled throughout the state both on the judicial circuit and to promote the presidential candidacy of Whig nominee William Henry Harrison, who eventually defeated incumbent Democrat Martin Van Buren. It was during this time that Mary first experienced Lincoln's frequent absences from home due to the demands of his career, absences that would continue to one degree or another for the next two decades.

Shortly after their engagement became official, however, Lincoln broke it off. His reasons for doing so are not clear. Some have speculated that Lincoln, who was beginning to show signs of severe melancholy (what in modern times might be viewed as clinical depression), simply could not cope with the prospect of committing to marriage. Others have argued that Lincoln, still struggling to pay his debts from New Salem, felt financially unable to support Mary in the lifestyle to which she had grown accustomed. Still others have suggested that Mary's wealthy father, Robert Smith Todd, and her aristocratic brother-in-law, Ninian

Edwards, felt that Mary could do much better than Lincoln, who still carried a reputation among Springfield's elite as a backwoodsman, and that those men exerted pressure on the young lawyer to break off the engagement by appealing to his sense of financial inadequacy. Predictably, Lincoln dealt with the broken engagement by "drown[ing] his cares among the intricacies and perplexities of the law," which included traveling thousands of miles around the state to further his growing law practice.

After the end of his fourth and final term in the legislature in 1841, Lincoln's law practice became his sole source of income, though he remained active in Whig politics. Earlier that year, he and Stuart had dissolved their partnership. Stuart had been elected to Congress and was contributing little to the law practice. Lincoln then formed a new partnership with Stephen T. Logan, a well-respected Springfield lawyer and distant cousin of Mary.

In the summer of 1842, more than eighteen months after the broken engagement, Lincoln and Mary began courting again. In the preceding months, they had seen each other occasionally, and with Lincoln's court cases and political activities being well known around town, she kept abreast of his career. They were formally reintroduced at a party hosted by mutual friends, and the spark that had existed once before became readily apparent again. By early November, they were engaged for the second time. After a hastily called wedding, perhaps to thwart any attempt for outsiders to talk them out of it, Lincoln and Mary were married on November 4. Lincoln presented Mary with a wide-band gold ring engraved with the words, "A.L. to Mary, Nov. 4, 1842. Love is Eternal."

The next day, the Lincolns took up residence in an eight-by-fourteen-foot room on the second floor of the Globe Tavern, a ramshackle building with a common dining room that doubled as a watering hole for Whig politicians and a polling place on election day. The widowed landlady, Sarah Beck, prepared the meals and charged the newlyweds $4 a week for room and board, but she was stingy and often complained about having to supply her guests with candles. For Lincoln, the new living quarters were a step up, having spent the previous five years sharing a bed with his best friend Joshua Fry Speed on the second floor of Speed's general store. For Mary, however, the Globe Tavern was a world away from both her father's L-shaped brick mansion in Lexington, where she grew up, and her sister's spacious home in an area of Springfield known as Aristocrat's Hill where she had been living in the years prior to her marriage.

Less than forty-eight hours after his wedding, Lincoln left Springfield on a four-day trip to handle nine trials in nearby Taylorville. After returning home for a few days, he left again until November 19. All in all, Lincoln was away from home working for ten of the first fourteen days of his marriage. If Mary thought that Lincoln would end or curtail his frequent work-related absences from Springfield after their marriage, she soon realized that would not be the case.

On August 1, 1843, three days shy of nine months after the wedding, their first son, Robert Todd Lincoln, was born. When the Lincolns first announced Mary's pregnancy, gossips in town whispered that Mary may have been pregnant before the wedding, thus explaining the hasty nuptials. The baby's gestation period, however, was consistent with a full term pregnancy commencing with their wedding night, if not any of the several days that Lincoln was home immediately following their wedding. Moreover, without the convenience of medically accurate pregnancy tests, several weeks likely passed after conception before the Lincolns knew that Mary was pregnant, a time period that would have taken them well past their wedding date before they could have discovered that she was carrying a baby that would reach full term in November. As late as March of 1843, more than four months after the wedding, Lincoln suspected that Mary was pregnant but was still not certain. Writing his best friend Speed, who had inquired about the possibility of a baby and suggested, perhaps jokingly, that their first born son be named after him, Lincoln said, "About the prospects of your having a namesake at our house, can't say exactly yet."

During Mary's pregnancy, Lincoln continued with his busy law practice and political activities, and as a result he was frequently absent from home. Following several important trials in early 1843, which occupied much of his time and attention, Lincoln in March tried to secure an endorsement by the local Whig party to run for a seat in Congress representing the Seventh Congressional District. When it became clear that his friend, Edward Baker, was the favorite, a disappointed Lincoln withdrew from the competition and instead reluctantly agreed to be a delegate to the forthcoming Whig convention that would formally nominate Baker. On April 5, as the summer term for the judicial circuit began, Lincoln left home for a month-long trek around the circuit. His absence meant that Mary would have to spend her first Easter Sunday as a married and pregnant woman without him. Since Lincoln had not yet joined a church and rarely attended weekly services anyway, he likely thought little of missing one of the most sacred days on the Christian calendar. But Mary, who was raised as a church-going Presbyterian, felt alone. Lincoln was also gone for several days in May and June, and on a hot Saturday morning in mid-July he traveled to Hillsborough to give a speech for the Whig congressional candidate. Two weeks later, shortly after having written Speed that "we are but two, as yet," Robert Todd Lincoln was born.

By the middle of the nineteenth century, it was becoming increasingly common for fathers to be present during the birth of their children. While some doctors allowed but did not encourage the husband's involvement, a growing number of them believed that the husband could play an important role in the delivery process by providing emotional and physical support to his wife. It is not clear whether Lincoln was present during Robert's delivery or whether he merely waited nervously downstairs at the Globe Tavern until he was called to Mary's bedside. Years after Lincoln's death, Mary told a friend that she remembered that "my darling husband was bending over me, with such love and tenderness when [Robert] was born." Mary could have been referring to Lincoln's presence at the birth or immediately thereafter, and there are no other known descriptions of the birthing scene. In any case, Mary delivered Robert in her small boarding room on the second floor. Lincoln was finally a father at thirty-four, nearly five years older than most first-time fathers of his generation.

The Lincolns named the boy after Mary's father, Robert Todd. In doing so, Lincoln broke with a family tradition of naming the eldest son after the paternal grandfather. Lincoln himself was named after Thomas's father, Abraham Lincoln, who was murdered by Native Americans on his Kentucky farm. Thomas's older brother, Mordecai, was named after his paternal grandfather, Mordecai Lincoln. But Lincoln was still trying to put distance between himself and his father, so naming the boy after Thomas was simply out of the question. Besides, Mary had never even met Thomas, a circumstance more attributable to Lincoln than to his father. Historically, naming rights were almost always the exclusive province of the father. As the nineteenth century progressed, however, wives were increasingly consulted, and in most cases the final decision was made by mutual agreement. In the case of the Lincolns, Mary's influence was obvious.

Robert Todd had remarried after the death of Mary's mother many years earlier, and while Mary dearly loved her father, she did not get along well with her stepmother, Elizabeth. Elizabeth had eight children with Robert, so Mary and her five siblings had to compete for their father's attention as he was raising his new family. Thus, Mary likely saw that giving her father a namesake was an opportunity to solidify her relationship with him, a relationship she clearly desired to have. Likewise, the increasingly ambitious Lincoln likely saw the Todd name as a more prominent heritage than anything Thomas could offer. As Robert grew, the Lincolns made him acutely aware of the fact that he was named after a Todd and not a Lincoln. "I was named for my maternal grandfather," he later wrote to a Lincoln biographer, "and not for any connection with any Lincoln bearing the name." Mary's father was elated by the decision. During a prayer with Mary, he said, "May God bless and protect my little namesake." Thomas would never meet his grandson.

Lincoln remained at home in Springfield for about a month after Robert's birth. During that time, he attended a local Whig convention and continued with his law practice, though he spent considerably less time than usual at the office. During that month he appeared to have worked on only one legal matter and authored no written correspondence to friends or acquaintances. Lincoln was likely helping Mary with the new baby and enjoying his son. A new mother often counts on her mother or mother-in-law to help with a newborn for a few days or weeks, but that was not the case with Mary. Mary's mother had passed away when she was six, and her stepmother was already busy with eight children of her own, three of whom were still under five years old. Lincoln's mother, too, had died when he was a child, and his stepmother back in Lexington was probably not even informed of Robert's birth in a timely manner, much less invited to come for a visit. Mary's sisters, who continued to believe that she had made a mistake in marrying Lincoln, offered no help. Thus, the Lincolns had only themselves and their friends. "Mrs. Lincoln had no nurse for herself or the baby," recalled the daughter of Harriet Bledsoe, another Globe resident. "Whether this was due to poverty or more probably to the great difficulty securing domestic help, I do not know." In any case, Harriet "went everyday to [Mary's] room in the hotel, washed and dressed the baby, and made sure the mother was comfortable and the room tidy for several weeks, till Mrs. Lincoln was able to do these things for herself." During that time, Mary was often so tired that she entrusted the baby's care to Harriet's six-year-old daughter, Sophie. Lincoln helped, too, carrying the screaming Robert around the room whenever the baby had a bout of colic and occasionally pushing him around the block in a baby carriage.

On September 6, five weeks after Robert's birth, Lincoln left again for the circuit. For the next two months, he traveled about Illinois, returning home only three times for a few days at a stretch to see his family and tend to business at his office in Springfield. During one of those return trips, Lincoln hired a nursemaid to help Mary during the day when he was out of town. Mary's father, who had traveled from Lexington to see his little namesake, insisted on giving the young couple $120 a year until Lincoln was more firmly established financially. Lincoln likely had mixed feelings about this financial assistance. While his income was modest but growing, he still carried the burden of the New Salem debt, and he clearly recognized that Mary had become accustomed to a lifestyle substantially more lavish than her present circumstances in a room on the second floor of a tavern. On the other hand, accepting the help may have wounded his own sense of masculinity by both undercutting his role as the financial provider for the family and robbing him of the ability to claim honestly that his success was entirely of his own making. Nevertheless, the Lincolns accepted the money, and immediately hired the day maid for about $1.50 per week.

When Lincoln finally returned home at the end of the fall circuit term in early November, his first order of domestic business was to find larger living quarters. The Lincolns had outgrown their small room at the Globe Tavern, and with Robert's frequent screaming and crying easily heard by the other tenants, they had overstayed their welcome. The Lincolns were ready to join the increasing number of city dwellers who owned a home of their own. After briefly renting a three-room frame cottage at 214 South Fourth Street, Lincoln in January 1844 signed a contract to purchase a five-room house on the corner of Eighth and Jackson Streets, not far from Lincoln's office. The seller was the Reverend Charles Dresser, who had married the Lincolns a little more than a year earlier. Lincoln paid $1,500 for the house, $1,200 of which was paid in cash and the remaining $300 represented the value of a small lot Lincoln owned on Adams Street that he conveyed to Dresser as part of the deal. The one-and-a-half story Greek revival wood frame home was painted a pale chocolate color and sat on a 152-by-50-foot lot, the typical size for residential lots in urban Springfield. There was no central heating—typical for homes of that era—so warmth was provided by the kitchen stove and fireplaces located in several of the rooms. Hauling in wood, stoking the flames, and cleaning out ashes were all part of daily chores in the wintertime. The backyard included a wood shed and an outhouse, and Lincoln was able to keep his horse and a milk cow pastured in an adjacent field.

A decade and a half after leaving his father's rural home, Lincoln was now comfortably settled into a middle-class lifestyle, with a steady career, a wife and child, and a home of his own. In contrast to his father, who constantly moved the family about, Lincoln would offer his home as a source of stability for Mary and the children. The house at Eighth and Jackson was the only home that Lincoln ever owned, and except for the White House, the only home that his children ever knew during his lifetime. Though Lincoln would always make a comfortable living, his lifestyle in Springfield remained modest. Commenting on Lincoln's election to the presidency in 1860, Ralph Waldo Emerson approvingly proclaimed, "This middle-class country had got a middle-class president, at last."

Mary immediately began to suitably decorate their new home. Among her first purchases were lamps for the parlor so that Lincoln could read or converse with her or his friends until well into the night. She also bought linens, kitchen utensils, and furniture. While having a day maid was helpful, Mary was used to being waited on by servants when she was a child, so she persuaded her husband that she needed live-in help to properly manage the household. Feeling more and more comfortable about their finances, in early summer of 1844 the Lincolns arranged for Harriet Hanks, the teenage daughter of Lincoln's cousin Dennis Hanks, to live with them in Springfield. The Lincolns provided room and board for Harriet and paid the tuition for her to attend a local finishing school. In exchange, Harriet served as a housemaid and babysitter. Mary, who was by now frequently exhibiting a short temper, clashed constantly with Harriet. While Harriet remained in the Lincoln home for about eighteen months, she was just the first of many domestic servants that Mary hired and then ultimately drove away with her unpredictable outbursts and often unreasonable demands.

As the inside of the home began to reflect a woman's touch, the outside suffered from lack of attention. Lincoln was not interested in domestic yard work. He planted some rose bushes in the front yard, but then neglected to nurture them. Other than the rose bushes, Lincoln never planted any trees or other decorative vegetation around the house. One neighbor observed that "he did not it seems care for such things," while another took it upon himself to beautify Lincoln's yard: "I have planted flowers in their front yard myself to hide nakedness—ugliness . . . have done it often."

During the first few months after moving into the new house, Lincoln stayed busy with his local law practice and traveled outside of Springfield only a few times, mostly for political meetings. He and Logan had dissolved their partnership the previous December after Logan decided that he wanted to practice with his son David. Lincoln asked William H. Herndon, a young law clerk in the office, to join him as the junior partner of the new firm of Lincoln & Herndon. The summer circuit term, which lasted from April 1 to July 31, kept Lincoln away from Springfield about half the time. For the second year in a row, Lincoln missed spending Easter Sunday with Mary. On August 1, the Lincolns hosted a party celebrating Robert's first birthday. All of Mary's relatives in Springfield attended, except for a cousin, whom Mary refused to invite because she allegedly said that Robert "was a sweet child but not good looking." Mary would always be extremely sensitive about how others perceived her children. Once after returning home from a walk downtown with baby Robert, Lincoln told Mary that he had met fellow attorney (and future political rival) Stephen Douglas on the street. Mary asked her husband if Douglas thought that Robert was pretty, and "when L[incoln] said he failed to notice or ask about Bob she became very indignant."

Shortly after his birthday, Robert—whom the Lincolns sometimes called Bob or Bobbie—took his first steps on the oak floors of the house at Eighth and Jackson. A few months later, he began muttering his first words. Until then, like most infants, Robert was largely stationary and only able to communicate by offering smiles and cries. Suddenly, Robert was mobile, and Lincoln took full advantage of his son's playfulness. "One of his greatest pleasures when at home was that of nursing and playing with the little boy," Harriet Hanks later recalled. One of Lincoln's law clerks recalled Lincoln telling of how "he was lying down at home, having left his boots in the second-story hallway, when all at once he heard a tremendous clatter on the stairs. He jumped up, hurried to the head of the stairs, and looking down, saw Bob getting up on all fours from the floor of the hallway below, unhurt but sadly bewildered. 'The youngster had got into my boots and in trying to walk around in them had fallen downstairs.' He looked so comical with the bootlegs reaching clear up to his little body."

It was also now easier for Robert to get into trouble, and for the first time Lincoln was faced with having to discipline his son. "He is quite smart enough," Lincoln wrote in a letter to Speed. "I sometime fear he is one of the little rare-ripe sort, that are smarter at about five than ever after. He has a great deal of that sort of mischief that is the offspring of much animal spirits." When Lincoln misbehaved as a boy, Thomas would "knock him a rod," a backwoods expression for whipping. Lincoln simply did not want to impose that form of punishment on his own son, so he relied on calm but stern scoldings to discipline Robert.

In the early years, Mary alone meted out the physical punishments, and Lincoln seemed content to let her do so. When Robert was about three, Lincoln wrote Speed, saying, "Since I began this letter a messenger came to tell me Bob was lost; but by the time I reached the house, his mother had found him, and had him whipped." Lincoln then added with a sense of amusement that "by now, very likely he is run away again." Margaret Ryan, one of the many young domestic servants who worked for Mrs. Lincoln, observed that Mary "would whip Bob a good deal," and another neighbor remembered that she "held a private-strapping party" after one of the boys came home covered in mud after falling into a puddle. Mary, who was described as "turbulent—loud—always yelling at children," once whipped Tad on his legs with a switch after accusing him, falsely it turned out, of stealing ten cents.

After a few years, though, even Mary stopped the spankings. Parents of the Lincolns' generation increasingly moved away from harsher notions of discipline in favor of a more affectionate treatment of their children. The emerging cultural shift saw the object of child rearing not as an exercise in breaking a will through intense moral or physical pressure but as a responsibility to shape character. There was an emerging belief that persuasion rather than force held better promise to bring about basic change in a child's character. The Lincolns, however, quickly developed a reputation around Springfield (and later in the White House) of going too far in indulging their children and being lax disciplinarians. Though they were indeed at one extreme in the indulgences granted to their children, they were also, in a sense, reflecting the spirit of republicanism that had taken hold in the country after the American Revolution. "The decay of patriarchalism is a natural corollary of political democracy," noted one historian, "for the government recognizes, not families, but individuals." For the Lincolns, permitting the boys to run wild and get into trouble was simply letting them be themselves.

Lincoln and Mary occasionally disagreed over issues of discipline. On one occasion after Robert committed some infraction, Harriet Hanks watched as Lincoln "undertook to correct the child and his wife was determined that he should not, and attempted to take it from him. But in this she failed. She then tried tongue lashing but met with the same fate, for Mr. Lincoln corrected his child as a father ought to do, in the face of his wife's anger and that too without even changing his countenance, or making any reply to his wife." In this instance, Mary seemed oblivious to the importance of showing a unified front when disciplining children, who usually learn to exploit parental disagreements to their advantage.

While the incident that Harriet witnessed also suggests that Lincoln was not averse to punishing Robert in some manner when he misbehaved, in fact Lincoln left most of the discipline to Mary. In this way, the Lincolns were fairly typical of middle-class households of their era, as mothers increasingly dominated the domestic sphere. Up through the eighteenth century, when most families lived on farms that provided both sustenance and income for the family, fathers assumed the primary obligation of both disciplining their sons and molding their character. Many people at that time believed that "mothers were too indulgent and thus were likely to ruin their sons. Consequently, women were discouraged from playing an active role in the lives of their boys after their early years of childhood." This paradigm shifted as families increasingly migrated to urban areas and established middle-class households. As fathers found employment outside of the home, mothers assumed greater domestic roles. No longer the center of economic productivity for the family, the house now served as exclusively "private space," and with fathers frequently absent as they developed their careers, mothers were expected to take over more and more child-rearing responsibilities. The Lincolns started their family just as the paradigm shift in domesticity firmly took root. The newly accepted division of responsibility for discipline suited Lincoln perfectly, for he could work hard all day while Mary struggled to keep the boys in line, then come home and be the hero that laughs and plays with them until bedtime.

By late summer of 1845, Mary was pregnant again. After the end of the fall circuit term in early November, Lincoln focused on his Springfield law practice and began planning a run for Congress. Two years earlier, a disappointed Lincoln had lost the Whig party nomination to his good friend, Edward Baker, who was eventually elected. In 1842, during a Whig convention in Pekin, Illinois, Lincoln, Baker, and John Hardin, whom Baker had succeeded in Congress, had put in place an informal plan known as the Pekin Agreement. According to that plan, each man, after securing the party nomination and being elected, would serve just one term in Congress, thus allowing all three to have a chance to go to Washington over a six-year period. Hardin served first, then Baker. Now it was Lincoln's turn.

From the outset, Baker intended to keep up his end of the bargain, telling Lincoln in November that "the track for the next congressional race was clear" for Lincoln and that he "would say so publicly in any manner." Much to Lincoln's chagrin, however, Hardin was making comments about abrogating the arrangement and running again. Lincoln found Hardin's wavering ironic, if not disturbing. When the three men first hatched the Pekin Agreement, Hardin had whispered to Lincoln that Baker was the one who would not likely stick to it, predicting that "if Baker succeeded [in getting elected] he would most likely hang on as long as possible." Yet now it was Hardin, not Baker, who was backing out of the arrangement. Lincoln first tried some back-channel efforts to have others urge Hardin to run for governor rather than for Congress again, but Hardin would not commit. Lincoln then began courting and counting votes among potential Whig delegates, though he was careful not to offend Hardin. "Let nothing be said against Hardin," Lincoln cautioned a friend in early December, "Let the pith of the whole argument be 'Turn about is fair play.'"

By mid-January, as Mary was starting to show, Lincoln planned a campaign tour, "a quiet trip through the towns and neighborhoods of Logan county, Delevan, Tremont, and on to & through the upper counties." After learning that Hardin had formally proposed to scrap both the Pekin Agreement and the established convention system of selecting the party nominee in favor of a direct-vote primary, Lincoln fired off a letter to his potential rival. He was polite but firm. "I am entirely satisfied with the old system," he wrote. In a lengthy second letter to Hardin sent in early February, Lincoln was somewhat more blunt. After detailing the history of the Pekin Agreement and defending his own recent actions to become the nominee, Lincoln ended the letter with a call to fairness and reason. "I believe you do not mean to be unjust or ungenerous, and therefore am slow to believe that you will not think *better* and think *differently* of this matter." Lincoln's letter worked. Just nine days later, shortly after Lincoln left Springfield to start campaigning, Hardin announced that he would not be a candidate. Hardin continued to argue in favor of a direct primary nomination process, but the party promptly rejected this suggestion and kept plans to hold the convention the following May. Lincoln's path to the nomination was now clear.

Lincoln stayed close to home during the final month of Mary's pregnancy. Save for a week of campaigning in early February, he remained in Springfield as Mary neared her delivery date. During that time, Lincoln sent copies of some of his favorite poems to a lawyer friend, Andrew Quincy Johnston, including William Knox's "Mortality." Lincoln even wrote a lengthy poem, entitled "My Childhood Home—I See Again," a fond recollection of a happy childhood that, not surprisingly, omitted any references to a father.

Lincoln's second son, Edward Baker Lincoln, was born on March 10, 1846. "We have another boy," the proud father joyously wrote his old friend Speed. "He is very much such a child as Bob was at his age—rather of a long order." Lincoln also offered a description of the two-and-a-half-year-old Robert, who by then had not developed the height that Lincoln expected given his length at birth: "Bob is short and low, and I expect, always will be. He talks very plainly—almost as plainly as any body. He is quite smart enough." Lincoln's observations about Robert were prescient. Robert in fact grew up to be short and plump, more like his mother than his father, and his keen intellect, bolstered by a Harvard education, carried him into both a cabinet post in the Garfield administration and later to the president's chair at the Pullman Railroad Company, where he enjoyed both social status and wealth. Lincoln was seeing the first signs that Robert was, in appearance and disposition, more Todd than Lincoln.

For the second time, Lincoln had an opportunity to name a child after his father, and for a second time he declined to do so. This time, Lincoln not only once again overlooked his good friend Speed, but he also went outside of both the Lincoln and Todd families altogether. With Mary's blessing, he named the boy after Edward Baker, the man who honored his agreement to step aside after one term in Congress in order to give Lincoln an opportunity to serve. While Lincoln's friendships with Speed, fellow circuit rider David Davis (whom Lincoln later appointed to the Supreme Court), and other local men are well documented, the record contains little to gauge the degree of closeness of the Lincoln-Baker friendship. Nevertheless, at a time when the ambitious Lincoln, whole-heartedly supported by Mary, needed a boost to get to Washington, Baker was there to provide it. So, Baker was amply rewarded with a namesake. Over the next two years, Baker frequently visited with little Eddy. Once again, Thomas would never meet his grandson.

Six days after Eddy's birth, Lincoln was in court in Springfield, where he had twelve cases called. He undoubtedly spent time in the preceding days preparing for those hearings. Lincoln was also in court for twelve of the next thirteen days, which left little time for him to help around the house. "Work, work, work," was how Lincoln's partner Herndon described Lincoln's commitment to his law practice. Recognizing Lincoln's aversion to hard labor that he had developed in his youth, Herndon observed that Lincoln "was not fond of physical exercise, but his mental application was untiring." Sometimes Lincoln would "study twenty-four hours without food or sleep . . . often walking unconscious, his head on one side, thinking and talking, to himself."

Less than two weeks later, as the summer circuit term began, Lincoln left for Jacksonville, Illinois, leaving Mary at home with the two children and the live-in maid. Between riding the circuit and campaigning for Congress, over the next seven months Lincoln was home in Springfield for fewer than eighty days. During that time, however, he secured the Whig nomination for Congress that he so desperately craved. Then, on August 3, 1846, he won a substantial victory over his Democratic opponent in the general election. Lincoln was now a Congressman-elect, and the only Whig in the Illinois Congressional delegation.

Since the new Congress would not convene until December of 1847, Lincoln had another year in which to continue his law practice before undertaking his official duties in Washington. That year was typical for Lincoln, as he was gone from Springfield riding the circuit for substantial periods of time throughout the summer and fall. Also, with his law practice flourishing, the Lincolns decided to expand their Springfield home, adding another bedroom and a pantry at the back of the house and moving the kitchen slightly from its original location. Lincoln was also making progress paying down the "national debt" from his New Salem years. Thanks to Lincoln's hard work and dedication to his law practice, he was finally gaining a degree of financial security for himself and his family.

By the time Lincoln and Mary began seriously contemplating his departure for Washington, Mary had grown tired of her husband's frequent absences from home and insisted that she and the boys accompany him to the capital to live during the eight-month legislative session. She remarked to a neighbor, James Gourley, that "if her husband had stayed home as he ought to she would love him more." Her loneliness inside the house occasionally turned to fear. One evening, before Eddy was born and while Lincoln was away, Mary frantically called out to Gourley and pleaded with him to come over to the house. She had earlier discovered that her young maid was sneaking men into the house to spend the night. "Come—do come and stay with me all night," Mary cried to Gourley, fearful of having strangers in the house. In general, Mary was an overanxious mother who had a tendency to overreact, and she often had difficulty coping with even small problems. Once when Robert was playing in the backyard, he got into the lime box next to the outhouse toilet and put some of the powdery substance in his mouth. Rather than taking immediate action herself, she screamed, "Robert will die! Robert will die!" until a neighbor came by and washed out the boy's mouth. The prospect of Lincoln being gone for many months in Washington was simply too much for her. Lincoln acceded to Mary's request, perhaps recognizing how little time he had actually spent with the boys over the past several months. Robert was four and Eddy, at nineteen months, was now walking and happily joining his older brother in trying Mary's patience. They needed to be together as a family.

To generate some income while they were away in Washington, the Lincolns decided to rent out their house to Cornelius Ludlum for $90 a year starting November 1. The lease expressly excepted the "North-upstairs room," where the couple stored their furniture. Before departing Springfield, the Lincolns each posed for a daguerreotype, the forerunner of modern photography, at the recently opened Daguerreotype Miniature Gallery near the courthouse square. Lincoln wore a black frock coat, silk vest, and a high-collar white shirt with a thick tie around the neck. His hair, usually in a tussle, was carefully parted and neatly slicked back. Mary wore a fancy dress with silk stripes, a lace shoulderette, and a cameo brooch. Lincoln looked distinguished, and Mary looked happy. Now they were ready to taste life in the nation's capital.

CHAPTER 3

Don't Let the Blessed Fellows
Forget Father

Since Congress would not convene until early December, Lincoln and Mary decided that the family would leave Springfield in late October in order to first visit Mary's family in Lexington before continuing the difficult trek to Washington. Lincoln had visited Lexington once before, in 1841, when he made a side trip there while staying at his friend Joshua Speed's house in Louisville. He was already known in the city because, after the election the previous year, the *Lexington Observer & Reporter*, a Whig organ, proudly announced that "the son-in-law of State Senator Robert S. Todd had been elected to Congress."

The family traveled first by stagecoach to St. Louis, where they met up with Speed. The October 28 issue of the local *Daily Era* newspaper, which printed the local hotel registers, reported the arrival of "A. Lincoln and family" and "Joshua F. Speed" at Scott's Hotel. From there, the family took a steamboat down the Mississippi to Cairo, then up the Ohio to the Kentucky River. They eventually landed at Frankfort, where they boarded a train to Lexington.

Also on the train was Joseph Humphreys, a nephew of Mary's stepmother Elizabeth Todd. Having never met before, the Lincolns and Humphreys made the entire train trip without meeting or realizing the family connection. When Humphreys, who was traveling alone and without luggage, arrived before the Lincolns at the Todd house, he reported the details of his journey to Mrs. Todd. "Aunt Betsy, I was never so glad to get off a train in my life. There were two lively youngsters on board who kept the whole train in a turmoil, and their long-legged father, instead of spanking the brats, looked pleased as Punch and aided and abetted the older one in mischief." As the Lincolns finally approached the Todd house, Humphreys looked out the window and, realizing who they were, exclaimed, "Good Lord, there they are now!" He quickly left the house and never returned while the Lincolns were there. Most parents have experienced the challenge of traveling long distances with young children, contending with unpredictable bouts of crying and screaming inside a tightly confined area and trying desperately to contain a child's natural tendency to wiggle and run about. Lincoln, already disinclined to punish the boys, and perhaps sensing the fun they were having on a mode of travel unavailable when he was their age, decided to join them in their antics rather than temper their amusement by reining them in, much to the chagrin of the other passengers.

After getting out of the carriage, the Lincolns walked joyously up the steps of the imposing redbrick mansion on Main Street where a crowd of Todds, most of whom had never met Lincoln before, waited to greet them inside. Mary held little Eddy and Lincoln carried Robert, while a cadre of servants unloaded their luggage from the carriage. Eleven-year-old Emilie Todd, Mary's stepsister, quietly watched the commotion unfold as the new arrivals entered the house. Wearing a full-length black coat and a fur cap with ear straps to protect his head from the winter cold, Lincoln entered the wide hallway and carefully set Robert down on the floor. Emilie was not sure what to make of the unusually tall Lincoln, who reminded her of the giant in the Jack and the Beanstalk fairy tale. She hid behind her mother until Lincoln turned, lifted her up, and said with a warm smile, "So this is little sister." She immediately took to her new relative, who had developed a disarming way of relating to children, both his own and those of others.

During their stay, Mary caught up on family gossip and Lincoln sat for hours in his father-in-law's large wood-paneled library exploring the vast collection of books that Mr. Todd had assembled. Lincoln's favorite book was *Elegant Extracts, or Useful and Entertaining Passages from the Best English Authors and Translations*. Using a lead pencil, he took the liberty of underlining several poems and passages that interested him. Meanwhile, Emilie took it upon herself to become Robert's playmate, and the two children noisily romped about the house. By now Lincoln was used to having children screaming and running about him, so he was able to focus on his reading while seeming totally oblivious to the antics of the children around him.

Three weeks after the family arrived at the Todd house, it was time to leave for Washington so that Lincoln could begin his work as a congressman. The first leg of the trip was by stagecoach to Winchester, Virginia. From there, the family of four took a train to Harpers Ferry, then another train to Relay Station, Maryland, then yet another train into Washington, where they finally arrived in the late evening of December 2. The entire trip from Lexington to the capital took about a week.

Immediately upon entering the city, the Lincolns took a room at Brown's Indian Queen Hotel. A few days later, they settled at a boarding house owned by Mrs. Ann G. Sprigg. Hardin and Baker had boarded there during their terms in Washington, and they recommended it to Lincoln. The house was in an ideal location for the couple. Sitting on a plot where the Library of Congress is now located, it was about twenty yards from Capitol Park, where Mary could take the boys to play, weather permitting. And, just as Lincoln could easily walk from home to his office in Springfield, he could leave the Sprigg house and be at the capitol building in less than five minutes. Though the location of the house was perfect for the Lincolns, the house itself was no match for their large home in Springfield and was even more crowded than the Globe Tavern, where they had lived until Robert was born. While six other congressmen (all Whigs) also roomed there, none brought their wives or children with them, making the Lincoln family seem oddly out of place. But Mrs. Sprigg's house was affordable and, most importantly, temporary, as the Congressional session was forecast to last only until midsummer.

Both Lincoln's work habits and his parenting methods changed little in Washington. Though he was home in bed every night, a welcome respite from riding the circuit that Mary undoubtedly appreciated, Lincoln worked long hours and often attended political and other meetings well into the evening. Just two days after arriving in the city, Lincoln left Mary with the boys and went out for a late evening of meetings with some fellow Whig legislators.

Soon after the Lincolns arrived in Washington, the first session of the Thirtieth Congress opened. Lincoln was active for a first-term congressman. Throughout his term, he missed only 13 out of 456 roll call votes. He served on several committees and spent a substantial amount of time answering correspondence and handling constituent requests. Lincoln was not afraid to take to the floor of the House chamber to make speeches, having gained confidence in public speaking from his time in the Illinois legislature and as an attorney in the courtroom. He spent considerable time mailing thousands of copies of his speeches to supporters at home and to other Whigs around the country. Samuel Busey, a physician and fellow boarder at Mrs. Sprigg's house, observed that Lincoln "attended to his business, going promptly to the House and remaining until the session adjourned, and appeared to be familiar with the progress of legislation." Lincoln enjoyed his work and was dedicated to doing a good job for the people who elected him.

Lincoln's commitment to his work kept him busy, and at times he felt torn between his work and his family. Lincoln later told Mary that "when you were here [in Washington] I thought you hindered me some in attending to business." Nevertheless, Lincoln made time to be with his family. When he took Robert on a tour of the Patent Office, the four-year-old boy was mesmerized by the model room gallery that displayed miniature replicas of various inventions. The tour was one of Robert's few memories of the family's stay in Washington while Lincoln was a Congressman. More than a decade later, when Robert was in Washington for his father's first inauguration, Robert would return to the Patent Office for another visit, as if to relive a happy childhood memory.

It was not just official business and politics, however, that kept Lincoln occupied. In his spare time he often dined and relaxed with fellow congressmen. He also participated in a bowling group that played games in an outdoor alley near the capitol. Washington offered Lincoln the same masculine culture that he found at home in Springfield and on the circuit, and he wholeheartedly embraced that culture, to some degree at the expense of time with his family.

Meanwhile, Mary tended to the boys and managed the domestic household. She opened accounts at several stores around town where she purchased items for herself and her sons. When Lincoln later discovered some unpaid accounts that Mary had run up, he gently chastised her. Mary's notoriously poor money-management skills caused Lincoln great distress throughout their marriage.

While the Lincolns seemed to get along well with Mrs. Sprigg, their failure to rein in the boys was noticed by those around them. Robert "was a bright boy," wrote fellow boarder Busey, but "he seemed to have his own way." Mary had several run-ins with other guests. Some of the conflicts undoubtedly resulted from the noise and frequent commotion that Robert and Eddy caused as they ran about the house. These conflicts must have been reminiscent of how tenants at the Globe Tavern back in Springfield had become frustrated by baby Robert's constant screaming and crying before the young family finally moved out. Other dustups probably had their roots in Mary's short temper and tendency to lash out. In a letter to Mary sent after she left Washington and took the boys back to Lexington, leaving her husband alone in the capital, Lincoln wrote candidly to his wife that "all the house—or rather, all with whom you were on decided good terms—send their love to you. The others say nothing."

Fewer than four months after settling in, and well before the projected end of the Congressional session, Mary and the boys left Washington and returned to Lexington, leaving Lincoln to room alone at Mrs. Sprigg's house. The precise reasons for her early departure are not known, but there are several possible explanations besides perhaps tiring of the constant run-ins with other guests at the house. With no family or close friends to help with the boys and Lincoln working long hours during the day and often late into the evening, Mary likely felt quite alone. Also, she may have grown tired of living in cramped quarters at the Sprigg house, and the thought of once again spending time at her father's comfortable mansion where she was waited on by a contingent of servants was simply too inviting. Finally, being married to a freshman congressman from a western state, she may not have been as readily accepted into the Washington social scene as she originally anticipated. At the time the Lincolns left for Washington, Lincoln's friend and fellow circuit rider David Davis wrote to his wife, "Mrs. L., I am told, accompanies her husband to Washington city next winter. She wishes to loom largely." Then a city of forty thousand residents, Washington boasted a heavy social calendar, but the best gatherings were usually limited to permanent residents and long-serving officials. Although President Polk invited the Lincolns and all other congressional families to New Year's Day festivities at the White House (then formally called the Executive Mansion), a more typical event for the Lincolns was their attendance at a performance of the Ethiopian Serenaders, a touring group of black-faced minstrels. The simple fact was that, despite Lincoln's status as a congressman, the more permanent Washington insider class considered the Lincolns very much outsiders and treated them accordingly.

The real significance of Mary and the boys leaving Lincoln alone in the capital, however, lies not in her reasons for returning to Lexington. Rather, Mary's departure was of lasting importance because it soon provided a revealing glimpse into both the Lincoln marriage and Lincoln's relationship with the boys. In the months immediately following Mary's departure from Washington, the Lincolns exchanged a series of letters that revealed a man who not only dearly missed his wife, but who also ached to see his young sons again. Had Mary not left her husband alone at Mrs. Sprigg's house, it is likely that the record would simply contain more stories from outside observers about rambunctious children and occasional outbursts of temper by their mother. Instead, the Lincolns left the more precious gift of firsthand accounts of their feelings toward each other and their children. These letters contain the first evidence from Lincoln's own hand of a growing emotional attachment between father and sons, as well as early indications that he was beginning to recognize that he often had competing obligations in career and family, and that to be successful at both sometimes required a difficult balancing act.

On April 16, just a few weeks after Mary left, Lincoln sat down and penned a letter to his wife. He was already missing his family and beginning to realize that his life outside of work made him a more complete person. "Having nothing but business—no variety—it has grown exceedingly tasteless to me," Lincoln wrote. "I hate to sit down and direct documents, and I hate to stay in this old room by myself." Mary had earlier written her husband telling him of Eddy's pronouncement that "father has gone Tapila." Lincoln reacted with typical parental amusement when a child mispronounces words as they learn to speak, in this case using the word "Tapila" instead of "capital." "Dear Eddy thinks father has 'gone tapila,'" Lincoln replied, probably with a gentle smile. He went on to explain that he had been unsuccessful in finding a particular pair of socks for Eddy that Mary had asked him to buy. "I went yesterday to hunt the little plaid stockings, as you wished," Lincoln began. "But I found that McKnight has quit business, and Allen has not a single pair of the description you give, and only one plaid pair of any sort that I thought would fit Eddy's little feet. I have a notion to make another trial tomorrow morning." There was Abraham Lincoln, the busy, traveling lawyer and congressman who, like many of his contemporaries, had ceded control of the domestic household to his wife so that he could focus on his career obligations, walking the streets of Washington alone in search of a pair of socks for his young son.

In his letter Lincoln next turned to Robert. He had earlier written to Mary about a dream he had involving something bad happening to Robert, but now his mind was more at ease: "I did not get rid of the impression of that foolish dream about dear Bobby till I got your letter written the same day." Then Lincoln asked, "What did [Bobby] and Eddy think of the little letters father sent them?" Regrettably, the "little letters" to which Lincoln referred have not survived, but the mere fact that Lincoln wrote them at all suggests a growing bond with the boys that he was both feeling and missing. Lincoln then pleaded with Mary to keep him forefront in the minds of the boys: "Don't let the blessed fellows forget father."

Mary replied to Lincoln's letter with a touching story about Eddy. Most parents have encountered a situation when their child either begs them to get a pet dog or cat or the child actually brings home a stray and then pleads with teary eyes for the creature to become part of the family. This dilemma often forces parents either to accede to their child's wishes against their own better judgment or to risk breaking their child's heart with disappointment. Fortunately for the Lincolns, their first pet encounter occurred at the Todd house in Lexington, where Mary's stepmother took responsibility for letting the boys down. "Our little Eddy has recovered from his sickness," Mary began her letter on a Saturday evening as the boys slept. "Dear boy, I must tell you a story about him, Bobby in his wanderings today, came across in a yard, a little kitten, your hobby, he says he asked a man for it, he brought it triumphantly to the house, so as soon as Eddy spied it—his tenderness broke forth, he made them bring it water, fed it with bread himself, with his own dear hands, he was a delighted little creature over it, in the midst of all his happiness Ma came in, she you must know dislikes the whole cat race, I thought in a very unfeeling manner, she ordered the servant near, to throw it out, which, of course, was done, Ed screaming and protesting loudly against the proceeding, she never appeared to mind his screams, which were long and loud, I assure you." Mary failed to intervene on behalf of Eddy and the cat, and she was likely relieved that her stepmother did the dirty work in disappointing the boys. At the end of the letter, Mary responded to Lincoln's earlier plea that the children remember him. "I must bid you good night," she closed. "Do not fear the children have forgotten you. . . . E[ddy's] eyes brighten at the mention of your name."

By mid-June, Mary had been gone for more than two months, the longest uninterrupted period of separation from her husband since their marriage. She told him in a letter that she was thinking of returning to Washington. Lincoln was excited. "I want to see you, and our dear—dear boys very much." Then, in what was at best an exaggeration and at worst an outright lie, Lincoln said, "Everybody here wants to see our dear Bobby." Lincoln ended the letter to Mary with an expression of love for the boys: "Father expected to see all you sooner; but let it pass; stay as long as you please and come when you please. Kiss and love the dear rascals." Mary did not come at that time. But a few weeks later, as Congress was nearing adjournment, Lincoln made plans to meet up with Mary and the boys for a family vacation in New England.

Lincoln's expression of emotion toward the boys in these letters is revealing. He was ambitious, liked his work, and logged long hours advancing his career, frequently at the expense of spending time with his family. After experiencing for the first time a long separation from Mary and the boys, however, Lincoln began to realize that conflicts between career and family could be quite real. As Stephen Frank noted in his work on nineteenth-century fatherhood, "ideals of masculine achievement were at odds with their desire to participate more fully in the emotional warmth they saw embodied in the lives of their wives and children." Absent fathers often expressed their feelings about their children in letters, with emotional outpourings that illustrated that "participation in the market economy opened a chasm between home and work." Just a few years before Lincoln traveled to Washington, Albert G. Browne, a busy and prosperous merchant from Massachusetts, wrote his wife while away on business that "more than a month has passed since I left you, my children, my friends. . . . Absent from you I know better how to appreciate my blessings." Lincoln's letters in the spring and summer of 1848 show similar feelings of longing for his wife and children as well as a growing realization that his family life needed to coexist with his career not only for the sake of Mary and the boys, but for his own sake as well. Yet Lincoln did not immediately change his ways. Indeed, several more years would pass before he began to meaningfully cut back on his travel in order to spend more time with his children.

Congress finally adjourned on August 14. Most congressmen immediately left for home in order to escape the oppressive summer heat and humidity of Washington. Lincoln, however, remained in town for about ten days working on campaign speeches that he planned to deliver in the Northeast on behalf of General Zachary Taylor, the Whig nominee for president. Lincoln had garnered the attention of prominent Whigs from around the country, particularly with his defiant challenge of President Polk's entry into war with Mexico, and he scheduled several speaking engagements at Whig rallies and conventions that would raise his political profile. With his longing for Mary and the boys still strong, Lincoln arranged for them to join him along the way. He had missed Robert's fifth birthday, which was the first time he failed to attend a birthday party for one of his sons.

Lincoln rendezvoused with Mary and the boys, probably in Massachusetts and probably sometime in September, just as he was gaining positive reviews from Whig newspapers that a year earlier had not heard of this obscure congressman from the west. The Lincolns eventually made their way into New York State, where they took in the magnificent sight of what Lincoln called the "mysterious power" of Niagara Falls. In an unfinished manuscript later found among his papers, Lincoln described the falls in a way that could have also described his own career at that time: "Never still for a single moment. Never dried, never froze, never slept, never rested."

By the first week in October, the Lincolns were in Chicago, having made the thousand-mile journey from Buffalo over the Great Lakes on the steamer *Globe*. The voyage was undoubtedly exciting for the boys, though it is likely that the Lincolns kept a close eye on them as they ran around the deck of the ship as it gently swayed up and down in the choppy waters. On October 6, Lincoln was the featured speaker at a Whig rally. The *Chicago Journal* reported that his two-hour speech was "one of the very best we have heard or read, since the opening of the campaign." The next day, the *Chicago Democrat* reported that "Hon. A. Lincoln and Family passed down to Springfield this morning on his way home from Congress." On October 10, two weeks shy of the anniversary of their departure for Washington, the Lincolns were finally home again in Springfield.

Since the lease of their house to Ludlum ran through November 1, the Lincolns were forced to find temporary lodgings until Ludlum vacated. Of all places, they once again chose to move into the Globe Tavern, which had been renovated and was under new management. Presumably, both Lincoln and Mary were satisfied with the updated accommodations, for they almost immediately decided to extend their stay at the Globe for a few months rather than move back to their own home. Since Lincoln would soon be leaving Springfield yet again to campaign for Taylor around Illinois, followed by a return trip to Washington for the second (but shorter) session of his congressional term, the Lincolns probably concluded that Mary would feel safer and more comfortable living around other people rather than being alone with the boys in her own house. Moreover, others would be responsible for keeping the fireplace going strong throughout the winter and cooking meals for her and the boys. Also, extending the lease on his house kept some extra income coming in.

Eleven days after returning to Springfield, Lincoln left for a week-long journey that included campaign speeches for Taylor and meetings with other lawyers on bar matters. After returning home for a few days, he left again for a week of campaigning as the election neared. On November 7, 1848, Taylor was elected president, though he failed to carry Illinois. Taylor's loss of Illinois was not surprising. Between 1828, when the Whigs fielded their first presidential candidate, and 1852, when they fielded their last, the Democratic nominee carried Illinois in every election, often by substantial margins. Nevertheless, Lincoln's efforts on behalf of Taylor did not go unnoticed by prominent Whigs throughout the country.

A month later, Lincoln was back in Washington to finish his term as the Thirtieth Congress convened for its second and final session. Lincoln had earlier decided not to seek reelection, honoring the Whig party's rotation program that started with the Pekin Agreement. Though Lincoln was personally popular and viewed as a workhorse within the Whig party, his position against war with Mexico was unpopular with many local Whigs. Thus, it is not certain whether Lincoln would have been renominated even if he wanted to run again. In any case, Lincoln chose to step aside in favor of his former law partner Stephen T. Logan, who went on to narrowly lose the seat to the Democratic nominee.

Congress finally adjourned on the morning of March 4, 1849, and Lincoln worked right up until the final vote. Now, Lincoln's brief term as a congressman was over. The next day, he watched Taylor deliver his inaugural address and take the oath of office. On March 7, he was admitted to practice before the United States Supreme Court, whereupon he immediately argued a case that had originated in Springfield before making its way up to the nation's highest court. The court, led by Chief Justice Roger Taney, later ruled against Lincoln's client. Taney would figure prominently in Lincoln's future. Less than a decade later, Taney wrote the pro-slavery majority opinion in the Dred Scott case, a ruling that infuriated Lincoln but gave him a tactical edge in subsequent debates with political opponent Stephen Douglas. A few years after that, Lincoln would take the presidential oath from an aging Taney. Then, during the Civil War, Taney ruled that Lincoln exceeded his constitutional authority as president when he suspended the writ of habeas corpus.

Lincoln remained in Washington for two weeks following Taylor's inauguration. During that time, he discussed patronage opportunities for Illinois Whigs with new members of the Taylor administration. Though out of office, Lincoln intended to remain a player in local politics. While his next successful political campaign would be for the presidency nearly twelve years later, Lincoln's prominence on the political stage was just beginning.

Between April 1848, when Mary and the boys left Washington, and April 1849, when Lincoln returned to Springfield after the end of his Congressional term, the Lincolns had been together as a family for less than eight weeks, and most of that time was spent on the New England trip and subsequent journey back to Springfield. Lincoln's service in Congress took a toll on his time with the boys. Now, however, they were back in their house at Eighth and Jackson. Feeling ever more confident about their finances, they further remodeled the house, installing stoves in the parlor rooms, building a retaining wall in front of the home, and replacing the wood on the front walkway with bricks.

As the construction was under way, Lincoln worked at his office, busily writing letters seeking appointments of various Whigs to federal offices. As the only Whig representing Illinois in the previous Congress, Lincoln felt that the Taylor administration should consult him and Baker on presidential appointments involving Illinoisans. Baker had recently been elected to a seat in Congress from a neighboring district, and now he was the only Whig in the Illinois delegation. When word reached Lincoln that Taylor was considering naming Justin Butterfield as a commissioner of the General Land Office, he was appalled. Butterfield had supported the aging Henry Clay over Taylor for the Whig presidential nomination. While Lincoln greatly admired Clay, he now saw the Great Compromiser as representing the older generation of Whigs and believed that new blood was necessary for the party to thrive. Moreover, Lincoln felt that Butterfield had failed to aggressively support Taylor in the general election. "That ought not to be," Lincoln complained to prominent Whig journalist Duff Green, who had boarded next door to Mrs. Sprigg's house and frequently dined there during Lincoln's tenure in Washington. "That is about the only crumb of patronage which Illinois expects," Lincoln lamented. In fact, Lincoln wanted the job for himself. With a return to Congress unlikely in the next election, Lincoln saw the appointment as his best route back to Washington. After discussing the position with Mary, she was supportive. The job paid $3,000 per year, more than his salary as a Congressman, and it offered the possibility of a four-year term, during which time Lincoln could make further connections in the capital. And, while the Lincolns would have to move again to Washington, the full-time nature of the office meant that they could get their own home there, avoiding the burdens of living with children at a boardinghouse.

With Mary's blessing, in mid-June Lincoln made a hasty trip to Washington to press his case. He was "armed with a half-bushel full of letters of recommendation." But it was too late. Thomas Ewing, the Secretary of the Interior, favored Butterfield, and he prevailed on Taylor to choose him over Lincoln. When Lincoln got word of the decision at his hotel room, he lay quietly on his bed for more than an hour, "his big feet sticking over the footboard," and then sighed to his roommate, "Well, I reckon the people will find some use to put me to yet." Lincoln later claimed that he never really wanted the Land Office job for himself, but rather sought the appointment as a matter of party patronage to demonstrate to those Whigs whom he felt represented the future of the party that their continued involvement would eventually be rewarded.

The Taylor administration soon presented Lincoln with a different but significant opportunity in government, but it was a position that, if he accepted, would take the family far away from Illinois and in the opposite direction of Washington. A few months after Lincoln lost out on the appointment as a commissioner to the General Land Office, Secretary Ewing realized that he had offended Lincoln, who was one of the most hardworking and reliable Whigs in Illinois. In an attempt to make amends, he offered Lincoln the governorship of the Oregon Territory. Oregon was headed for statehood, and the governorship was a natural steppingstone to a possible United States Senate seat, which would return Lincoln to Washington in a position of prominence. According to William Herndon, Lincoln's law partner, "when he brought the proposition home to his fireside, his wife put her foot squarely down

on it with a firm and emphatic 'No.' That always ended it with Lincoln."
Herndon never liked Mary, and the feeling was mutual. Accordingly, in
scrutinizing Herndon's voluminous writings about Lincoln, care must be
taken when considering his critical comments about Lincoln's wife. Nevertheless, in this instance, it is not difficult to imagine Mary's determined
opposition to uprooting the family to move to the far western frontier,
two thousand miles away from her cozy home in Springfield. Moreover,
Eddy continued to experience bouts of sickness, and Mary undoubtedly
worried about how his health would fare in the unfamiliar and uninviting
environment.

Lincoln had his own reasons to hesitate at the appointment. Oregon
was heavily Democratic, and the chances of him succeeding there as a
Whig were remote. He was already well known in Whig politics in Illinois and somewhat known to active Whigs on the East Coast. Though
at times he thought his political career was over, Lincoln knew that he
could continue to be influential within the party apparatus. Most importantly, however, he liked his law practice, which was now providing
financial security. In fact, he turned down an offer to join a law firm in
Chicago, preferring his Springfield practice and riding the circuit to having to, in his words, "sit down & die in Chicago."

Though Mary and the boys would certainly have moved to Oregon
with Lincoln, they likely would have made occasional trips back to
Springfield and Lexington. This meant separations both longer in time
and greater in distance than the one that Lincoln so lamented while he
was in Washington and Mary was in Lexington. Also, Mary's father
had died suddenly in July at age fifty-eight, devastating her and leaving
Lincoln as the only close male figure in her life. Mary needed her husband more than ever. Thus, she may indeed have put her foot down over
the Oregon governorship opportunity as Hendon later described. But
Lincoln also knew that the move and periodic separations would have
created severe hardships on his family.

In the end, he declined the appointment. Lincoln wanted to continue
his career in politics and in law, but he had a family, too. He needed to
nurture both. "I respectfully decline Governorship of Oregon," Lincoln
said in a telegraph to Ewing, without offering any explanation for his

decision. He had his reasons, though. Lincoln told his friend Anson Henry that his reasons for declining the Oregon governorship were "private ones." Indeed they were. In the span of just six years, Lincoln had gone from being a committed bachelor who was socially awkward around women, to being a married man and doting father of two young boys whom he adored and who in turn adored him. He ultimately chose to put his family first and thus determined that he would simply need to find another path to advance his political career.

CHAPTER 4

Of Such Is the Kingdom of Heaven

THE LOSS OF A CHILD IS EVERY PARENT'S WORST NIGHTMARE. AFTER months or years of nurturing, teaching, laughing, crying, hoping, and praying, there is suddenly a vast and painful emptiness. The bereaved parents are forced to cope with the insufferable truth that, here on earth, they will never see their child again, never hear him laugh, never see him smile, never hear his voice, never watch him sleep, never share his dreams, never witness him grow and learn and flourish. A profound sense of helplessness descends upon them, and no words of condolence or acceptance of warm embraces from family and friends can fill the enormous void that now rests deep inside the body and soul. In their grief, the parents sometimes turn to God, sometimes turn away from God, and sometimes do a little of both. All the while, they face the daunting reality that their own lives must somehow, some way, go on. There may be other children to raise, and there is work to be done and lives to live.

In early 1850, Abraham and Mary Lincoln experienced such a loss. They responded to that loss in a manner typical of both nineteenth-century parents and modern parents: they were heartbroken, devastated. Standing at the dawn of the twenty-first century looking back, if there was anything extraordinary about the way the Lincolns and other nineteenth-century parents dealt with those tragedies, it is that so many of them both deeply felt their grief and candidly expressed their suffering despite some long-established cultural, religious, and social pressures not to do so. Due in part to high infant mortality rates, particularly during the colonial period, parents were often taught and encouraged to refrain from forming strong emotional attachments to their infant children that would lead to "loving a child too well." This way of thinking promoted a defense mechanism designed to lessen a parent's sorrow in the event of the child's premature death. Moreover, religious teachings counseled parents to quietly accept the loss of a child as God's will. "We should find it difficult to part with our little Boy who is just Seven months old," wrote Chicago merchant Thomas Carter in 1842. "But we do not know how Soon we may be obligated to part with him. And it is our duty to be ready for any event, and not complain at any of the dealings of a Kind & merciful Providence. It is well for us to feel that 'all things work together for good to them that love God.'" Two decades earlier, New York businessman George Borrowe wrote of the death of his baby son, "We endeavor to bear the affliction with resignation to [God's] will; but it has been the most trying period of our lives."

Despite outside pressures to develop defense mechanisms to lessen their sorrow and mute their grief upon a child's death, nineteenth-century parents, including the Lincolns, increasingly rejected these colonial-era cultural pressures and let their natural feelings dictate their behavior. Shortly after the death of his seventeen-month-old daughter Fanny in 1848, Henry Wadsworth Longfellow wrote, "I feel very sad today. I miss very much my dear little Fanny. An inappeasable longing to see her comes over me at times, which I can hardly control." As sociologist Shawn Johansen noted, "the expression of emotions at the time of death and sickness increased and intensified as the nineteenth century progressed. The rise in strong and impassioned laments, the dread of death anniversaries, the remembrance through cemetery monuments, the idealization of the dead, and other manifestations of this trend indicate that middle-class nineteenth-century Americans were changing their view of death."

At the time Lincoln declined the Oregon governorship in late September 1849, he was out riding the circuit, practicing the profession that he loved so much. He returned home shortly thereafter for a few days before leaving again, this time traveling to Bloomington and Mount Pulaski to try some cases before heading home as the circuit season drew to a close. Sometime after October 18, the Lincolns left for Lexington.

Mary and her siblings needed Lincoln to handle some litigation involving their late father's estate. The request for help from the Todd family had arrived some weeks earlier, but the Lincolns waited to depart until a massive cholera epidemic that claimed lives from Indiana to New Orleans had safely abated. That epidemic struck Lexington with a vengeance, and not only killed Mary's father the previous July, but also felled many physicians in the area and hundreds of other city residents.

Robert was now six and Eddy nearly four. Though Eddy had suffered frequent bouts of sickness since birth, he was now well and ready for the trip. The entire family was looking forward to spending a few weeks with the Todds, though it would be a working vacation for Lincoln. Like their journey to Lexington two years earlier, the trip itself was full of fun and amusement for the family. While steaming down the Mississippi, one of the passengers was caught playing various pranks on other travelers. In good fun, the victims arranged for a mock arrest and trial of the perpetrator, with Lincoln acting as the judge. The verdict rendered and any corresponding sentence imposed by Lincoln has been lost to history, but the entire Lincoln family undoubtedly enjoyed the theatrics of the event.

After changing boats at Cairo, the Lincolns steamed up the Ohio. Along the way, their boat challenged another northbound steamer to a friendly race. Just when Lincoln's boat had established a commanding lead, it began to run short of fuel. The pilot quickly hitched to a nearby flatboat loaded with wood, and Lincoln immediately took charge. "Come on, boys," he yelled, as he jumped down and began pitching wood up to the deck as Robert and Eddy shouted encouragement. It was too late. The other boat steamed by with its passengers cheering their victory and laughing at their vanquished opponents. The race, undertaken in the spirit of fun, broke up the monotony of the long voyage.

After arriving by train in Lexington, the Lincolns traveled to Buena Vista, the Todd family's summer house on the Leestown Pike, about eighteen miles outside of the city. This time they decided to stay at Buena Vista rather than the stately brick mansion on Main Street where they had resided during their last trip. Buena Vista was a "tall, rambling, frame house, surrounded by large locust trees, situated on a beautiful knoll." Views from either of the two porticos were magnificent. A tiny brook meandered nearby, bordered by hemp fields. Lincoln commuted daily by buggy into town to tend to his legal work, while Mary and the boys stayed in the country, enjoying the fresh autumn air. There was plenty of room for the boys to play, and one cousin recalled how Robert "scampered about on ponies, slid down the ice-house roof and romped with the dogs."

Mary's family immediately noticed a pleasant change in Lincoln's appearance. Two years earlier, when Congressman-elect Lincoln visited the Todds on his way to Washington, he was awkward in dress, at least compared to lawyers in Lexington. Now, after having served his term in Washington and having gained confidence as his law practice became ever more successful, Lincoln upgraded his wardrobe, most likely with Mary's assistance. As Mary's cousin Dr. A.T. Parker recalled, "wearing a black frock coat and pantaloons of broadcloth, satin vest and black cravat of the choker style and a tall moleskin hat, with a short, circular blue cloak, the Springfield lawyer did not suffer in comparison with the best dressed members of the Lexington bar."

After tending to the Todd legal matters, Lincoln and his family returned to Springfield on November 15, having been away from home for nearly a month. He immediately went back to work at his office to catch up on both legal and political matters that had accumulated while he was gone. The fall circuit term was already over, so for the next four months he would mostly be home in Springfield. Everything seemed to be going well for him. He had finally paid off his "national debt." His law practice was thriving. Mary had made a comfortable home, and his two boys were at ages where their boundless energy allowed them to walk and talk and play for hours on end.

Then, on December 11, Eddy fell ill. It was nothing new, for he seemed to have been born with a weak immune system and thus experienced frequent bouts of illness nearly all of his life. He always soon recovered, however, and was then able to keep up with his older brother as they wreaked havoc among those around them. Though always concerned about Eddy's health, the Lincolns did not see him as an invalid and never hesitated to take him on their long and difficult journeys to Lexington and Washington. As a result of those trips, including the side trip to New England, the well-traveled Eddy was away from Springfield for just over a quarter of his life.

All children, of course, get sick from time to time. Over the years the Lincolns were frequent customers of the Corneau & Diller drugstore in Springfield. There they purchased a variety of nostrums designed to treat various ailments, including "Castor Oil," "Calomel," "Ox Marrow," "Cough Candy," "Syrup Ipecac," and even "Vermifuge," which was used to treat worms. This time, however, nothing was working for Eddy. His symptoms included high fever, severe coughing, chills, and exhaustion. The family summoned Dr. William Wallace, Mary's brother-in-law, who wrote prescriptions for what he thought was diphtheria. But diphtheria typically passed in two to three weeks, and well after that time frame Eddy was still not getting better. To alleviate Eddy's cough, Mary applied to Eddy's chest, at Wallace's recommendation, Winston's Balsam of Wildcherry, a patent medicine containing cough-suppressing opium.

In early January, Lincoln was spending more and more time at Eddy's bedside and around the house. The increasingly cold winter weather required him to constantly keep the fireplaces burning. He left Herndon, who had by then blossomed into a very capable lawyer, alone at the office to handle the bulk of the work. For the entire month of January, Lincoln's work schedule included just three days of argument before the Illinois Supreme Court and writing a few letters on political matters. Mostly, though, he was at home. "Mr. Lincoln was always very solicitous when his boys were sick," a Springfield doctor once observed. "His sympathy was almost motherly."

As Eddy's condition worsened, Mary received some painful news. On January 21, her maternal grandmother, Elizabeth Porter Parker, died in Lexington. The elderly Mrs. Parker, who had been a widow for fifty years, was in feeble health when the Lincolns visited her a few months earlier and finally died at her home on a chilly Monday night. The strain on Mary was unbearable. Within the last six months, she had lost both her father and grandmother, and now her beloved Eddy was seriously ill. Those around her began to notice that "when engaged in thought, [she was] pulling out one hair at a time from her head."

Then, at 6:00 a.m. on February 1, fifty-two days after he first fell ill, Eddy Lincoln died in his bed at the house at Eighth and Jackson. He was thirty-seven days shy of his fourth birthday. The eyes that brightened at the mention of Lincoln's name were now closed forever. Grappling to understand Eddy's death themselves, the Lincolns had the unenviable task of having to somehow explain it to six-year-old Robert. Ruth Painter Randall later wrote about Robert's memory of "the strangeness of the day. Rain pattered on the roof of the cottage, inside the rooms were darkened, kind neighbors came to help make arrangements, speaking in hushed voices, and . . . the sound of his mother's uncontrollable weeping. . . . His father's face was haggard and filled with deep lines. People sat up all night beside the form of [Eddy's body] that was so strangely still."

Though originally diagnosed by Dr. Wallace as diphtheria, the cause of death was likely pulmonary tuberculosis, then known as consumption. It was an illness that had no known effective treatment at the time and in fact was a leading cause of death in America, with half its victims being under the age of five. Its course was dreadful, with symptoms that included high fever, chronic coughing, and exhaustion, together with substantial weight loss that made it appear that the body was wasting away or being "consumed." Eddy's congenitally weak immune system, which had allowed so many other episodes of illness to develop, simply could not overcome this debilitating ailment.

Within hours after Eddy died, word had traveled around Springfield about the tragic loss. Though raised a Presbyterian, Mary had been attending the local Episcopal Church with her sister and brother-in-law since she moved to Springfield years before marrying Lincoln. The pastor of that church, Dr. Charles Dresser, who had married the Lincolns and sold them their house, was out of town when Eddy died. Dr. James Smith, pastor of the local First Presbyterian Church, heard the news of Eddy's death from a lady in town and rushed to comfort the Lincolns. Although Mary's uncle, John Todd, had helped found First Presbyterian in the 1830s, Dr. Smith had been in Springfield less than a year and had only a "general acquaintance" with the Lincolns. Dr. Smith's visit with the grieving parents that day, however, "resulted in great intimacy and friendship between them," and they asked him to speak at the funeral, which was to be held in the parlor of the Lincoln home at 11:00 the next morning.

As the somber funeral got under way, friends and neighbors, as well as those members of Mary's family who resided in Springfield, packed into the small parlor room at the front left of the house where Eddy lay peacefully in a small wooden casket. Noticeably absent were Lincoln's father and stepmother. Even if Lincoln had notified them immediately upon Eddy's death, they could not have made the three-day trip from Coles County, Illinois, in time to attend the service. But, as evidence of Lincoln's emotional distance from his father, more than three weeks elapsed before Lincoln advised them of Eddy's passing. Even then, he did so only indirectly through a letter to his stepbrother, John D. Johnston, without any special request to inform Thomas about the death of his grandson. Though still deeply in mourning over Eddy's death, Lincoln was almost casual in breaking the news. At the end of a letter rather than the beginning, Lincoln wrote Johnston: "I suppose you had not learned that we lost our little boy. He was sick fifty-two days & died that morning of the first day of this month." Then, without even mentioning Eddy's name, he added, "It was not our first, but our second child."

Following the funeral service at the Lincoln home, the stream of mourners quietly filed out of the house and into the bitter cold, where they slowly made their way to Hutchinson's Cemetery about twelve blocks away. Several men had earlier used pickaxes and shovels to break the frozen ground and dig a small grave at Lot No. 490. As the gathering of people stood in a circle around the casket, Dr. Smith, a large Scotsman known for his temperance, spoke with an accent from his native land as he offered the traditional burial reading from the Book of Common Prayer:

> *Man, that is born of woman hath but a short time to live, and is full of misery. He cometh up, and is cut down like a flower; he fleeth as it were a shadow, and never continueth in one stay. In the midst of life we are in death: of whom may we seek for succor, but of thee, O Lord, who our sins are justly displeased? Yet, O Lord God most holy, O Lord most mighty, O holy and most merciful Saviour, deliver us*

not into the bitter pains of eternal death. Thou knowest, Lord, the secrets of our hearts; shut not thy merciful ears to our prayer; but spare us, Lord most holy, O God most mighty, O holy and merciful Saviour, thou most worthy judge eternal, suffer us not, at our last hour, for any pains of death, to fall from thee. For as much as it hath pleased Almighty God of his great mercy to take unto himself the soul of our dear brother here departed, we therefore commit his body to the ground; earth to earth, ashes to ashes, dust to dust; in sure and certain hope of the Resurrection to eternal life, through our Lord Jesus Christ; who shall change our vile body, that it may be like unto his glorious body, according to the mighty working, whereby he is able to subdue all things to himself.

Eddy's tiny casket was then lowered into the ground. At the end of the burial service, the Lincolns stayed behind for a few minutes after the others left the cemetery. When Lincoln finally returned to his home, where some of Mary's family had already congregated again, he "came into the room and picked up a card which lay on the table. It was the last prescription written by the doctor for the child. He looked at it—then threw it from him and bursting into tears left the room." He would later tell his friend and fellow lawyer Oscar Harmon of Danville, in whose home Lincoln often stayed while riding the circuit, that if he "had twenty children he would never cease to sorrow for that one." Lincoln was grieving. Mary was, too. While Lincoln could turn to his work to distract him from his grief, however, Mary had no such outlet. For the next several weeks, Mary "lay prostrate, turning away from food urged upon her." Though Mary was a Christian and attended church regularly, she, like many other nineteenth-century parents, rejected the teaching that Eddy's death should be seen as a positive part of God's greater plan. Two years after Eddy died, she confessed to a friend, "I grieve to say that even at this distant day, I do not feel sufficiently submissive to our loss."

Five days after Eddy's funeral, as the bitter winter in Springfield continued unabated, a twenty-four-line poem appeared in the *Illinois Daily Journal* newspaper. It was submitted "By Request," with no name attached.

Little Eddie

Those midnight stars are sadly dimmed,
That late so brilliantly shone,
And the crimson tinge from cheek and lip,
With the heart's warm life had flown—
The angel death was hovering nigh,
And the lovely boy was called to die.

The silken waves of his glossy hair
Lie still over his marble brow,
And the pallid lip and pearly cheek
The presence of Death avow.
Pure little bud in kindness given,
In mercy taken to bloom in heaven.

Happier far is the angel child
With the harp and the crown of gold,
Who warbles now at the Saviour's feet
The glories to us untold.

Eddie, sweet blossom of heavenly love,
Dwells in the spirit-world above.

Angel boy—fare thee well, farewell
Sweet Eddie, we bid thee adieu!
Affection's wail cannot reach thee now,
Deep though it be, and true.
Bright is the home to him now given,
For "of such is the kingdom of Heaven."

For years, the question of who wrote and submitted the poem for publication has been one of the great unsolved mysteries among Lincoln historians. The absence of any draft written in Lincoln's own hand or of his contemporary or subsequent acknowledgment of authorship caused many to stop short of declaring him the author. One historian flatly declared that Mary was the author, perhaps with help from her husband, while others have suggested that some friend or family member may have penned the poem.

The evidence that Lincoln could have been the author was certainly compelling. Lincoln enjoyed reading poetry and that by the time of Eddy's death he had already written some poetry of his own. It is therefore not surprising that he might have used poetry to express his grief in the wake of this profound personal loss. Indeed, Lincoln advocated "the importance of learning, early in life, sentiments expressed in verse," particularly verses contained in the Bible. A young boy from Springfield whom Lincoln had befriended recalled that "he said that as a man grows older lines which he learned because of their pleasant sound come to have a meaning; just as old saws show their truth later in life. 'It is a pleasure,' he said, 'to be able to quote lines to fit any occasion,' and he noted that the Bible is the richest source of pertinent quotations." Orville Browning, one of Lincoln's closest friends, once recalled an episode when he visited Lincoln in the White House "and found him in a spell of deep melancholy. . . . After talking to me awhile about his sources of domestic sadness, he sent one of the boys to get a volume of Hood's poems. It was brought to him and he read to me several of those sad pathetic pieces—I suppose because they were accurate pictures of his own experiences and feelings. Between his reading and our talking, I gradually got him into a more comfortable frame of mind, and by [the] time I left him, he seemed quite cheerful and happy again."

The tenor of "Little Eddie" is similar to that of William Knox's "Oh, Why Should the Spirit of Mortal Be Proud," a favorite of Lincoln's. While the rhyme scheme of "Little Eddie" (abcbdd) differed from Lincoln's earlier poems, including "My Childhood Home I See Again" (abab), as a novice poet Lincoln would probably not haven been concerned about developing a consistent style, particularly if he was writing it in the days following his son's death. Some have suggested that references in the poem to heaven and the "Saviour" would have been out of character for a man who seemed to eschew matters of religion. Yet Lincoln's aversion to spiritual matters related primarily to organized religion, not necessarily the fundamental principles of Christianity. Moreover, as will be seen, Eddy's death marked the beginning of Lincoln's movement toward a greater religious faith, so it would have been plausible that the poem represented his first effort to express that faith in a meaningful way, having listened carefully to the comforting words of Dr. Smith. It is also worth noting that Lincoln spent time at his office in the days immediately following Eddy's death. This gave him the opportunity to have some quiet time away from Mary and Robert that would have allowed him to concentrate on such a literary undertaking. Lincoln's presence there is noteworthy, for it was in his office that he did most of his writing and thinking. It is therefore rather easy to imagine him sitting in his office, surrounded by books and papers, quietly writing a final tribute to his little boy, then walking it down the street to deliver it to the local newspaper with a request that it be published. It would have been a quiet way for Lincoln to both express and share his grief.

While Mary, like her husband, enjoyed reading poetry, there is no evidence that she ever wrote a poem of her own, and it is highly unlikely that her first effort would have been undertaken during that very trying time in her life. She was in a state of utter devastation for weeks after Eddy's death, crying uncontrollably and refusing to eat. Thus, while Lincoln went back to work a couple of days after Eddy's death, Mary was largely inconsolable in the days immediately following Eddy's passing. It seems quite unlikely, therefore, that she would have been able to sit down and concentrate long enough to write a poem. The eminent historian Jean H. Baker, who wrote one of the most important biographies of Mary, argued that Mary was indeed the author of the poem. Baker based her conclusion largely on her view that the language of the poem was infused with a strong sense of maternity in both its feminine lexicon and motherly endearments (such as referring to Eddy as "pure little bud," "angel child," and "angel boy"). But such phrases were not exclusively in the province of the female vocabulary at the time. Lincoln himself often referred to his late mother as "angel mother," and he previously used terms of endearment to refer to the boys, such as "my dear, dear boys" and the "blessed fellows." Baker allowed the possibility that the poem could have been a joint effort between Lincoln and Mary. Given Mary's severe state of mourning at that time, however, it seems somewhat improbable that Mary would have collaborated with Lincoln to write a poem in the days following Eddy's death.

In 2012, Samuel Wheeler, a research historian at the Abraham Lincoln Presidential Library and Museum, published an article concluding that "Little Eddie" was written by the poet Mary E. Chamberlin under the pseudonym Ethel Grey. Wheeler argued that Grey wrote the poem (with the title "Eddie") in 1849, a year before Eddy's death, and that it was published soon thereafter in a St. Louis newspaper, though evidence of such publication has not yet been found. The poem, with some slight variations, was then included in Grey's first book of poems titled *Sunset Gleams from the City of the Mounds*, published in 1852. Wheeler asserted that Grey did not know the Lincolns and that the poem was not in any way about Eddy Lincoln, who died a year after "Eddie" was supposedly first written in 1849. According to Wheeler, Grey intended it as a more general poem about the loss of a child. *Sunset Gleams* contained many other poems about children and death. Wheeler's research and analysis is convincing, though it would have been completely irrefutable had he been able to find evidence of the St. Louis publication prior to Eddy's death. Nevertheless, with publication of the poem in Grey's book in 1852, two years after Eddy's death, in order to conclude that the poem originated in Springfield in the days following Eddy's death, one would have to believe that Grey, who had no connection to that city or to the Lincolns, plagiarized the poem from Lincoln, Mary, or another local author. Although *Sunset Gleams* was Grey's first book, given that Grey went on to become a widely published poet and fiction writer, that belief seems farfetched. It is also worth noting that if Grey rather than Lincoln indeed wrote the poem, her authorship helps explain why the name in the title was spelled "Eddie." In all of Lincoln's letters, he spelled his son's name "Eddy," but the newspaper that printed the poem spelled it "Eddie."

In any case, assuming Wheeler is correct as to Grey's authorship, the mystery still remains as to who requested that the poem be published in the local Springfield newspaper following Eddy's death. Wheeler speculates, probably correctly, that someone in Springfield—perhaps Lincoln, perhaps *Illinois Daily Journal* editor Simeon Francis, or perhaps a family friend of the Lincolns—had seen and remembered the poem in the still unknown St. Louis publication and decided to have it reprinted after Eddy's funeral in order to provide some comfort to the Lincoln family.

Several weeks after Eddy was buried, the Lincolns purchased a tombstone for his grave at Hutchison's Cemetery. The white marble slab, which was twenty-four inches wide by forty-eight inches high and two inches thick, was engraved as follows:

EDWARD B.
Son of
A. & M. LINCOLN
DIED
Feb. 1, 1850.
Age
3 years 10 months 18 days.
Of such is the kingdom of Heaven

Authorship aside, the poem had an impact on the Lincolns. The final line of Eddy's tombstone—"Of such is the kingdom of Heaven"—was also the final line of the poem. Those words are a slight variation of a portion of the Gospel of Mark in the New Testament, which reads in part, "Suffer the children to come unto me, and forbid them not: for such is the kingdom of God."

The tombstone also reveals the depth of the loss that the Lincolns were feeling. In specifying Eddy's age right down to the day (three years, ten months, and eighteen days), the Lincolns chose not to simply state his age in a whole number or leave it for the reader of the tombstone to calculate Eddy's age by giving the dates of both his birth and death. Rather, the Lincolns precisely counted the years, months, and days that Eddy lived, as if to proclaim that every single one of those days was a precious gift to the parents who loved him so dearly. In doing so, the Lincolns were ahead of their time. In the nineteenth century, the tombstone was seen merely as "a marker of the border of mortality." It was intended to be informational rather than memorial in nature. After observing various tombstones on a stroll through an old cemetery, essayist Joseph Addison wrote that "most of them recorded nothing else of the buried person, but that he was born upon one day, and died upon another; the whole history of his life being comprehended in those two circumstances that are common to all mankind. I could not but look upon those registers of existence, whether of brass or marble, as a kind of satire upon the departed persons; who had left no other memorial of them, but that they were born, and that they died." In later commenting on Addison's observations, Ruth Moore correctly pointed out that "such an inscription is not at all a satire on the departed person, but upon his relatives or friends who had not wit enough to place a better epitaph upon his tomb." By the twentieth century, however, tombstones were considered the "last physical evidence of the dead and the literal picture of the survivors' emotions." In counting the treasured days that they spent with Eddy and offering a biblical phrase that connected Eddy to both heaven and the poem that they either wrote or accepted as a gift, the Lincolns rejected the contemporary usage of tombstones and offered Eddy's marker as a means of conveying their emotions in a manner more typical of twentieth-century memorials: it was a testimonial to their grief.

In the days after the funeral, Lincoln became increasingly concerned about Mary's refusal to take food. "Eat Mary, for we must live," he implored his wife. Unlike Lincoln, Mary had no outlet to which she was able to divert her grief. She could only stay home, where every time she looked at Robert she was reminded of Eddy. Lincoln, however, had his work, and an office where he could go to escape from the constant reminders of his loss. Though devastated by Eddy's death, Lincoln knew that somehow, some way, life must go on. He had a family to support, and as the senior partner in his firm, he needed to manage his law practice and tend to the needs of his clients.

Just seventy-two hours after Eddy was laid to rest, Lincoln was back at work. He spent two days arguing a case before the Illinois Supreme Court, which he eventually lost. Within days after that, he was once again in the thick of Whig politics, lobbying for the appointment of a friend as a United States Marshal. For the next several weeks, Lincoln kept a busy schedule, but he was still mourning Eddy. "We miss him very much," Lincoln wrote his stepbrother, John D. Johnston. Years later, when he became president and received almost daily reports of young soldiers being killed in battle during the Civil War, Lincoln could sympathize with what the parents of the fallen men were going through.

In the aftermath of Eddy's death, Lincoln's faith began to strengthen, though it would take many years and the death of a second son for it to reach a greater maturity. Lincoln's father, Thomas, could never interest his son in religion, and Mary rarely prevailed on him to attend Sunday services with her. During his campaign for Congress, rumors circulated that Lincoln was not a Christian, a fact that, if true, would likely have been fatal to his prospects of winning the election. Lincoln rebutted the rumors with a handbill that read in part, "A charge having gotten into circulation . . . in substance that I am an open scoffer at Christianity, I have by the advice of some friends concluded to notice the subject in this form. That I am not a member of any Christian Church, is true; but I have never denied the truth of the Scriptures; and I have never spoken with intentional disrespect of religion in general, or of any denomination of Christians in particular." Lincoln was simply ambivalent in matters of faith, neither denying nor embracing the basic tenets of Christianity. Put another way, if his faith at the time of Eddy's death existed at all, it was weak at best. Dr. Smith found Lincoln "very much depressed and downcast at the death of his son, and without the consolation of the gospel."

But the loss of his son would soon have an impact. In the months and years following Eddy's death, Lincoln invoked God's name more frequently in his letters and speeches and began to read the Bible more regularly. That Lincoln believed in God and looked to God for strength is without question. What is debatable is whether Eddy's death prompted Lincoln to expressly accept Christianity. Up to that time, Lincoln had a general reservation about joining a particular church that required adherence to its own set of man-made doctrines and had difficulty separating his instinctive lawyerly desire for argument and proof from the more amorphous notion of accepting scripture teachings based almost exclusively on having faith in their essential truth. "I have never united myself to any church," Lincoln wrote, "because I have found difficulty in giving my assent, without mental reservation, to the long, complicated statements of Christian doctrine which characterize their articles of belief and confessions of faith. When any church will inscribe over its altars, as its sole qualification for membership, the Saviour's condensed statement of the substance of both law and gospel, 'Thou shalt love the Lord thy God with all thy heart, and with all thy soul, and with all thy mind, and thy neighbor as thyself,' that church will I join with all my heart and my soul." Lincoln never found such a church. Although in the coming years he increasingly attended Sunday services, he never became a member of any church. He was not alone in his aversion to formal church membership, however. In Lincoln's time, only about one in four Americans actually joined a particular church, though many more attended services regularly.

Many early Lincoln contemporaries and biographers, alarmed at the absence of any speech or writing from Lincoln in which he expressly accepted Christianity, sought to affirm that Lincoln was a committed Christian. As one story goes, rather than merely accepting Christianity as a matter of faith, Lincoln resorted to his lawyerly penchant for examining the relative merits of conflicting arguments, relying on a book titled *The Christian's Defence, Containing a Fair Statement, and Impartial Examination of the Leading Objections Urged by Infidels Against the Antiquity, Genuineness, Credibility, and Inspiration of the Holy Scripture*, written by Dr. Smith, the man who officiated at Eddy's funeral and who had offered Lincoln "loving and sympathetic ministrations." The book, first published in Cincinnati in 1843, seemed perfectly suited for Lincoln's analytical mind, as it presented "arguments for and against the divine authority and inspiration of the Holy Scriptures." It was a product of a series of debates between Dr. Smith and Charles G. Olmsted held in Columbia, Mississippi, in the spring of 1841. Containing more than six hundred pages, *The Christian Defence* drew on a standard legal work, Starkie's *A Practical Treatise on the Law of Evidence*, in analyzing various arguments.

Smith described Lincoln's views on religious matters before reading the book. "I found him an honest and anxious inquirer. He gradually revealed the state of his mind and heart, and at last unbosomed his doubts and struggles and unrest of soul. In frequent conversations I found that he was perplexed and unsettled on the fundamentals of religion, by speculative difficulties, connected with Providence and revelation, which lie beyond and above the legitimate province of religion. I placed in his hands my book."

For several weeks, according to Dr. Smith, Lincoln studied *The Christian Defence* and, being the lawyer that he was, "examined and weighed the evidence, pro and con, and judged the credibility of the contents of revelation. The result," Dr. Smith, continued, "was the announcement by [Lincoln] that the divine authority and inspiration of the Scriptures was unanswerable." Lincoln's brother-in-law, Ninian Edwards, confirmed Lincoln's conversion of faith. "Mr. Lincoln said to me, 'I have been reading a work of Dr. Smith on the evidences of Christianity, and have heard him preach and converse on the subject, and I am now convinced on the truth of the Christian religion.'"

Whether Lincoln actually professed his firm belief in Christianity at that time remains in doubt. Robert remembers Lincoln keeping *The Christian Defence* in a bookcase at the house at Eighth and Jackson, and described Dr. Smith as "a very close friend of my father's," a friendship that clearly blossomed only after Eddy's death. Nevertheless, Robert also wrote to William Herndon shortly after Lincoln's death, "I do not know of Dr. Smith's having 'converted' my father from 'Unitarian' to 'Trinitarian' belief, nor do I know that he held any decided views on the subject as I never heard him speak of it." Even Mary said, after her husband's death, that "he was not a technical Christian."

The record from Lincoln's own hand tends to support Robert and Mary. In all of his surviving letters and speeches, Lincoln often mentioned God in such a way as to make clear that he believed in that Supreme Being, but he never once stated expressly that he was a Christian and only occasionally made reference to a "Saviour." Dr. Smith and others likely embellished the record somewhat to assist Lincoln's rise in the American memory by preventing him from being portrayed as a mere Deist in a predominantly Christian nation. Nonetheless, Lincoln's faith in God and his interest in studying Christian scripture strengthened considerably following Eddy's death, and while Lincoln may not have experienced an overt conversion to Christianity, he quite clearly increasingly sought guidance from God. Indeed, Mary later said that after Eddy's death, Lincoln's "heart, was directed towards religion." And, although shortly after Lincoln's death Robert had told Herndon that he never heard his father speak of any decided views on the subject of Christianity,

Robert later told Lincoln biographer John W. Starr Jr. that "the views of his father's opinions on the subject [of Christianity] which he considered most satisfactory were those given by Isaac N. Arnold in his biography of President Lincoln." Arnold had indeed concluded that Lincoln was a Christian, but that conclusion was based primarily on Lincoln's frequent invocation of God's name in speeches and writings, reading of the Bible, and devotion to prayer, rather than any overt acceptance of Christianity.

The most probable explanation of Lincoln's religion is that he tended toward Christianity but simply preferred not talking about it much with others and was particularly put off by its ceremonial aspects. He was not an evangelist, and he did not want to be evangelized. "He believed in God as much as the most approved Church member," wrote fellow circuit rider Leonard Swett shortly after Lincoln's death. "Yet he judged of Providence by the same system of great generalization as of everything else. He had in my judgment very little faith in ceremonials and forms." And he deeply respected other people's right to practice their faith as they saw fit.

Prior to Eddy's death, Mary had regularly attended the Episcopal Church, and Robert, as a toddler, attended Sunday school there. Impressed with Dr. Smith's handling of Eddy's funeral, shortly thereafter she began attending First Presbyterian regularly. With Lincoln's blessing, in April 1852, Mary became a member of that church and was finally baptized. Lincoln, who until that time rarely attended services, now occasionally joined his wife at church on Sundays, but "was not constant in his attendance at public worship." While he continued to study and learn more about the Christian faith, he was not yet ready to commit to regular church attendance and never formally became a member of any church. It was customary in that era for members to rent pews in a church, thereby reserving the same seats from week to week. Shortly after Mary joined First Presbyterian, Lincoln asked Thomas Lewis, a fellow lawyer and elder at the church, if there were any pews to rent. "Yes," replied Lewis, "and a very desirable one, vacated by Governor Madison, who had just left the city."

"What is the rent?" Lincoln asked.

"Fifty dollars, payable quarterly," Lewis answered.

"Put it down to me," Lincoln said, as he handed Lewis $12.50 as a down payment. The Lincoln family now had exclusive rights to pew number twenty, set in a choice location on the left side, seventh row from the front, and adorned with a black haircloth cushion.

Eddy's death at the tender age of three left Lincoln with a broken heart and a feeling that there was a void in his spiritual life. Perhaps with the help of Dr. Smith and *The Christian Defence*, and certainly with his increased study of the Bible, Lincoln began to fill that spiritual void as he began to develop a deeper relationship with God. But it was his willingness to openly grieve about his tragic loss that is most revealing about Lincoln the father. Like others in his generation were beginning to do, Lincoln broke free from long-standing cultural expectations that parents suppress their sorrow and internalize a child's death as simply being God's will. Instead, Lincoln openly displayed and shared his grief in his words and actions. But he also knew that his life needed to go on. And it did.

CHAPTER 5

Growing Ambition, Growing Family

IN THE AFTERMATH OF EDDY'S DEATH, LINCOLN TURNED TO BOTH work and God. Work filled up his time and attention, thus diverting his mind away from the constant reminders of his late son that permeated the house at Eighth and Jackson. In God, Lincoln found comfort knowing that Eddy was in a good place, and by opening up to religious faith, he began to fill the spiritual void he felt in the days and weeks following Eddy's passing. Yet there remained an emptiness in his domestic life. Lincoln was forty-one and had only one child, while most married men his age already had several children. He and Mary quickly decided that they wanted another child.

Nineteenth-century parents commonly sought to have another baby shortly after experiencing the death of an infant or toddler. They did not seek to "replace" a child, for like all parents they recognized the inherent uniqueness of each little soul. Rather, there was a sense that having another baby would lessen their pain, breathe new life into the disheartened home, and in some cases, give the gift of a little brother or sister to a surviving sibling. Less than two months after Eddy's funeral, Mary was pregnant again.

Throughout Mary's third pregnancy, as during her first two, Lincoln kept busy both at the office and on the circuit. Eddy's funeral was on February 2, and between mid-February and the end of March, Lincoln worked nearly every day. Then, on April 1, Lincoln left home to begin the summer circuit season. He returned for a week in late April but then left again for the entire month of May. Sarah Davis, wife of Lincoln's good friend and fellow circuit rider David Davis, "was a little critical of Lincoln, whom she adored, for staying out on the circuit when Mary was expecting." In July, a Whig party committee selected Lincoln to deliver a eulogy in Chicago on President Taylor, who had died suddenly in Washington. Lincoln closed the eulogy by reciting his favorite poem by William Knox, "Oh, Why Should the Spirit of Mortal be Proud." Later, after the fall circuit season ended in early November, Lincoln headed back to Springfield, where he remained until the following April.

William Wallace Lincoln was born on December 21, 1850, just over ten months after Eddy's death. The Lincolns called him Willie. For the third time, Lincoln had an opportunity to name a son after his father, Thomas, and for the third time he declined to do so. The Lincolns named the boy after Mary's brother-in-law, William Wallace, a local physician who had tended to Eddy when he was ill and then delivered Willie. Once again, Thomas would never meet his grandson.

By Christmas Eve, just three days after Willie's birth, Lincoln was back at work. He took Christmas day off to be with the family; then on the twenty-sixth he argued a case before the Illinois Supreme Court and proceeded to work every day for the remainder of the year. A few weeks later, Lincoln received a letter from Harriet Hanks Chapman, daughter of his cousin Dennis Hanks. Harriet reported that Thomas Lincoln was ill and that Lincoln's stepbrother, John D. Johnston, wondered why Lincoln had not replied to two of his earlier letters informing him of his father's declining condition. Harriet's letter finally prompted Lincoln to write back to Johnston. He acknowledged receipt of both letters but explained that "although I have not answered them, it is no[t because] I have forgotten them, or been uninterested about them—but because it appeared to me I could write nothing which could do any good." He apparently did not believe that visiting Thomas or even sending words of comfort and encouragement would do any good, either. Though Lincoln went on to assure Johnston that he would help pay for any medical care that Thomas required, he added that he was simply too busy to make the three-day trip to Thomas's bedside. "My business is such that I could hardly leave home now, if it were not, as it is, that my own wife is sick-abed. (It is a case of baby-sickness, and I suppose is not dangerous.)"

Lincoln closed the letter with both a call for Thomas to make peace with God and an implicit acknowledgment of his estrangement with his father: "I sincerely hope Father may yet recover his health; but at all events tell him to remember to call upon, and confide in, our great, and good, and merciful Maker; who will not turn away from him in any extremity. He notes the fall of a sparrow, and numbers the hairs of our heads; and He will not forget the dying man, who puts his trust in Him. Say to him that if we could meet now, it is doubtful whether it would not be more painful than pleasant; but that if it be his lot to go now, he will soon have a joyous [meeting] with many loved ones gone before; and where [the rest] of us, through the help of God, hope ere-long [to join] them." Five days later, Thomas Lincoln died.

Lincoln did not attend his father's funeral, which took place on a cold January day at Johnston's house. As a practical matter, Lincoln likely could not have received news of the death and made the two- to three-day trip to Thomas's home in time for the burial. Nevertheless, given the emotional distance he had fostered over the years between himself and his father, it is doubtful that Lincoln would have attended the service even if he could have traveled there in time.

Within weeks after Eddy's death, Lincoln had arranged for a poetic tombstone made of white marble to be placed on his son's grave, but he never provided a proper marker for Thomas. A decade after Thomas died, when he was the president-elect on his way to be sworn into office as president, Lincoln visited Thomas's grave for the first time, "and with his pen-knife cut the initials 'T.L.' on a bit of oak board and placed it at the head of the grave." That board was soon stolen by a souvenir hunter. Nearly three years after Lincoln's assassination in 1865, Mary wrote Sarah Bush Lincoln, Thomas's widow and Lincoln's stepmother, telling her, "My husband a few weeks before his death mentioned to me, that he intended *that* summer, paying proper respect to *his* father's grave, by head & foot stone, with his name, age & and I propose very soon carrying out his intentions." Mary did not follow through, however, and Thomas's grave remained unmarked until Lincoln's son Robert paid for a permanent tombstone sometime after 1880, long after Lincoln's own death.

Two years after Thomas's death, Lincoln delivered a eulogy in Springfield for his longtime hero, Henry Clay, who had recently died. Lincoln observed that Clay's lack of education, "however it may be regretted generally, teaches us at least one profitable lesson; it teaches that in this country, one can scarcely be so poor, but that, if he *will*, he *can* acquire sufficient education to get through the world respectably." Lincoln seemed, at once, to be speaking of both his own ambition and acquired respectability and Thomas's lack of the same.

Lincoln was away from home during much of Willie's infant years. Between April 2, 1851, when the summer circuit term began, and the end of that calendar year, Lincoln was gone from Springfield about half the time, 134 out of 264 days. The following year, when Willie was about one and a half, Lincoln was absent even more. "Mr. Lincoln is so much engaged [on the circuit] that he will not find time to go home," wrote Lincoln's friend David Davis to his wife, "so before he gets home he will have been absent six (6) weeks."

Though Mary disliked Lincoln's frequent absences from home, there was a trade-off. As his career boomed, the Lincolns became very comfortable financially. Lincoln was making well in excess of $2,000 a year, a very nice sum at the time. He was handling more and more cases on behalf of railroad companies, which not only paid very well but also provided interesting and challenging legal issues for him to resolve, mostly relating to land titles and taxation. As they gained financial security, the Lincolns continued to make improvements to their home and upgrade their lifestyle. In June 1852, shortly after returning home from the summer circuit term, Lincoln paid $260 in cash for a fancy carriage made by Obed Lewis. Lincoln took pride in his carriages, which served as a symbol of his success, much as an automobile does today. Once when someone asked to borrow his carriage, Lincoln joked, "there are only two things I will not loan, my wife & my carriage." In fact, he occasionally lent both his horse and his carriage to N. W. Miner, a neighbor and minister who often needed transportation to visit nearby towns.

On April 4, 1853, when Robert was almost ten and Willie two and a half, another son, Thomas Lincoln, was born. The Lincolns had actually hoped for a girl. A few months after the boy's birth, Sarah Davis wrote to her husband David, "Is Mr. Lincoln with you on the circuit? And has he become reconciled to his little son?" Years later, Mary told fourteen-year-old Julia Taft Bayne, a playmate of the boys, "I wish I had a little girl like you, Julia." The boy was born with a slightly cleft palate, a disability that eventually resulted in a minor speech impediment in the form of a lisp that stayed with him throughout his life.

Though Lincoln finally chose to name a son after his father, who had now been dead for more than two years, he never called the boy by his given name. Soon after the birth, Lincoln observed that the baby had a large head and a small body and tended to squirm around like a tadpole, so he nicknamed him "Tad." Lincoln had given his other three sons nicknames, too, but all were common derivatives of their real names. Robert was "Bob," Edward was "Eddy," and William was "Willie." In this case, however, Lincoln bypassed "Tom" or "Tommy" in favor of "Tad." When referring to his fourth son by name, both in speech and in writing, Lincoln always called him Tad or Taddie, but never Thomas. It was as if Lincoln simply could not bring himself to endure any constant reminders of his now-deceased father. Lincoln transferred his own aversion to using the boy's real name to his son. Tad's playmate, Julia Taft Bayne, later observed, "Tad hated to be called Thomas. It was his grandfather's name and I never called him by it unless I was angry."

The thirty-day period leading up to Tad's birth was one of the busiest in Lincoln's law practice. During that time he handled scores of cases. Just two days before Mary delivered her youngest son, Lincoln and Herndon had thirteen cases called before the court in a single day. Then, less than a week after Tad was born, Lincoln left for the summer circuit term, leaving Mary behind with the three boys, including the newborn Tad. He would not return home for nearly two months. Though Lincoln later spent the entire summer in Springfield, he left again for two months during the fall circuit term. The next year, 1854, was much the same story. Lincoln was gone the entire time between April 5 and June 10, and in the ninety-seven-day period between August 26 and November 20, he was away from home for all but twenty days. Though relieved of any domestic duties while on the road, he did not use his time away to sleep late or slack off. One court clerk noted, "Lincoln had a habit of coming there mornings before court to read or study."

As Lincoln's family grew, so did his ambition. Though his law practice was booming, he still had his eye on politics. In June 1852, Lincoln had been appointed as an Illinois member of the Whig national committee, and thereafter he occasionally spoke out on current political issues. By 1854, the growing debate over slavery dominated the national political scene. Early in the year, Congress debated the Kansas-Nebraska Act, which would repeal the Missouri Compromise of 1820 and allow slavery to extend into otherwise free territories under the notion of "popular sovereignty," by which the people of each territory could decide for themselves whether or not to allow slavery. The Kansas-Nebraska Act eventually passed and became law in May, but the debate over its wisdom raged on. By August, Lincoln earnestly joined the discussion in opposition. Now back in the political fray, Lincoln decided to run for office again. "I have really got it into my head to try to be United States senator," he wrote to a friend.

At that time, senators were selected by state legislatures, not by popular vote. If those opposed to the Kansas-Nebraska Act gained a majority in the Illinois legislature in the November 1854 elections, Lincoln reasoned, then he would have a chance to win the senate seat that was up for selection by the legislature in early 1855. Lincoln shared his senatorial ambitions with only a small group of friends.

Unaware of Lincoln's plans, party leaders asked him to stand for election to the Illinois House of Representatives. They believed that his name on the ballot would assure victory for a Whig slate of candidates in Sangamon County, but their request posed a dilemma for Lincoln. The Illinois constitution prohibited sitting members of the legislature from being elected to the United States Senate. Thus, a victory in the election would likely eliminate him from consideration for the senate seat that he really desired. Nevertheless, out of loyalty to the Whig party, he reluctantly agreed to run and on November 7 won the election. Forces opposed to the Kansas-Nebraska Act, largely Whigs, also won a slim majority in the General Assembly. Ambitious for the senate seat, Lincoln announced shortly after the election that he was declining to accept his election, a decision that rendered him eligible for consideration for the senate seat but which infuriated some of his local supporters.

When the General Assembly met in February, fifty votes were needed to secure election to the senate. On the first ballot, Lincoln had forty-five votes; the incumbent Democrat, James Shields, had forty-one; Lyman Trumbull, an Anti-Nebraska Democrat, had five; and Democrat Joel Matteson, the current governor, had one. As the balloting continued, Lincoln's and Shield's support declined substantially while Trumbull's and Matteson's increased. Lincoln believed that Governor Matteson was misleading various legislators into believing that he was "as good Anti-Nebraska as anyone," including Lincoln. Concerned that Matteson might use his position as governor to offer various forms of patronage to gain support of members who were opposed to the Kansas-Nebraska Act, Lincoln threw his support to Trumbull, who was finally elected on the tenth ballot.

Lincoln blamed his loss on Matteson's "double game." "I regret my defeat moderately," Lincoln wrote a friend. "I have to content myself with the honor of having been the first choice of a large majority of the fifty-one members who finally made the election." Though disappointed, Lincoln knew that the entire experience raised his political profile throughout Illinois. Moreover, he knew that he would have an opportunity for a senate seat again in 1858, when incumbent Senator Stephen A. Douglas, an architect of the Kansas-Nebraska Act, would stand for reelection.

After the election, Lincoln resumed his law practice. One of his first tasks was to apologize to a New York law firm that had sent him a collection bond to handle for one of its clients: "When I received the bond, I was dabbling in politics; and, of course, neglecting business," a contrite Lincoln wrote. "Having since been beaten out, I have gone to work again." And so he did, with his usual zest. Though he spent substantial time away from home during the 1855 summer and fall circuit seasons, the increasing availability of rail lines made it easier for him to return home on weekends, which he now chose to do more frequently than in past years.

Lincoln's client list became more and more impressive, anchored by a number of railroads that provided both steady work and good pay. When

Lincoln won an important tax case for the Illinois Central Railroad that saved the company substantial amounts of money, he sent the client a bill for $2,000. The railroad balked, and after several other lawyers told Lincoln that his fee was too low, Lincoln increased the fee to $5,000 and resubmitted a bill. After Lincoln prosecuted a collection lawsuit in which the amount was adjudged reasonable, the railroad paid the bill. Though disgruntled by the amount of the fee, the client was impressed enough with Lincoln's skill as a lawyer that it continued sending him legal work.

As the younger boys grew out of infancy, Lincoln began spending more time with them. "Lincoln would take his Children and would walk out on the Rail way out in the Country—would talk to them—Explain things Carefully—particularly," one neighbor later said. One hot August day in 1860, as Lincoln was in the midst of his presidential campaign, *Farmer's Advocate* owner-editor Jeriah Bonham visited Lincoln at an office he occasionally used at the statehouse in Springfield and found Willie and Tad playing with their casually dressed father. "'Tad' was spinning a top, and Mr. Lincoln, as we came in, had just finished adjusting the string so it would give the top greater force when it was whirled off on the floor. He said he was having a little season of relaxation with the boys, which he could not always enjoy now, as so many callers and so much correspondence occupied his time."

Sometimes, however, he did not completely take his mind off of work. Once, Lincoln walked to his office using one hand to pull a wagon carrying Willie and Tad and the other to hold a book in which he was engrossed. One of the boys fell out of the wagon, but Lincoln continued walking, totally oblivious to his baby son's wailing. Though at the time Mary gave her husband a severe scolding, the episode later became a funny family story that always brought a laugh when told. One neighbor observed that "on a winter's morning he might be seen stalking towards the market house, basket on arm, his old gray shawl wrapped around his neck, his little boy Willie or Tad running along at his heels asking a thousand boyish questions, which his father, in deep abstraction, neither heeded nor heard." Tad and Willie seemed to naturally crave physical contact with Lincoln in a way that Robert never did. When Lincoln was working at home, Tad would burst into the room looking for something and "having found it, he threw himself on his father like a small thunderbolt, gave him one wild, fierce hug, and, without a word, fled from the room before his father could put out a hand to detain him."

Lincoln often took Willie and Tad on errands with him and exercised great patience as he tried to accomplish the chore at hand. "He was a frequent visitor at the [*Illinois State*] *Journal* office," wrote one observer. "Sometimes he had with him his two small boys, who would often slip out into the work room, just back of the editorial room, when Mr. Lincoln would find that the boys had gone, he would go and find them leading them back by the hands; this would occur two or three times at each visit when the boys were with him."

Lincoln also helped get the boys dressed, fed, and tucked into bed, though often these were done at Mary's urging. One day as Lincoln started to walk toward his office, Mary shouted, "Come back here now and dress those children or they won't be tended today. I'm not going to break my back dressing up those children while you loaf at the office talking politics all day." On another occasion, during the 1860 presidential campaign, a visitor to the Lincoln home heard Mary direct Lincoln to "come and put this child to bed!"

Having previously exercised little control over Robert and Eddy, the Lincolns continued their lack of discipline over Willie and Tad, which became legendary in Springfield. Occasionally Lincoln brought the boys to the office, much to the annoyance of his partner, William Herndon. "The boys were absolutely unrestrained in their amusements," Herndon later lamented. "If they pulled down all the books from the shelves, bent the points of all the pens, overturned ink-stands, scattered law papers over the floor, or threw the pencils into the spittoon, it never disturbed the serenity of their father's good nature. Frequently absorbed in thought, he never observed their mischievous but destructive pranks . . . and even if brought to his attention, he virtually encouraged their repetition by declining to show any substantial evidence of parental disapproval."

One day Lincoln and Judge Samuel Treat were playing chess in Lincoln's office, a "small poorly furnished room filled with law books and newspapers." One of the boys came with a message that Mary wanted him home for dinner. Lincoln told the boy he would be there soon, but then lost track of time as the game continued. About a half hour later, the boy returned again to call his father home, but the two men were so deeply engrossed in their game that they failed to acknowledge the little messenger. Angered at being ignored, the boy approached the men, lifted his foot, and kicked the board, causing the chessmen to scatter about. "It was one of the most abrupt, if not brazen, things I ever saw," Treat later recalled, "but the surprising thing was its effect on Lincoln. Instead of the animated scene between an irate father and an impudent youth which I expected, Mr. Lincoln without a word of reproof calmly arose, took the boy by the hand, and started for dinner. Reaching the door he turned, smiled good-naturedly, and exclaimed, 'Well, Judge, I reckon we'll have to finish this game some other time.'"

Mary later summed up what she said was Lincoln's approach to parenting, which seemed to implicitly draw contrasts with his own childhood experience: "He was very indulgent to his children—chided or praised for it always said 'It is my pleasure that my children are free—happy and unrestrained by parental tyranny. Love is the chain whereby to lock a child to his parent.'"

When Lincoln was running for president in 1860, artist Thomas Hicks came to Springfield to paint his portrait. They decided to have the sitting in Lincoln's temporary office in the state capitol building in the center of town. As Hicks worked, seven-year-old Tad and a friend slipped into the room. Positioned where Hicks could see them but Lincoln could not, the boys started their mischief. As Hicks later told the story, "The little fellows got among my paints. They took the brightest blue, yellow and red. Then they squeezed from a tube into their little palms, a lot of red, and smeared it on the wall; then they took the blue and smeared it in another place, and afterward they smeared the yellow." After they had created a "brilliant wall decoration" and further smeared themselves with the paint, Lincoln realized what was happening. He said "with the mildest tone and with greatest affection, 'Boys! Boys! You mustn't meddle with Mr. Hicks's paints; now run home and have your faces and hands washed."

Occasionally Lincoln rebuked the boys for bad behavior and used threats of spankings, rather than the actual physical punishment itself.

Herndon once described the scene of a formal dinner party at the Lincoln home: "Tad would dash into the room with a bacon ham in his hands swinging it . . . among silks—gold—tinsels & lace. . . . [T]he ladies and gentlemen would give Tad a wide birth [sic], parting to let him through." Though Lincoln mildly chided the boy, "he would fail to see disgust on the faces of those present and annoyed at Tad." Mary once said that when the boys were "slow to obey," Lincoln would sometimes break off a switch from a tree or bush, but "he never touched them with it." Another time, Robert and his friends tried to train some dogs to stand on their hind legs by tying ropes around their necks and pulling them firm over a rafter. When Lincoln saw what was happening, he "seized a stave from an ash barrel . . . as a handy instrument for restoring order. The boys fled and Mr. Lincoln released the long-suffering animals."

Willie, too, was not immune from engaging in mischief. During the 1860 election, Lincoln received a number of gifts from well-wishers, including boxes of cigars. Ten-year-old Willie smuggled some cigars and matches out to the carriage house and invited Tad and two neighborhood boys to join him. After talking it over, the group thought it better to experiment with the contraband farther away from the house, so they scurried down the street and slipped into Mrs. Niles's barn. "We proceeded to light the cigars and have a good smoke, our first offence," wrote one of the boys years later. "A sicker lot of boys there never was. Our wails of woe soon brought Mrs. Niles out and she took us into her house, fixed us up as best she could in the way of allaying our sufferings and sent for our respective mothers. My recollection of this distressing episode is that there was no scolding on the part of the mothers, but undeserved sympathy." Lincoln likely found amusement in the whole affair.

Tad could be especially problematic in church, a public setting where he was supposed to sit still and quiet for an hour or so and where the Lincolns could not, without making a scene, impose any immediate discipline for bad behavior. When Tad acted up during services, the best Lincoln could do was lift him up and scurry up the aisle and out of the church before his screams and protestations turned too many heads. On one occasion when Tad began to disrupt the service, Lincoln quickly picked him up, walked out of the church, and headed home, with a wiggling

Tad "slung over his father's arm like a pair of saddlebags." Along the way, Lincoln encountered a group of friends and good-naturedly explained his predicament. "Gentlemen, I entered this colt, but he kicked around so I had to withdraw him."

Tad frequently found himself up in his father's arms, sometimes for fun and sometimes as a result of a temper tantrum. After Tad descended into such a tantrum, Lincoln, using his oversized arms, would pick him up and hold him out at arm's length, all the while laughing as the boy tried in vain to kick him in the face. Once when the Lincolns were hosting a dinner party, Tad tiptoed downstairs in his red flannel pajamas and, peeping through a door, complained about being excluded from the gathering. Lincoln, experiencing the common problem of a child refusing to stay in bed after being tucked in, promptly picked up his somewhat embarrassed son and carried him about the room laughing as he introduced him to the guests before putting him back in bed. On another occasion, Lincoln was in his Springfield office discussing politics with Henry Guest Pike and Lyman Trumbull. Pike later recalled that "the door opened and a boy dashed in, running as hard as he could. He was Tad. His father stood up and opened wide his arms. Tad came running. When he was about 6 feet away he jumped and caught his father around the neck. Lincoln wrapped his arms around the boy and spanked him good, both of them laughing and carrying on as if there was nobody looking at them."

Lincoln enjoyed holding Tad, and his physical strength allowed him to carry his son even when the boy was fully capable of walking on his own. "Why, Mr. Lincoln, put down that great big boy," remarked a neighbor when she saw Lincoln carrying Tad on the sidewalk. "He is big enough to walk." Lincoln just smiled and said, "Oh, don't you think his little feet get too tired?" Willie, too, occasionally found himself up in his father's arms. Once when Mary was preparing to give him a bath, the naked toddler ran off when Mary turned her back for a moment. Willie flew past Lincoln, who was on the front porch, and streaked down the street and into a field. Lincoln watched in amusement, but Mary was horrified at the sight of her son parading around the neighborhood without clothes. She implored her husband to chase down the boy, which he did, hoisting him up on his shoulders for the triumphant return home.

When Robert and Eddy were in Lexington, Mary's stepmother had foiled their attempt to adopt a kitten. Back in Springfield, however, Robert, Willie, and Tad successfully adopted several pets. They occasionally took in cats, which were Lincoln's favorite animal, as well as goats, which Lincoln did not like. Mary described cats as Lincoln's "hobby," and the future president would often get down on the floor to talk to and play with them for long periods of time. Eventually the family got a dog, a mixed yellow Labrador on which they bestowed the rather unoriginal name "Fido." Herndon saw Lincoln's willingness to shelter animals as an extension of his lack of parental discipline. If the Lincoln boys "wanted a dog-cat-rat or the Devil," Herndon wrote scornfully, "it was all right and well treated—housed—petted—fed—fondled &c &c."

Lincoln often attempted to teach the boys various lessons and occasionally helped to right some wrongs. Once Lincoln was visiting with his friend, George T. M. Davis, as Robert and Tad stood nearby. "Tad, show Mr. Davis the knife I bought you yesterday," Lincoln directed his son. "It's the first knife Tad ever had," Lincoln explained to Davis, "and it's a big thing for him." When Tad hesitated, Lincoln asked if he had already lost it.

"No, but I ain't got any," Tad replied sheepishly.

"What has become of it?" Lincoln pressed.

After a long pause, Tad fessed up, as he looked away from Robert. "Bob told me if he was me, he'd swap my knife for candy."

Lincoln laughed, then turned to Robert. "Bob, how much did you pay for that candy?" When Robert told his father the price, Lincoln sought to make him see that he'd taken advantage of his little brother. "Why, Tad's knife cost three bits . . . ; do you think you made a fair trade with Tad?"

"No sir," replied an embarrassed Robert, as he took the knife from his pocket and handed it to Tad.

"I guess, Bob," Lincoln continued, "that's about right on your part and now, Tad, as you've got your knife, you must give back to Bob the candy he gave you for the knife."

"I can't," replied Tad, "cause I ate up all the candy Bob give me, and I ain't got no money to buy it."

Lincoln did not let Tad off the hook. "Bob must have his candy back to make things square between you," he said. The trio pondered the problem for a moment, then Lincoln handed Tad one bit.

"Come on, Bob, I'll get your candy back for you," Tad said joyfully, as the boys headed for the store.

Lincoln had a great curiosity about mechanical objects and liked to tinker with anything that had moving parts. In 1849, he obtained a patent on a device used to help barges float over shoals and obstructions, making him the only president to have secured a patent on an invention. To satisfy his curiosity, he would often "take one of his boys' toys to pieces, find out how it was made, and put it together again. Tad . . . on more than one occasion had cause to bewail, loudly, his father's curiosity." One day Lincoln noticed that the wood-framed clock on the fireplace mantel had stopped working. On further inspection and investigation, he discovered that Tad had removed the back and disassembled all of the intricate workings. Unable to reassemble the many parts, the boy merely placed them back inside the frame and closed it up. Tad may have hoped that he would not be found out, but just in case, he was surely ready to point out that his father often took apart his toys without permission, so turnabout was fair play.

Lincoln also had to deal with children begging for money, unearned by any chores, so they could buy candy, toys, or items of perceived great need for the youngster.

"Father I want twenty-five cents," Willie once demanded.

"My son," Lincoln replied, "what do you want of twenty-five cents?"

"I want to buy some candy," Willie answered honestly.

"My son, I shall not give you twenty-five cents, but I will give you five cents," Lincoln replied. Lincoln reached into his pocket, pulled out a five-cent silver coin, and placed it on the table. A disappointed Willie turned and walked away, leaving the money behind. "He will be back in a few minutes," Lincoln said to John S. Bliss, a Wisconsin journalist who was interviewing Lincoln and witnessed the entire exchange.

"Why do you think so?" inquired Bliss.

"Because as soon as he finds I will give him no more he will come and get it," Lincoln said confidently. A few minutes later, Willie quietly walked in the room, picked up the coin, and walked away without saying a word. Lincoln's comments to Bliss suggest that he had faced this situation before, and thus he could predict the final outcome. Though in this case he was unable to just say "no" to the boy's request altogether, Lincoln attempted to teach his son the necessary lesson that money should be neither freely given nor spent frivolously.

As a lawyer, Lincoln respected the importance of being careful and accurate in his work, traits that he first learned during his days as a surveyor. Lincoln sought to pass on those qualities to Robert: "Driving toward Springfield . . . he recalled he had surveyed the neighborhood they were driving through. He stopped the buggy several times, and each time, with a chuckle, asked Bob to go into the woods and at a certain distance and find a blazed tree, which he had more than twenty years ago marked as a survey corner. 'And he never made a mistake,' said Bob." Lincoln's lessons stuck with Robert, who was "scrupulously careful" and had "the same love of precision" as his father.

The 1850s were Robert's formative years. During that decade, Robert grew from young boy to teenager. Robert's serious demeanor, which he clearly inherited from his mother's side of the family, stood in marked contrast to Lincoln's jovial personality. This may have caused Lincoln to favor spending time with Willie and Tad. While history records numerous stories of Lincoln frolicking with Willie and Tad during the later Springfield years, Robert seemed to stand more quietly in the background, surfacing only for more serious matters such as educational pursuits, baby-sitting duties when his parents went out for dinner, washing dishes and other chores, and even participation in a junior military company.

When Lincoln lent his horse and carriage to local minister N. W. Miner, "Bob . . . used to clean the carriage and harness the horse for me and he did well," Miner later recalled. As a teenager, he joined the Springfield Cadets, a military company whose primary purpose was to march in parades, such as the annual event celebrating George Washington's birthday. Robert was Fourth Corporal and wore a handsome dark blue uniform patterned after the official dress of the United States Army. Since younger children typically require more attention from their parents than older siblings, the age difference between Robert and his younger brothers resulted in a degree of separation from them. "In the grouping of the children in their activities, we find Willie and Tad in close and constant association, while Robert stood apart," observed one biographer. "Those men with whom I have talked of their Lincoln associations have referred to themselves as playmates of Robert or playmates of Willie and Tad, but never as playmates of Robert and the younger boys."

It was Robert's education rather than playtime, however, that dominated recollections of his youth. Since there were no free public schools available in Springfield, the Lincolns arranged for Robert to attend private schools. "I have a dim recollection of being under the slipper-guardianship of a school mistress [named Ms. Corcoran] until 1850," Robert later wrote. The term "slipper-guardianship" referred to a teacher who was not afraid to use her shoe as a weapon of discipline with her pupils. When Robert was seven, the Lincolns enrolled him in an academy run by Abel E. Estabrook, not far from the house at Eighth and Jackson. Three years later, Robert entered Illinois State University, a private preparatory school. Despite its name, the school was neither a university nor affiliated with the State of Illinois. Tuition was about $100 per year. Having just turned eleven, Robert was the youngest of fifty-two students. By attending summer classes, he achieved freshman status at thirteen.

Though some of his classmates were studious, Robert did not strenuously apply himself and his grades were merely average. "This 'University' had, I believe, four instructors, Dr. W. M. Reynolds being the President," Robert later recalled. "The government was very easy, and we did just what pleased us, study consuming only a very small portion of our time. The Classes were divided as at College; and when I left I was about to enter the Senior Class." While Robert may have taken his studies lightly, a number of serious students attended the school with him, including John Hay, who later became Lincoln's private secretary and then secretary of state under Presidents William McKinley and Theodore Roosevelt. Though Robert may have lacked frolicking time with his father, it appears that Lincoln, when he was home, took time to help his son with schoolwork. When Robert began to study Latin, one classmate recalled, "his father studied it with him, going around the house declining Latin nouns as he did the chores of paterfamilias."

While Lincoln helped Robert with his studies, Mary took it upon herself to teach her son some social graces that her husband lacked as a young boy, such as "helping the ladies out of the carriage in the manner befitting a young gentleman." Mary arranged dance lessons for the boy and introduced him to fine literature. Robert also spent much time with Mary's stepsister Emilie, who lived with the Lincolns for six months in 1855 and brought with her the quiet and dignified manners of the South. More and more, Robert emulated the Todd disposition rather than that of his father. That is not to say, however, that Robert refrained from all mischief. Once Robert took Lincoln's carriage for a drive into the country without asking for his father's permission. Along for the ride was Robert's friend, Josiah Kent. The buggy broke, and Robert managed to quickly get it to a blacksmith, who repaired and painted over the damage. Kent later recalled that, before the paint dried, "Bob threw dust on [the paint] to make it look old so [Lincoln] would not notice & never heard anything from it."

Robert became interested in the legal profession at a young age, perhaps hoping to follow in his father's footsteps or just to find some common ground on which they could better relate. Lincoln took Willie and Tad to his office to do nothing more than play and have a good time, but with Robert he engaged in more substantive interaction to teach the boy about his work as a lawyer. When the local newspaper began coverage of a prominent trial in Boston in which a doctor was accused of murder, Robert followed the case with great interest, no doubt peppering his father with technical questions. Judge David Davis, who traveled the circuit with Lincoln, disapprovingly described to his wife Robert's interest in the case: "Poor Dr. Webster was hung yesterday. . . . Lincoln says that his little boy has been counting the days that Dr. Webster had to live, & Thursday he said that Thursday was the last night he had to live. Rather singular that the event should so mark itself, . . . on a child of seven years."

Willie followed Robert and attended Mrs. Corcoran's "slipper guardian" school. He "was very studious and took delight in discussing the problems of the day with the other boys." Willie also excelled in math. He had as a hobby copying and creating railroad timetables and once created an accurate schedule for an imaginary train traveling from Chicago to Washington. His greatest strength, however, lay in his ability to write, which he revealed in two early letters. In 1859, Lincoln needed to try a case in Chicago and decided to take nine-year-old Willie with him. They traveled by train and stayed at the Tremont Hotel. Writing playmate Henry Remann back in Springfield, Willie found Chicago "a very beautiful place... We had a nice little room to ourselves," which had "two little pitcher[s] on a washstand, the smallest one for me and the largest one for father. We have two little towels on top of both pitchers. The smallest one for me, the largest one for father." Willie reported that he and his father attended "two theatres the other night," and that they went to "an exhibition on Wednesday before last." In another surviving letter, stained with chocolate, Willie described the improving condition of Springfield roads following some wet weather, perhaps in anticipation of his father's return from the circuit. The letter concluded with, "I have not any more to say so I must bring my letter to an end."

Because Tad suffered from the speech impediment caused by his slightly cleft palate, he could not even read by the time the Lincolns reached the White House when he was eight years old. Viewing Tad's inability to properly articulate words as a learning disability that would prevent him from keeping up with his peers, the Lincolns did not push education on the boy during the Springfield years. To their friends, however, they explained their rationale differently. "Let him run," Lincoln said. "There's time enough yet for him to learn his letters and get pokey. Bob was just such a little rascal, and now he is a very decent boy." That explanation was disingenuous. If the Lincolns really favored de-emphasizing education in favor of play time, they would have applied the same philosophy to Willie, which they did not do. Nor had they taken that approach with Robert, whom Lincoln cited as an example of the success of their philosophy. Although Robert was a marginal student, at least he went to school, as did Willie. In reality, the Lincolns predicted that Tad would have trouble in school and did not want to place him in an environment where he would be subject to ridicule by his peers.

Their fears were not without some foundation. "I love you, Johnny," Tad once told his cousin, John Grimsley, "because you are nice to me and don't tease me." Nevertheless, the problem with the Lincolns' approach was that the very difficulty they wished to avoid only got worse as time went by. "You would not like to go to school without knowing how to read," Mary once told Tad after he refused her efforts to get him to read on his own, seemingly oblivious to the notion that by sending him to school he *would* learn how to read. After Lincoln's death, Mary still fretted about putting twelve-year-old Tad in school out of fear that he would be so far behind that other students would make fun of him.

As the 1850s progressed, Lincoln's political profile continued to rise. Though he lost his senate race in 1855, he remained politically active. Shortly after the election, the Whig party disintegrated, having been beset by internal divisions over slavery. By 1856, the Republican party, largely made up of former Whigs who lived in the Northern and Western states, as well as former members of the fading Free Soil party, had become the dominant opposition party to the Democrats. That summer, the nascent party nominated John C. Frémont of California for president. A delegate from Illinois placed Lincoln's name in nomination for vice president, proclaiming that he was "a prince of good fellows, and an Old-Line Whig." Another supportive delegate argued that Lincoln's nomination would put Illinois in Frémont's column and suggested that his Kentucky roots would add further strength to the ticket. An informal ballot showed former Senator William L. Dayton of New Jersey leading Lincoln 253 to 110, with a small number of votes scattered among thirteen other nominees. When the Lincoln forces realized that Dayton was the clear favorite, they withdrew Lincoln's name and threw their support to Dayton, who was eventually nominated. Lincoln himself never took seriously his chances of actually being nominated. He was on the circuit in Urbana during the convention and did not even find out that his name had been proffered for vice president until after Dayton had already been nominated. When told that he had been considered for the ticket, he replied with dismissive humor. "I reckon that ain't me; there's another great man in Massachusetts named Lincoln, and I reckon it's him." In fact, there was no contender from Massachusetts named Lincoln, and he knew it. He also knew that he was now a nationally known figure within the Republican party. His political ambitions still had life.

The summer circuit term, which ordinarily ended in early June, was extended for a couple of weeks so that additional cases could be heard in Urbana. It was while he was in Urbana that Lincoln received word of the vice-presidential proceedings. He returned home on June 27 but left a week later to attend a large political rally in Princeton, about 125 miles north of Springfield, where he spoke to a crowd of about ten thousand. Though not on the Republican ticket, Lincoln intended to campaign hard for Frémont. In the six years since Eddy died, Lincoln had mostly been home during the two-month break between the summer and fall circuit terms, which allowed him to spend more time with the boys, though his Springfield law practice still kept him quite busy. The summer of 1856, however, would be different. In mid-July, Lincoln left for Chicago where he expected to spend two weeks working on "a little business in court." While based in Chicago, however, he made side trips to Dixon, Sterling, Galena, and Oregon City, where he made political speeches on behalf of Frémont. Lincoln returned to Springfield on July 28, where he dabbled in some legal work for a week before leaving again.

Though the fall circuit term began on August 1, Lincoln decided to forego riding the circuit for the first time since he began practicing law nearly a decade earlier. Lincoln's interest in the political campaign had overtaken, at least temporarily, his interest in practicing law, and he devoted nearly all his time and travels in the months preceding election day to campaigning around the state on behalf of Frémont and other Republican candidates. He thrived on the campaign trail. "His eyes were full and bright," wrote one observer, "and he was in the fullness of health and vigor." Newspapers, which were highly partisan organs vocally supporting one party or the other, covered Lincoln as he crisscrossed the state. "Never was he so powerful, so strong in argument, so convincing in logic," wrote one Republican newspaper. But a Democratic reporter countered that Lincoln's speech was the "same old stereotyped one he got up some time since about tearing down the fence and letting in the cows, &c., &c. To those who have heard it before, it was very dry and prosy, and with those who have heard it, it made no impression whatsoever." On one occasion when both Lincoln and Trumbull spoke, a Democratic paper attempted to sow some discord within Republican ranks by exploiting the senate battle that had occurred between those two men the previous year. "Mr. Trumbull's speech contrasted very unfavorably with that of Lincoln, and made some of the Republicans regret the bargain which sent Trumbull to the senate instead of Lincoln."

Election day saw a large turnout, despite bad weather and muddy streets. "We heard of a number of fights upon the streets, between drinking rowdies," reported the *Illinois State Journal*, "but around the polls, everything was quiet and decorous." Despite Lincoln's tireless effort during the campaign, Frémont lost to Democrat James Buchanan both in Illinois and nationally. Former President Millard Fillmore, who had been a Whig but was now running on the anti-Catholic, anti-immigrant Know-Nothing ticket, siphoned some votes away from Frémont but not enough to make a difference in the race. With the campaign over, Lincoln returned to his law practice. For the next eighteen months, he fell back into the routine of riding the circuit, practicing in Springfield, and being a family man. Yet he had become a leading figure in the Republican party, and he was especially popular in Illinois. By 1858, he once again saw a possible path to power.

Lincoln had lost a United States Senate election to Lyman Trumbull four years earlier. At that time, neither party nominated candidates prior to the legislative elections, so when the balloting began in the General Assembly, several candidates were in contention. Though Whigs held a narrow majority, they were concerned that Democrats might be able to engineer some defections, so they quickly rallied around the better-known Trumbull. In 1858, the other United States Senate seat from Illinois was up for election, and the Republican party decided to nominate a single candidate who would go head-to-head against the powerful and popular Democratic incumbent, Stephen A. Douglas. Now, because each party selected its candidate in advance, when the people went to the polls to vote for their state legislators they would be indirectly voting for one of two United States Senate candidates. On June 16, the state Republican convention met in Springfield and unanimously adopted a resolution "that Abraham Lincoln is the first and only choice of Republicans of Illinois of the U.S. Senate." Hours after receiving the nomination, Lincoln delivered a speech in which he uttered the famous line, "A house divided against itself cannot stand."

Lincoln knew that Douglas, the chief sponsor of the Kansas-Nebraska Act that Lincoln so vigorously opposed back in 1854, would be a formidable opponent. The two men knew each other well. Douglas, nicknamed the "Little Giant" due to his small physical stature (five feet, four inches tall and weighing ninety pounds) but large intellect, lived in Springfield and ran in some of the same social circles as Lincoln. As a young man, he had even courted Mary. One issue would dominate the campaign: the extension of slavery into the new states that were created from the previously unorganized western territories. While both men abhorred slavery, neither supported mandatory abolition. Douglas favored popular sovereignty: letting new states decide for themselves whether or not to allow slavery. Lincoln opposed the extension of slavery into any new state.

On July 24, Lincoln wrote Douglas, challenging him to a series of debates. Douglas promptly wrote back, accepting the challenge and proposing that the debates be held in seven different cities throughout the state, each in a congressional district where neither candidate had yet campaigned, between August 21 and October 15. On July 28, before Lincoln received Douglas's reply, the two men dined together. Three days later, Lincoln wrote Douglas accepting his proposal for the seven-city tour.

The debates soon captured the imagination of the entire nation and solidified Lincoln's standing as a leading national figure in Republican politics. The debate schedule, coupled with regular campaign events, meant that Lincoln was away from home for most of the summer and fall. Mary, who remained ambitious for her husband, was supportive: "Mr. Douglas is a very little, *little* giant by the side of my tall Kentuckian husband, and intellectually my husband towers above Douglas just as he does physically." Lincoln was home in Springfield for only two Sundays during the entire debate schedule. For the final debate at Alton on October 15, a large crowd from Springfield, including Robert, traveled by train to hear the candidates. Robert brought the rest of the Springfield Cadets to march in the festivities surrounding the event.

On election day in Springfield, "the rain fell almost incessantly throughout the entire day, and the streets were in a horrid condition." Soon the results were in, and it was yet another defeat for Lincoln. Democrats established a solid majority in the General Assembly, thus ensuring victory for Douglas when the legislature would meet early the following year to select the next senator. "The emotions of defeat, at the close of a struggle in which I felt more than a merely selfish interest . . . are fresh upon me," a disappointed Lincoln wrote to a friend. He put everything he had into a campaign in which he believed the issues at stake went beyond his own political ambitions.

For the third time in four years, Lincoln had to resume his law practice following months of campaigning and political involvement. Lincoln had not practiced law for nearly four months, and during that period he'd had virtually no income and had incurred substantial expenses traveling around Illinois. He was feeling the pinch just weeks into the campaign. "I am now in need of money," Lincoln wrote in July to another attorney with whom he had tried a case on behalf of Dr. Charles Sprague: "Suppose we say the amount shall be $50—? If the Dr. is satisfied with that, please get that money and send it to me." By the time the campaign was over, Lincoln was in deep trouble with his finances, and he knew it. Norman B. Judd, a member of the Republican National Committee, wrote Lincoln shortly after the election reminding him that he owed the committee money for expenses advanced on Lincoln's behalf during the campaign. Lincoln pled poverty and asked for more time. "I am willing to pay according to my ability," a dejected Lincoln wrote, "but I am the poorest hand living to get others to pay. I have been on expenses so long without earning any thing that I am absolutely without money now for even household purposes. . . . [M]y loss of time and business, bears pretty heavily upon [me]." Lincoln needed to get back to work, so after spending a week or so writing supporters and urging that the fight over slavery must go on, he was practicing law again. "This year I must devote to my private business," he wrote in response to an invitation to speak at an agricultural meeting, "our own Sangamon circuit court will be in session at that time."

His mind, however, was not completely off politics. In just four years, he had made two runs at a United States Senate seat, been considered for the vice-presidential nomination, debated a leading figure in the Democratic party in events that garnered national attention, and attained national standing within the Republican party and among anti-slavery forces. On the surface, he told friends and acquaintances that he was probably through with politics. "I am glad I made the late race," he wrote his friend Anson G. Henry. "It gave me a hearing on the great and durable question of the age, which I could have had in no other way; and though I now sink out of view, and shall be forgotten, I believe I have made some marks which will tell for the cause of civil liberty long after I am gone."

Three weeks later, however, he was upbeat. Once again, in defeat he saw an opportunity to fight another day. Writing to one of his disappointed supporters, Lincoln urged him to cheer up. "You will soon feel better. Another 'blow-up' is coming; and we shall have fun again." His loyal supporters were on board. Indeed, only days after his defeat in 1858, one such supporter was already thinking of the 1860 presidential election: "He is one of the best men God ever made. Can't we make him President or *vice*." Lincoln himself would not take that possibility seriously until late 1859. As that off-election year began, however, although Lincoln knew that he needed to nurture his law practice and personal finances back to life, he stayed deeply involved in the political arena, keeping up correspondence with Republican leaders and giving speeches in Iowa, Ohio, Indiana, Wisconsin, and Kansas. And, in the fall, he needed to tend to an important family matter involving Robert.

CHAPTER 6

Bob Promises Very Well

ROBERT'S TEACHERS AT ILLINOIS STATE, ALL OF WHOM WERE PROTES-
tant ministers, emphasized a classical education. But Robert and his parents eventually realized that the rather lax governance of the school was
not in Robert's best educational interests. "I became aware that I could
never get an education in that way," Robert later wrote about his experience at that school. Of course, to the extent that Robert viewed the education at Illinois State as inadequate, he bore some of the blame himself.
Robert went through a period where he frequently skipped class, forcing
his father to visit the school "to see what could be done to get Bob to
attend classes regularly again." His grades were average, with his highest
scores coming in Greek and his lowest in composition and declamation.
Though elected as a member of the Philomathean Society, he rarely went
to meetings and was once fined for his lack of attendance.

In the fall of 1859, Robert turned sixteen, the age at which many
young men left home for college. One of Robert's other friends from
Springfield, Clinton Conkling, left for Yale at that age. John Hay, who
was a few classes ahead of Robert at Illinois State, left for Brown University shortly before his seventeenth birthday, and George Latham, a
classmate at Illinois State, left for an East Coast preparatory school at
sixteen and applied to Harvard a year later. So, shortly after his sixteenth birthday, Robert decided to take the entrance examination at
Harvard.

It is not clear whether attendance at Harvard was Robert's or his
father's idea. In an autobiography that he wrote as a young man, Robert

said that he himself had "resolved to enter Harvard College." According to one contemporary, however, Robert told Springfield attorney Frederick W. Lehmann that it was indeed his father who urged his attendance at Harvard. Lincoln was determined "to give his eldest son Robert the schooling he himself lacked," wrote another biographer, and "decided to send Bob to Harvard." It is certainly plausible that Lincoln wanted his son to have the opportunity that he himself never had to attend one of the country's finest institutions of higher learning, an opportunity that Lincoln's own father could not and would not give to him. Lincoln likely recalled that when he was sixteen, he had learned about a school established by Robert Owen at an experimental utopian colony about sixty miles away from his home in Indiana. "There's a school and thousands of books there and fellers that know everything in creation," cousin Dennis Hanks recalled Lincoln saying when he learned of Owen's social experiment. Thomas, however, could not afford the $100 in tuition, and it is doubtful that Thomas would have let Lincoln attend even if he had the money, since he needed his son on the farm and saw little value in education anyway. "Abe might just as well wished for a hundred moons to shine at night," Hanks recalled, adding that Lincoln's father Thomas "didn't set no store by them things."

Regardless of who initiated the idea that Robert attend Harvard, in the end it was probably a joint decision that he enroll there. Robert had seen his older friend, John Hay, go east to Brown and knew that Conkling was headed for Yale. With his father gaining recognition among party regulars in the East, Robert must have appreciated what a Harvard education could mean for his own future. Moreover, having adopted the Todd disposition of manners and refinement, Robert likely saw Harvard as providing an opportunity to establish the social connections and acceptance that eluded Lincoln in his early manhood. For his part, Lincoln must have urged his son to get the education that he never had. Whatever leniency he was willing to grant his sons in their early education, Lincoln surely recognized that a college education, especially at a prestigious institution like Harvard, was important for, if not expected of, the son of a prominent lawyer and politician. Thus, for both Lincoln and his son, the prospect of Robert attending Harvard seemed like a good idea.

Shortly after Lincoln's death in 1865, Robert gave a description of his relationship with his father at the time he left home to take the Harvard entrance exam. "My Father's life was of a kind which gave me but little opportunity to learn the details of his early career. During my childhood and early youth he was almost constantly away from home, attending courts or making political speeches. In 1859 when I was sixteen and when he was beginning to devote himself to practice in his own neighborhood, and when I would have both the inclination and means of gratifying my desire to become better acquainted with the history of his struggles, I went to New Hampshire to school and afterward to Harvard College, and he became president. Henceforth any great intimacy between us became impossible. I scarcely even had ten minutes quiet talk with him during his Presidency, on account of his constant devotion to business."

Lincoln biographers have seized upon this statement to conclude that Robert felt a deep and permanent distance with his father. It is as if finding such a distance would enhance Lincoln's reputation as a hardworking lawyer and politician by suggesting that Lincoln sacrificed his family in pursuit of his career ambitions. For example, the eminent Lincoln historian David Herbert Donald wrote in 1995, "Robert's principal memory of his father during [the Springfield] years was of his loading his saddlebags in preparation for going out on the circuit." But there is no evidence that Robert made that specific statement. It appears that Donald merely expanded upon previous statements made by Lincoln biographer Frederick Trevor Hill and Lincoln scholar Wayne C. Temple. Hill wrote in his 1906 biography of Lincoln, "The Hon. Robert Lincoln told the writer that he distinctly remembers seeing his father start out on horseback, with his saddlebags, to accompany the judge on the circuit." Citing that very quotation from Hill's book, Temple wrote in 1960, "One of the first sights which Robert Todd Lincoln could recall was that of his father leaving home with saddlebags and a horse to follow the circuit." Somehow, Robert's saddlebag story morphed from a "distinct" memory as described by Hill, to a "first" memory as described by Temple, to the "principal" memory of his childhood as described by Donald.

Moreover, Robert's statement in the wake of his father's death clearly exaggerated the paucity of time that Lincoln spent with him both before and after he became president. In fact, as will be seen, Robert made frequent visits to Washington to see his father, often discussed his schooling and future plans with him, was occasionally consulted by his father on matters relating to the war, and frequently accompanied Lincoln on official business away from the White House. The record is full of interaction and conversations between Lincoln and Robert, both before and after Lincoln became president.

So why would Robert want to paint a picture that seemed to create distance between him and his father, or at least give the impression to biographers that he spent so little time with him? Robert made the statements minimizing his interactions with his father at a time when he was fending off requests for intimate details of his late father's life. By suggesting to others that he spent so little time with his father that he did not know much about him, he was able to curtail further inquiry by curious biographers. "While it is true," Robert wrote shortly after Lincoln's death, "that the details of the private life of a public man have always a great interest in the minds of some—it is after all his works which make him live—& the rest is but secondary." Robert was well aware that not long after Lincoln's death, biographers were hunting for information about Lincoln's reported romantic relationship with Ann Rutledge and were working mightily to paint the widow Mary in a rather unsympathetic light in order to make Lincoln seem all the more remarkable for tolerating her for so many years.

When Robert discovered that Lincoln's former law partner, William Herndon, was collecting a significant amount of personal information about his father to include in a biography, Robert pleaded with Herndon not to reveal sensitive matters. "All I ask is, that nothing may be published by you, which after *careful consideration* will seem apt to cause pain to my father's family, which I am sure you do not wish to do." When Herndon continued to press, Robert tried again. "One of the unpleasant consequences of political success is that however little it may have to do with that success, his whole private life is exposed to a public gaze—that is part of the price he pays. But I see no reason why his wife and children should be included—especially while they are alive." So, Robert refused to assist biographers in telling the story of Lincoln the father, and by such refusal he left the impression that there was a deep and permanent distance between him and his father. Now, however, nearly a hundred years after Robert's death, by assembling the rich trove of letters, diaries, and testimonies of Lincoln and his contemporaries, we are able to gaze into the lives of Lincoln's children and their relationships with their father, not for the purpose of exposing intimate details that might cause the pain that Robert feared, but to more fully understand and appreciate one of the most important figures in American history.

In late August 1859, Robert boarded a train and traveled from Springfield to Cambridge to take the Harvard entrance examination. He carried with him a letter of introduction that Lincoln had secured from Charles B. Brown, a recent Harvard graduate and clerk in Lincoln's law office. The exam, held on September 1, covered sixteen subjects, including history, geometry, algebra, mathematics, and Greek and Latin grammar. Students were also required to translate long sentences from English into Latin, including the following: "Let there be friendship for King Antiochus with the Roman people: let him depart from the cities on this side of Mount Taurus; let him carry forth no arms from those towns from which he may depart; if he has carried any forth, let him return them." One of the history questions asked, "For what do you remember the year 218 BC?"

Robert failed fifteen of the sixteen subjects on the exam and was denied admittance to Harvard. Reluctantly, he telegraphed the news to his father. No letter survives that reveals Lincoln's reaction to his son's setback. A year later, however, after Robert's friend and Illinois State classmate George Latham also failed the Harvard entrance exam, Lincoln wrote Latham a letter of encouragement that may give some clues to what he had said to his own son upon his rejection from Harvard.

> *I have scarcely felt greater pain in my life than on learning yesterday in Bob's letter, that you had failed to enter Harvard University. And yet there is very little in it, if you will allow no feeling of discouragement to seize, and prey upon you. It is a certain truth, that you*

can enter, and graduate in, Harvard University; and having made the attempt, you must succeed in it. "Must" is the word. I know not how to aid you, save in the assurance of one of mature age, and much severe experience, that you can not fail, if you resolutely determine, that you will not. . . . In your temporary failure there is no evidence that you may not yet be a better scholar, and a more successful man in the great struggle of life, than many others, who have entered college more easily.

Again I say let no feeling of discouragement prey upon you, and in the end you are sure to succeed.

"[I] imagin[ed] that there would be no trouble in [entering Harvard], in which idea it is necessary to say I was very much mistaken," Robert later reflected. "On being examined I had the honor to receive a fabulous number of conditions which precluded my admission. I was resolved not to retire beaten, and acting under the advice of President Walker, I entered the well-known Academy at Exeter, N.H." Robert's own reaction to his failure evidences not only a mature introspection over his lack of preparation at Illinois State, but also suggests that his father may have indeed given him the same advice offered to George Latham the following year.

Phillips Exeter Academy was an established preparatory school nestled in the rolling hills of Exeter, New Hampshire. Founded in 1783, it counted among its alumni Daniel Webster, Lewis Cass, and historian George Bancroft and was considered by some to be "the best-endowed institution of its class in the State of New Hampshire, if not in the country." On September 15, 1859, less than two weeks after failing the Harvard entrance exam Robert, with his father's approval, enrolled at Phillips Exeter along with 133 other students.

He arrived with a plan that he believed would soon lead him back to Harvard and allow him to catch up with his peers who passed the exam on their first try. He soon suffered yet another disappointment, however. The faculty recognized his inadequate education, as partly evidenced by his failure of the Harvard exam, and placed him in the pre-freshman class. Robert instantly knew that this decision would effectively prevent him from entering Harvard as a sophomore the following year as he had hoped and instead meant that at best he would have to begin there as a freshman. "I went to Exeter," he wrote, "hoping to enter the Class preparing to enter college, the next July, as Sophomores. The worthy Principal, Dr. Soule, soon convinced me of the vanity of my aspirations and I was obliged to enter the Subfreshman Class."

Lincoln promptly paid the $24 annual tuition and periodically sent Robert extra money for expenses and spending money. Robert shared a room with Springfield friend George Latham, who had also decided to attend Phillips Exeter for a year before attempting the Harvard entrance exam, though he ultimately failed that exam and eventually enrolled at Yale.

Having suffered the consequences of his lack of effort at Illinois State, Robert finally decided to buckle down. He later described his year at Phillips Exeter as being "devoid of excitement and full of hard work." Yet he had his share of fun. He was a "very popular young fellow, a gentleman in every sense of the word," one of his classmates recalled, and he was very popular with the girls. Moreover, Robert participated in some college pranks of the type that most parents hope their children will have sense enough to avoid but which cause little surprise when the miscreants are caught participating in the antics. One night Robert and some classmates crept through town unhinging and carrying off fence gates and performing other acts of mischief. He soon found himself, he later recalled with mature amusement, in "a flight from Justice, who pursued me in the shape of a policeman all over the flourishing village, for having, in the company with others, committed sundry depredations on the property of various denizens." The policeman eventually apprehended the boys, who were then brought before Dr. Gideon Soule, the principal of Phillips Exeter. Recognizing that Robert's behavior might prove embarrassing to his father, who was by then being mentioned as a possible presidential candidate, Soule offered to dismiss Robert from the entire affair. Robert refused and stood with his comrades to face his punishment. Fearing the worst—suspension or expulsion—the boys were greatly relieved when Soule merely ordered them to pay for the damages. "Filthy lucre," Robert wrote, "also the root of all evil, proved a great blessing in the present case." It is not known whether Lincoln ever found out about the incident or supplied the money for Robert's share of the damages, but given Lincoln's penchant for good stories and his philosophy that his boys should have a good time, if he did learn of Robert's involvement he likely reacted with a mixture of disappointment and amusement.

Upon Robert's departure for college, Lincoln realized that his son was likely gone from home for good, so he made even more determined efforts to spend time with him. Those efforts began with a visit to Robert at Exeter in early 1860. The visit grew out of an invitation Lincoln received to speak at Plymouth Congregational Church in Brooklyn, New York. Abolitionist preacher Henry Ward Beecher, who led the church, asked Lincoln to speak in February 1860 as part of a series of lectures sponsored by the church. Lincoln had by that time become fairly well known as an anti-slavery orator and, accordingly, was in demand by groups wishing to promote that cause. Previous speakers in the series included abolitionists Francis P. Blair and Cassius M. Clay. Beecher offered Lincoln $200 for the speech, a generous fee at the time. Lincoln accepted on the condition that he "be allowed to speak on a topic of his own choosing."

New Hampshire judge Elwin L. Page later wrote that the opportunity to travel east "appealed to the father, not the politician," as Lincoln also saw the trip to New York as a chance to visit Robert, who was just a modest train trip away from the big city. In early January, Lincoln had written Robert promising that when a large fee from a case he had just won came in, he would make the trip to Exeter. A week later, a disappointed Lincoln wrote again saying that the client was unable to pay and that the trip would need to be postponed until he was able to collect some more money. Days later, however, Beecher's invitation arrived, along with the offer of the $200 fee. Lincoln promptly wrote Robert informing him of his intention to visit immediately after delivering the speech in New York. Robert had been gone from home for nearly two months when Lincoln accepted the invitation, rivaling the long periods of time that Lincoln was away while riding the circuit.

After spending $100 on a new suit at Woods & Henckle, a local tailor shop, on February 23 Lincoln boarded a train in Springfield and headed for New York. When Lincoln arrived there two days later, he took a room at the Astor House, an elaborate hotel at 217 Broadway that featured indoor plumbing and commanded $2 per night. Later in the day he visited Henry C. Bowen, editor of the New York *Independent*, who informed him that the Young Men's Central Republican Union had taken over sponsorship of his speaking engagement and that the venue had been changed from Beecher's church in Brooklyn to the Cooper Union in Manhattan. Many people considered the Cooper Union building, which still stands today at the convergence of Third and Fourth Avenues and Seventh Street, as one of the most elegant auditoriums in the world. The next day Lincoln attended church services, spent some time touring the city, and worked on his speech.

On the morning of February 27, Lincoln sat for a photograph at Matthew Brady's studio on Broadway, not far from his hotel. Brady was the most famous photographer in the country, having photographed nearly all of the major political figures of the time. While at the studio, Lincoln met the eminent statesman and historian George Bancroft, an alumnus of Phillips Exeter. Lincoln told Bancroft that he was on his way to the school to visit his son, who "already knows much more than his father." Though his new black suit, which hung well below his waist like a frock coat, was somewhat ill fitting, Lincoln still looked fresh and distinguished. In Mary's absence he managed to neatly comb his hair, though it was not slicked back as in previous photographs taken in Springfield when Mary assisted with his grooming. Yet Brady still found him difficult to photograph. "When I got him before the camera," Brady later recalled, "I asked him if I might not arrange his collar, and with that he began to pull it up. 'Ah,' said Lincoln, 'I see you want to shorten my neck.' 'That's just it,' I answered, and we both laughed." Standing tall and erect, Lincoln looked a bit younger than his forty-eight years, though that was largely due to Brady touching up the negative to remove some lines from his face and correct a roving eye.

That evening Lincoln delivered his speech at Cooper Union. It was a triumph of substance over style. One observer recalled that many in the audience expected the westerner "to be something weird, rough, and uncultivated," and in physical appearance they got what they expected:

"The long, ungainly figure, upon which hung clothes that, while new for the trip, were evidently the work of an unskilled tailor; the large feet; the clumsy hands, of which . . . the orator seemed unduly conscious; the long, gaunt head capped by a shock of hair that seemed not to have been thoroughly brushed out made a picture which did not fit in with New York's conception of a finished statesman." Nevertheless, his speech electrified the crowd. Concluding with the words, "Let us have faith that right makes might, and in that faith, let us, to the end, dare to do our duty as we understand it," Lincoln left to a standing ovation. The next day numerous newspapers hailed the speech, and soon it was reprinted into pamphlets and distributed by Republican operatives who saw Lincoln as a possible presidential nominee later that year. In fact, Lincoln's Cooper Union speech would play a key role in Lincoln both securing the Republican nomination the following May and then winning the general election in November.

The next morning Lincoln traveled east. Word of his Cooper Union address had already reached New England. He first stopped in Providence, where Rhode Island residents flocked from nearby towns and rural areas to hear him speak before a capacity crowd at Railroad Hall. Up in New Hampshire where Lincoln was scheduled to go next, George W. Benn, a local Republican leader in Dover, fired off a hastily drafted letter to Robert, asking if his father would be willing to speak in that city. Benn did not even know Robert's name, only that Lincoln had a son at Exeter. He addressed the letter "To _____ Lincoln, son of A. Lincoln." Robert immediately replied in a polite letter promising to forward the request to "Mr. Lincoln," who would have to "answer for himself, though I have no doubt he will be happy to comply with your kind invitation should his time permit." Robert, keenly aware of his father's political ambitions, instinctively knew that Lincoln would gladly make unscheduled speeches even though the primary purpose of the trip to New Hampshire was for them to spend time together. In fact, even before leaving Providence and unbeknownst to Robert, Lincoln had agreed to make speeches in Concord and Manchester, New Hampshire, both easy train rides from Exeter.

Lincoln arrived in Exeter on February 29. Robert met him at the station and took him back to his room at a house owned by Mrs. S. B.

Clarke, where they spent the night. The next morning, Lincoln, Robert, and Robert's roommate George Latham took the train to Concord, where Lincoln delivered a speech. Robert soon realized that, although his father ostensibly came to see him, Lincoln simply could not leave his work behind and focus exclusively on his son. After spending the night in Concord, the party left for Manchester, where Lincoln delivered another speech after checking into the City Hotel at the corner of Elm and Lowell Streets. After leaving Manchester, Lincoln dropped off Robert and Latham at Exeter and went on to Dover, promising to return the next day. Just as Robert had earlier predicted, Lincoln had accepted Benn's invitation to speak at Dover.

Lincoln returned to Exeter on March 3. He spent some time in Robert's room, where he wrote several letters declining invitations to speak. "I have already spoken five times, and I am engaged to speak five more," a weary Lincoln wrote Isaac Pomeroy, a member of the Young Men's Working Club of the Republican Party of Newark, New Jersey, who had invited him to speak there. "By the time these engagements shall be fulfilled, I shall be so far worn down, and also will be carried so far beyond my allotted time, that an immediate return home will be a necessity with me. At this very sitting I am declining invitations to go to Philadelphia, Reading, and Pittsburgh in Pa. You perceive I treat you no worse than I do others." After spending part of the afternoon with Robert, Lincoln delivered a speech to the faculty and students at Robert's school. One of the students later recalled the event: "Mr. Lincoln's legs were so long he had trouble disposing of them and twisted them about under the chair to get them out of the way. One of the boys leaned over and whispered: 'Look here! Don't you feel kind of sorry for Bob?' We didn't laugh. We were sympathetic for 'Bob' because his father didn't make a better appearance. The girls whispered to each other, 'Isn't it too bad Bob's got such a homely father.'" Whatever embarrassment Robert may have felt was, however, soon relieved. Lincoln "rose slowly, untangled those long legs from their contact with the rounds of the chair, drew himself up to his full height of six feet, four inches, and began his speech. Not ten minutes had passed before his uncouth appearance was absolutely forgotten by us boys, and, I believe, by all of that large audience. . . . There was no more pity for our friend Bob; we were proud of his father."

The next day, Sunday, gave father and son some quiet time together. Though it was true, as later reported, that "during his days in Exeter, Lincoln was seen much in Robert's company," in fact the two were often on the go and rarely had moments to relax together except at night. On that Sunday, however, they finally got their chance. Early in the morning, Lincoln took some time to catch up on his correspondence, including writing a letter to James Briggs, an aide to Henry Ward Beecher, in which he acknowledged receipt of the $200 speaking fee. Lincoln also wrote to Mary. He described the speaking itinerary he kept with Robert in New Hampshire and inquired about the health of Willie and Tad, whom Mary had reported as being sick in an earlier letter to Robert. Then, in a bit of fatherly deference, he reported to Mary, "This is Sunday morning; and according to Bob's orders, I am to go to church once to-day." He closed by describing his remaining speaking schedule and complaining about how busy he had been on the trip. "I have been unable to escape this toil. If I had foreseen it, I think I would not have come east at all." Later that morning Lincoln and Robert attended church at the Second Church of the New Parish, and then took a leisurely walk back to Robert's room at Hemlock Square, at the corner of High and Pleasant Streets, where they continued to talk.

That evening, Lincoln and his son dined together and then joined some of Robert's classmates for an evening of fun. "Into the chatter Lincoln entered with true boy-like spirit," wrote one of Robert's friends. "When he talked with Bob, or the boys gathered around, the deep seams of his face broke into a series of twinkling lines." When Robert mentioned that Henry Cluskey played the banjo, Lincoln immediately requested that the boy bring out the instrument and entertain the group. Lincoln enjoyed the music so much that he pointed to the banjo and joked, "Robert, you ought to have one."

After spending the night in Robert's room, Lincoln left by train the next morning. Over the next several days, Lincoln delivered speeches in Connecticut and Rhode Island, then returned to New York. On March 12, Lincoln boarded a train and headed home to Springfield. On the day of his departure, the *New York Tribune* summed up his eastern trip: "Mr. Lincoln has done good work and made many warm friends." Though no record survives that reveals what Lincoln and Robert discussed during their time together at Exeter, it was likely a combination of politics, family, and school.

When Robert later wrote, "I went to New Hampshire to school and afterward to Harvard College, and he became president. Henceforth any great intimacy between us became impossible," his failure to mention Lincoln's visit to Exeter made it appear that he did not fully appreciate the time they had together. As noted earlier, however, Robert wrote these words in an attempt to fend off prying biographers. In later years, Robert acknowledged that his father came east to see him because he was worried about his well-being. In doing so, Robert jokingly took credit for Lincoln's ascension to the presidency. Robert noted that had he not failed the Harvard exams—a failure that caused great concern on the part of his father—Lincoln might not have made the effort to travel east to make the Cooper Union speech and thus may not have been elected president.

Nearly ten months passed before Robert saw his father again. During that time, Lincoln secured the Republican presidential nomination, defeating the initial favorite, Senator William Seward of New York, on the third ballot. Though the convention was held in Chicago, news of Lincoln's nomination quickly reached the East Coast. Robert's classmate, Albert Blair, was the first to see the news when he bought a copy of the *Boston Journal*. With the newspaper in hand, Blair quickly set out to tell Robert. Finding him in a bowling alley "much frequented by him . . . Blair flourished the paper and yelled 'Bob, your father got it!'"

"Good," replied Robert, as he slapped his hip. Then, with the humor of a college student wholly dependent on his parents for financial support, he added with a smile, "I will write home for a check before he spends all of his money in the campaign."

Robert took time from his studies to help his father's campaign locally in Exeter. He could have stayed on the sidelines, concentrating on academics so as to ensure his admittance to Harvard, but he did not. Lincoln's visit to Exeter earlier in the year drew the young man closer to his father. Though Robert knew that Lincoln's election to the presidency would make it difficult for them to spend more time together, he also knew how important the presidency was to his father. So, Robert wholeheartedly embraced Lincoln's candidacy. He joined a Republican group called the "Wide-Awakes," who were known for participating in torchlight parades, and helped hang a large "Lincoln & Hamlin" banner in town. He preferred to stay in the background, however, and balked when Frank Fuller, a Republican activist from New Hampshire, asked him to read the Declaration of Independence at a large Fourth of July celebration. "I'll do it if father is willing," Robert told Fuller, perhaps feeling that he was being asked not for his own qualifications but solely because he was the son of Abraham Lincoln. Fuller then telegraphed Lincoln with the request. Perhaps not fully appreciating his son's preference to stay out of the limelight, Lincoln promptly replied, "Tell Robert to take every occasion to read that immortal document, and the bigger the crowd, the louder he must holler." Robert reluctantly complied and "entered into the spirit of the occasion with all the fervor of youth."

Robert excelled at Phillips Exeter. Amos Tuck, a resident of Exeter and founder of the Republican Party in New Hampshire, told Lincoln's friend and fellow circuit rider Judge David Davis that Robert "has behaved himself as the son of Abraham Lincoln might be expected to do. He stands at the top of the ladder as a scholar, and is a singularly discreet, well behaved, brilliant and promising young man." Robert himself described his time at Exeter as "a very valuable year." Robert graduated from Phillips Exeter in June of 1860. Busy with his presidential campaign, Lincoln was unable to attend the commencement ceremonies. Whatever disappointment Robert may have felt at his father's absence may have been somewhat ameliorated by good news that came from Cambridge: after retaking the Harvard entrance exam, he passed and was accepted into the freshman class at Harvard. "After the commencement," Robert later wrote, "I was able to inform my father that I had succeeded in entering [Harvard] College without a Condition—quite a change from the previous year." Lincoln was proud of his son's achievements, and he recognized that those achievements were all the more remarkable in light of the lax parenting that he and Mary practiced before sending Robert east to school. "Our eldest boy, Bob, has been away from us nearly a year at school," Lincoln wrote a friend in early July, "and will enter Harvard University this month. He promises very well, considering we never controlled him much."

Up to the time that Robert had left home for college, Lincoln's parenting of the boy had been, in some ways, the polar opposite of his own father's way of raising him. Where Thomas was a disciplinarian, Lincoln was permissive to a fault; where Thomas undertook no efforts to educate his son, Lincoln made schooling available and offered encouragement. Where Thomas forced physical labor on his son and felt disappointment when the boy later rejected the frontier life, Lincoln did not push hard work on his son and did not steer him in one direction or another toward a particular career. Lincoln saw that his son was developing into a mature young man who was on a straight pathway to success, starting with attendance at a prestigious university. He knew that Robert would undoubtedly have an easier entrée into the professional world than he had, which must have given him some degree of satisfaction. Lincoln also knew that he had only a limited ability to impact his son's career success. In Thomas's time, fathers could more easily transmit their status position to their sons, whether in the form of a particular skill or through an inheritance of productive land and property. While Lincoln was capable of arranging introductions so that his son could meet certain people who might benefit the boy's career, it would be up to Robert to get the education necessary to make the introductions worth arranging.

Robert was already gone from the house for a year by the time he headed for Cambridge. Lincoln likely remembered that he himself had little contact with his own father once he had left home. With Robert well on his way to adult independence, Lincoln realized that he would need to make greater efforts to remain close with his son in the future, a task all the more difficult because of the possibility that he might assume the presidency. In the years ahead, Lincoln continued to build on the Exeter experience.

Lincoln also knew that he still had two other boys at home who were approaching their formative years, so there was still an opportunity to spend more time with them than he had with Robert in his early years. If he could win the presidency, that opportunity might be appreciably easier to seize. Having both his home and office in the White House would allow Lincoln to see the boys throughout the day, and because he could keep his overnight travel to a minimum, he would likely be home almost every night. Thus, Washington held the promise that Tad and Willie might enjoy an entirely different paternal experience with their father than Robert had known in Springfield.

CHAPTER 7

So Much Bliss

THE 1860 PRESIDENTIAL ELECTION WAS A FOUR-MAN RACE. LINCOLN, OF course, was the Republican party nominee. The regular Democratic party nominated Stephen A. Douglas, the same man who had defeated Lincoln for the United States Senate seat from Illinois two years earlier. Southern Democrats, unhappy with Douglas, bolted their party and created a new party known as both the Southern Democratic Party and the Constitutional Democratic Party. They nominated President James Buchanan's pro-slavery vice president, John C. Breckenridge of Kentucky. A group of former Whigs, who wished to avoid secession by de-emphasizing the slavery issue, formed the Constitutional Union Party and nominated former Tennessee Senator John Bell. On November 6, 1860, Abraham Lincoln was elected president. Though he garnered just 40 percent of the popular vote in the four-man race (to 30 percent for Douglas, 18 percent for Breckenridge, and 12 percent for Bell), Lincoln handily won the all-important Electoral College with 180 votes, compared to 72 for Breckenridge (all from Southern states), 39 for Bell, and just 12 for Douglas.

In the months between his election in November 1860 and his inauguration in March 1861, Lincoln kept busy assembling his administration and monitoring events in the South, where rebellion was in the air. He also spent time getting his personal affairs in order, selling some furniture and arranging for the house to be rented. He decided to leave Fido in the care of a neighbor, much to the disappointment of Willie and Tad, but agreed to let the mutt pose for a photograph at a studio in

Springfield so that the boys could bring to Washington a fresh reminder of their cherished pet.

In January, Mary traveled to New York City where she went on a shopping spree that plunged the family into debt. Eager to cater to the wife of the president-elect, merchants tempted her with the finest clothes, hats, scarves, and jewelry, and extended her credit on the assumption that her husband would make good on the debts. Mary had never been particularly careful with money. Now, as she undertook the role of the president's wife (the term "first lady" would not be commonly used until after 1877), she exhibited an increasing compulsion to shop. In doing so, she spent money that the Lincolns did not have. Though she managed to keep her husband in the dark about the extent of her personal debts during his presidency, those obligations eventually caught up with her after Lincoln's death and resulted in great public embarrassment to her and her children.

Robert joined his mother in New York, having arranged for a brief leave of absence from Harvard in addition to the normal winter break. He did so in order to be with his family for the unique experience of seeing his father leave Springfield and assume the duties of the presidency. Bad weather and poor communications left Lincoln uncertain as to when Mary and Robert would arrive by train back in Springfield. A *New York Herald* reporter wrote that "dutiful husband and father that he is, he had proceeded to the railroad depot for three successive nights in his anxiety to receive them, and that in spite of snow and cold." When mother and son finally arrived on January 25, Lincoln was "delighted" and found his wife in "good health and excellent spirits."

On February 6, five days before the family was to depart for Washington, the Lincolns hosted a reception at their house. In 1856 they added a full second floor to the home and expanded the formal dining room, but it was still too small to accommodate the seven hundred guests who wanted to greet the nation's next president, many of whom were the "political elite of Illinois and the beauty and fashion of the era." "Such a crowd, I seldom, or ever saw at a private house," wrote Mercy Conkling, whose son Clinton had left for Yale at the same time Robert traveled east to take the Harvard entrance exam. "It took about twenty minutes to get in the hall door. And then it required no little management to make your way out." Robert "figured quite largely," Mercy observed. "While I was standing near Mr. L he came up, and in his humorous style, gave his hand to his father, saying: 'Good evening *Mr. Lincoln!*'" Then, in a touching moment of intimate banter between Lincoln and his eldest son, Lincoln "gave him a gentle slap in the face."

Shortly after 7:30 a.m. on February 11, one day before Lincoln's fifty-second birthday, he and Robert walked together to the Great Western Railroad depot in Springfield. It was time for Lincoln to say goodbye to his friends and neighbors. Standing on the platform of the cold and drab station, its planks covered in mud from the shoes of well-wishers who walked through the dirt streets in a light rain to attend the send-off, Lincoln gave a moving farewell address that paid homage to his family, his friends, the city in which he came of age, and the God who gave him comfort in the wake of Eddy's death and whose help he would seek in the difficult years ahead:

> *My friends—No one, not in my situation, can appreciate my feeling of sadness at this parting. To this place, and the kindness of its people, I owe every thing. Here I have lived a quarter of a century, and have passed from a young man to an old man. Here my children have been born, and one is buried. I now leave, not knowing when, or whether ever, I may return, with a task before me greater than that which rested upon Washington. Without the assistance of that Divine Being, who ever attended him, I cannot succeed. With that assistance I cannot fail. Trusting in Him, who can go with me, and remain with you and be every where for good, let us confidently hope that all will yet be well. To His care commending you, as I hope in your prayers you will commend me, I bid you affectionate farewell.*

With that, Lincoln and Robert boarded the train, which pulled away promptly at 8:00 a.m. driven by a powerful Rogers locomotive. Also on board were Mary's brother-in-law, Dr. William Wallace, for whom Willie was named; Lincoln's former law partner Edward Baker, for whom his late son Eddy had been named; Robert's high-school friend George

Latham; Lincoln's newly hired secretaries John Hay and John Nicolay, who were only slightly older than Robert and who would befriend the president's oldest son in the coming years; and a number of other friends and political supporters.

For security purposes, Lincoln and Robert initially planned to travel separately from Mary and the younger boys, who were scheduled to leave several days later. As the prospect of civil war loomed heavily over the country, Lincoln's security detail had received numerous reports of death threats being made against the president-elect. Back in November, Lincoln received an anonymous telegram from Pensacola, Florida, informing him, "You were last night hung in effigy in this city." Over the coming months Lincoln would be given the same treatment in a number of other cities. In early January, Mary received an anonymous package from South Carolina, which had recently seceded from the Union, containing a canvas painting of Lincoln "with a rope around his neck, his feet chained and his body adorned with tar and feathers." Just hours after Lincoln left Springfield, General Winfield Scott, who was the general-in-chief of the army, changed his mind about the travel arrangements and sent a telegraph from Washington recommending that the family travel together. "Mrs. Lincoln was not to leave for some days after his departure," wrote Mercy Conkling to her son, "but a dispatch from Gen. Scott, determined her to leave the evening of the same day. The General thought it would be safer for him to be surrounded by his family." With that, Mary, Willie, and Tad immediately boarded an evening train. Informed of Scott's recommendation, Lincoln reluctantly agreed to the arrangements.

During a stop in Indianapolis, as he disembarked the train, Lincoln entrusted seventeen-year-old Robert with his black gripsack satchel that contained, unbeknownst to the boy, the only copy of Lincoln's inaugural address. Lincoln later described the address as "my certificate of my moral character, written by myself." While still in Springfield, Lincoln had publicly requested a two-week period of "the utmost privacy" so he could work on the address, and he let it be known that "no further invitations will be issued to prominent politicians to visit the President-elect, and none are desired here." After arriving at the hotel, Robert was invited by a group of boys his age to go out for an evening on the town. He hastily deposited the bag with a worker at the hotel, not realizing its valuable contents. When later that evening Lincoln could not find the bag among his belongings, he sent an aide to locate Robert and bring him back to the hotel. Under questioning from his father, who revealed the contents of the bag to the boy for the first time, Robert explained "with bored and injured virtue" that he thought he had given the bag to "a waiter of the hotel or to some one, he couldn't tell whom." A sharp exchange followed. Lincoln's friend, Ward Hill Lamon, who witnessed the event, said that he had never seen Lincoln "so much annoyed, so much perplexed, and for a time so angry. He seldom manifested a spirit of anger toward his children—this was the nearest approach to it I had ever witnessed." After frantically searching a pile of miscellaneous baggage in the custody of the hotel, Lincoln and Lamon located the missing bag. Lincoln likely expected a greater degree of responsibility from his college-age son, while Robert was probably frustrated that his father had failed to tell him of the importance of the contents so that he might have treated the bag with a more appropriate level of care.

Mary and the two younger boys caught up with Lincoln and Robert the next morning in Indianapolis, and for the next ten days the family would be together on the train. As the train made its way east traveling at about thirty miles an hour, Willie and Tad ran about the cars, wreaking havoc on the rest of the passengers. Mary had anticipated that the boys would be a handful, so she brought along a nurse to help keep them in check. It was to no avail. A reporter observed that one of the boys played tricks on other passengers by asking, "Do you want to see Old Abe?" When the excited passenger said, "Yes," the boy would point to someone else on the train and then giggle at the victim's disappointment. As each day came to an end, however, the boys settled down when bedtime approached. During a layover in Cincinnati, Lincoln attended a reception late into the evening. When he finally returned to his room, "he found a fretful little boy [Tad] waiting for his father to put him to bed. Lincoln took him lovingly in his arms, carried him to the adjoining room, gently undressed him, and laid him down. This had evidently been the custom at home and it was to be continued in the White House."

As the Lincoln family neared Harrisburg, Pennsylvania, rumors of assassination plots had multiplied. Lincoln's security forces finally decided to separate him from his family and secret him into the capital on a separate train. Lincoln left in the middle of the night, and Robert did not learn of his departure until the next morning. The family was reunited in Washington on February 23, when they all checked into Willard's Hotel.

For the next ten days, Lincoln met with political leaders, polished his inaugural address, and attended numerous receptions in his honor. Lincoln, his secretary John Nicolay, and Robert occasionally took predawn walks along the streets of Washington. Robert also did some sightseeing on his own, including a visit to the Patent Office where he once again toured the model room that he so fondly remembered seeing with his father thirteen years earlier. This time he was also able to see the wooden model of his father's patented invention that lifted boats over shoals and obstructions.

The morning of inauguration day, March 4, was cold and cloudy. Lincoln and Robert arose at 5:00 a.m. Having already practiced reading his inaugural address several times, Lincoln asked Robert to read it aloud back to him so that he could hear the speech as the audience would hear it. Robert, who was much relieved that the once-misplaced document had been found, obliged.

By 1:00 p.m., as the inaugural ceremonies got under way, the skies had cleared and the temperature had warmed. Lincoln was escorted to a wooden canopy built on the east portico of the capitol to protect the key participants from any rain. Lincoln sat in the front row, near outgoing President Buchanan and Chief Justice Roger Taney. To the left of the canopy sat the associate justices of the Supreme Court and key members of Congress, including Senator Stephen Douglas, the Democrat whom Lincoln had defeated for the presidency. Behind them sat the diplomatic corps and various other dignitaries. Mary, Willie, and Tad sat behind the diplomatic gallery, along with wives of the various dignitaries. Robert, along with Lincoln's young secretaries John Hay and John Nicolay, was given a choice seat just to the right of the canopy, not far from his father.

Promptly at 1:30 p.m., Lincoln was introduced to the gathered crowd by his old friend Edward Baker, now a senator from Oregon. As was the custom at the time, the president-elect delivered his inaugural address before being sworn in. When Lincoln rose to deliver his address, he could not find a place to put his stovepipe hat, so Douglas graciously reached out and took it so that Lincoln could continue with the ceremonies. "If I cannot be President, I can at least be his hat-bearer," Douglas joked. When Lincoln completed his speech, he took the oath of office from eighty-three-year-old Taney, "whose black robes, attenuated figure, and cadaverous countenance," wrote one observer, "reminded me of a galvanized corpse."

Though Lincoln was the center of attention during the inaugural events, the press paid some attention to his family. One reporter picked up on what many back in Springfield had known for years: that Robert and his father were quite different in many respects, including in manners and appearance. The reporter mistakenly attributed the differences to Robert's brief time at Harvard rather than the years back in Illinois where Robert was influenced by Mary and the rest of the more refined Todd family: "The effect of a residence within the improving influence of genteel, well dressed and well behaved Boston is plainly noticeable in his outward appearance, the comparative elegance of which presents a striking contrast to the loose, careless, awkward rigging of his Presidential father." Two days after Lincoln's inauguration, Robert left for Cambridge. During the campaign, Robert had been dubbed "the Prince of Rails," a play on the Prince of Wales, the future king of England who had visited America a year earlier. Robert's unwelcome nickname at once combined his father's image of a hardworking rail-splitter with the fact that Robert was the son of a possible future president. Robert's departure from Washington was noted in the papers. The *New York Herald* reported, "Bob, the Prince of Rails, starts for Cambridge tomorrow. He is sick of Washington and glad to get back to his college."

Meanwhile, the rest of the family settled in at the White House. The first order of business for the family was to inspect the house, "and this was most faithfully done by the irrepressible 'Tad' and observant Willie, from dome to basement, and every servant interviewed by these same young gentlemen, from 'Old Edward,' the door keeper, Stackpole, the messenger, to the maids and scullions." A "short, thin, humorous Irishman," Edward would prove invaluable to the Lincoln family, for he could "be trusted equally with state secrets, or with the diplomatic management of the President's unpredictable young son Tad." Fifteen presidents had preceded Lincoln, but only one, John Tyler twenty years earlier, raised young children while living in the White House. Thus, the constant presence of children would be a new experience for the entire domestic staff. In the words of John Hay, the boys "kept the house in an uproar."

Within days after moving in, Mary met Mrs. Horatio Nelson Taft, whose husband was chief examiner of the Patent Office. When Mary learned that the Tafts had two sons about the same ages as Willie and Tad, she seized on the opportunity for her boys to have new playmates. "Send them around to-morrow, please, Mrs. Taft," Mary pleaded. "Willie and Tad are so lonely and everything is so strange to them here in Washington." Mrs. Taft complied, and the next day, her sons, Horatio Nelson Taft Jr., known as "Bud," who was eleven, and Haslet Cook Taft, known as "Holly," who was eight, showed up at the White House, along with their older sister, sixteen-year-old Julia. The children became fast friends, which was important not only for their own pleasure but because years later Julia, who maintained a diary, wrote and published *Tad Lincoln's Father*, a priceless record that provides a touching and intimate look at the Lincoln family inside the White House. Julia became, for a short time, the daughter the Lincolns never had. She saw Lincoln as "a good, uncle-like person . . . smiling and kind." He called her a "flibbertigibbet," which he said meant "a small, slim thin thing with curls and a white dress and a blue sash who flies instead of walking."

Willie paired with Bud, and Tad with Holly. Over the next year, the forces of mischief, destruction, and fun at both the White House and the Taft home were doubled. On the first day they played together, Bud and Holly returned home looking like they "done been huntin' coons in the brush." The boys soon found that the roof of the White House served as an ideal setting for various activities. At one point when Washington was racked by fear that Confederate forces were on the verge of invasion, the boys set out to defend the White House with a garrison of broken rifles and a log representing a cannon. "You should see the fort we've got on the roof of our house," Tad bragged to Julia. When Lincoln came by to review the forces, he presented them with a flag. Willie's and Tad's interest in military matters pleased Lincoln, and he occasionally brought one or both boys with him when he reviewed military exercises.

Lincoln soon arranged for Willie, Tad, Bud, and Holly to be outfitted in marching uniforms. Julia once reported that the four boys "took a vacant room in the attic for an 'old Capitol Prison' and shut up my little black cat and the neighbor's dog as prisoners of war. The cat spent the time on the shelf, while the dog rushed about with yelps and barks until their protestations became so loud that my mother ordered their release." At the Taft house, where the president's sons often made "themselves quite at home," Tad and Bud found some real firepower in the form of a loaded musket and, according to Julia, "succeeded in firing it out the window. It nicked the corner of Mrs. Bartle's house, next door, the bullet whistling over the head of their old mammy, who was washing some clothes in a tub."

The boys also managed to insert themselves into more formal functions. At a military funeral, Tad and Holly "perched themselves on the back of General Scott's chair. And when he rose, of course they fell back into the arms of some members of his staff." On another occasion rain prevented Bud and Holly from going home after a long day of playing at the White House. The Lincolns decided to let all of the boys attend a state dinner planned for that evening. Bud and Holly had to change into clothes belonging to the Lincoln boys, though they were all dressed casually. Mrs. Taft, a consummate Washington insider and stickler for proper etiquette, was shocked that the boys were allowed to attend without formal attire. But the boys thought that Lincoln himself was not dressed up enough. "I tell you," Tad said to Mrs. Taft, "those 'bassadors were all tied up with gold cords; they glittered grand." "Pa looked pretty plain with his black suit," Willie added, "but Ma was dressed up, you bet."

The boys also injected themselves into another formal gathering, though this time without an invitation. In May, Tad and Holly barged into a cabinet meeting and began blasting the room with their toy cannon. Lincoln, being the commander-in-chief of the Army and Navy, immediately took charge, stopping the meeting and escorting the boys out of the room so that order could be restored. The meeting did not resume, however, until Lincoln finished comforting Holly, "who had pinched his fingers with some contrivance." When Secretary of the Navy Gideon Welles later told Horatio Taft, Holly's father, about the incident, Taft "was greatly disgusted with these tidings and stored up a lecture to be administered to Holly on the crime of disturbing cabinet meetings." Lincoln, on the other hand, apparently gave no such lecture to Tad, whose penchant for interrupting cabinet meetings became legendary during Lincoln's presidency.

Once Tad and Bud enlisted Julia's help in finding a missing doll. Julia soon spotted the doll in the sitting room, but Lincoln was also there "stretched out in his large chair. His head was lying back, his eyes closed, his hands and feet extended, and such a worn and weary look upon his face that I closed the door softly and went back and told Tad, 'Your father is just going to sleep and he is dreadfully tired. I saw [the doll] under his chair, but don't you dare disturb the President.'"

Ignoring Julia's demand, Tad turned to her little brother and said, "Come on, Holly. Let's go down just as still and give our Indian war whoop." Julia reported with disgust that the boys "went down, as still as a load of bricks, and I heard their wild whoops below."

Willie and Tad also got into plenty of trouble without the help of the Taft boys. "One day Tad broke a large mirror in the vestibule where the Marine Band used to play at receptions" Julia later recounted. Someone had given him a new ball, which he threw up and caught in reckless disregard of his surroundings. In due time it landed against this mirror, resulting in a terrifying shattering of glass. Tad kicked a piece of the mirror on the floor while the rest of the group watched in a speechless horror. "Well, it's broken," Tad said casually. "I don't b'lieve Pa'll care."

Willie was more worried, however. "It is not Pa's looking glass," he said. "It belongs to the United States Government." Tad was unmoved. After rushing to the kitchen and performing the customary ceremony of throwing salt over his shoulder to prevent seven years of bad luck, Tad moved on to other things.

On another day, Tad ate all the strawberries from the garden that were being grown for use at a state dinner. Major John Watt, the White House gardener, was furious. Willie immediately tattled to Mary about the incident, but she did nothing. Julia then told Watt that Mrs. Lincoln was already aware of the infraction and suggested that he control his anger because Tad "is the Madam's son, remember." Watt snarled back, "The Madam's wildcat." As another young playmate later recalled, when she told Lincoln that Tad had teased her and pulled her hair, the boy's father "would dry my tears and tell Tad he should be ashamed for teasing such a little girl," while Mary's reaction "was often short-tempered and bitter-tongued."

Watt was not the only member of the White House staff who was victimized by the boys' antics. Shortly after the family moved in, Tad and Willie discovered the White House bell system located in the garret. The boys would periodically ring all the bells in all the offices at the same time, causing panicky clerks and messengers to scurry about trying to determine who needed what. Once the workers realized the source of the confusion, they uttered some choice words about the offending rascals.

Lincoln went along with some of the boys' mischief. One day the four boys went to the attic where they found a trunk containing Mrs. Lincoln's clothes. They decided to put on a circus and charge five cents admission. When Julia arrived she found Tad using shoe polish to make a black face, and "Willie was struggling with a lilac silk of his mother's. The gown had a long train and was cut in the expensive Victorian décolleté. I pinned it up so he could manage it, then straightened the bonnet. . . . [Bud] was wearing a white morning dress of Mrs. Lincoln's pinned around him in billowy folds." Julia asked if Lincoln knew what they were doing. "Yep," Tad replied. "Pa knows and he don't care, neither. He's coming up when those generals go away." The fun was brought to a temporary halt when Lincoln's secretary, John Hay, rushed up to the attic and angrily grabbed the president's spectacles, which the boys had taken without permission. Julia soon left and saw Lincoln in the hallway after he had finished meeting with his generals. "Having a great time up there, eh?" Lincoln inquired. "Yes sir," she replied. "They are making a dreadful noise, and they have Mrs. Lincoln's things on and they look horrid." Lincoln then "threw back his head and laughed heartily. . . . 'Come, Julie, let's go up and see it. How much is it?' 'Five cents,' I answered." Lincoln then proceeded upstairs to attend the circus.

After Tad was given a soldier doll that he named Jack, he and Willie would repeatedly accuse Jack of sleeping at his post or desertion, hold a mock court-martial, sentence the doll to be shot, and then carry out the execution with a toy gun. They then buried the doll with full military honors in the rose garden, much to the consternation of gardener Watt. One day when Watt "arrived and looked at the yawning grave amid his rose bushes in helpless anger," he said to the boys with resignation, "Boys, why don't you get Jack pardoned?" The boys thought that was a splendid idea and immediately took Jack to their father. With Lincoln's secretary, John Hay, looking on, the president told the boys that they needed to state their case. "Well you see, Pa," Tad began, "most everyday we try Jack for being a spy or deserter or something and then we shoot him and bury him, and Julia says it spoils his clothes, and Major Watt says it digs up his flowers, and so we thought we'd get you to fix us up a pardon." After listening to Tad's plea, Lincoln rendered his verdict. "Yes, Tad, I think you've made a case. It's a good law that no man shall twice be put in jeopardy of his life for the same offence and you've already shot and buried Jack a dozen times. I guess he's entitled to a pardon." After signing a pardon and handing it to Tad, Lincoln turned to Hay, who assisted Lincoln with requests for real pardons, and said, "And I only wish, Hay, they were all that easy." Julia later wrote that less than a week later, she found Jack "hanging with a cord around his neck from a tree in the rear of our garden. Tad said he was proven to be a spy."

Lincoln also liked to frolic with the boys. "Once I heard a terrible racket in another room," Julia wrote, "and opening the door with the idea of bestowing some sisterly 'don't' upon my young brothers, whose voices could be heard amid the din, beheld the President lying on the floor, with the four boys trying to hold him down. Willie and Bud had hold of his hands, Holly and Tad sprawled over his feet and legs, while the broad grin of Mr. Lincoln's face was evidence that he was enjoying himself hugely. As soon as the boys saw my face at the door, Tad called, 'Julie, come quick and sit on his stomach.'" The boys enjoyed these moments with their father. When they were ready for more fun and Lincoln needed to focus on his work, "Willie used to say mournfully, 'Pa don't have time to play with us now.'"

Lincoln's willingness to frolic with the boys when he had time is noteworthy, as it shows Lincoln fulfilling a widespread nineteenth-century fatherhood role. The term "frolic" was commonly used to describe the playful moments when men entered "into the spirit of childhood." As middle-class fathers joined the urban workforce in the mid-1800s, mothers increasingly took over domestic responsibilities for discipline and moral instruction. As a result, "nineteenth-century fathers were left to cultivate the playful aspect of parent-child relations." Lincoln represented this relatively new form of fatherhood, which developed much earlier than most people today might think. As one historian observed, "Strikingly modern scenes of fathers rolling on the carpet with children, carrying them on their shoulders, entertaining them with toys and playthings—in short, routinely initiating or responding to demands for play—belie the one-dimensional stereotypes of work-obsessed and emotionally aloof Victorian patriarchs." Though Lincoln, who worked long hours and exhibited great ambition both in the legal profession and in politics, can fairly be described as work-obsessed, he nevertheless made time to frolic. The record seems to suggest that he did so much more with Willie and Tad than with Robert, which again is why some biographers have concluded that Robert felt a distance from his father. It is true that there are fewer descriptions of Lincoln frolicking with his eldest son than with Willie and Tad. But since Robert was a child during Lincoln's less-prominent years in Springfield, there were fewer opportunities for observers to see and record their intimate interaction together. Moreover, Robert's more stoic personality, even though he was just a boy, perhaps made him less eager to roll around with his father.

Lincoln could be tender as well as playful. "When the President came into the family sitting room and sat down to read, the boys would rush at him and demand a story," Julia recalled. "Tad perched precariously on the back of the big chair, Willie on one knee, Bud on the other, both leaning against him. Holly usually found a place on the arm of the chair, and often I would find myself swept into the group by the long arm which seemed to reach almost across the room." This was Lincoln the father at his best. The busy president was likely seeking quiet, alone time in the sitting room in order to get some important work done, but he patiently put aside his own books and papers to read to the boys and their friends.

Lincoln was often called upon to soothe the hurt feelings of the boys. Tad had befriended a group of soldiers at a large encampment situated between the White House and the War Department. Tad frequently pilfered fruit, flowers, newspapers, and books from the White House and brought the items to the soldiers. Tad's generosity was "a frequent source of grief to the [White House] care-takers, who did not relish having their treasures despoiled for men." One morning Lincoln came to breakfast and found Tad "dissolved to tears." When Lincoln asked what was wrong, Tad sniffled out "Why! Faver, such ungrateful soldiers! When I gave them tracts [newspapers], and asked them to read them, they laughed loud and said they had plenty of paper to start fires with, and would rather have a posey." Lincoln then "took him in his arms, pressed him tightly to him, kissed him, and tried to console him." While Lincoln may have provided the comfort that Tad needed at that moment, "it was days before the men saw their little friend's laughing face again, as he could not readily forgive ridicule."

Just as he had done with Eddy when he was sick, Lincoln took time away from the office to tend to Willie and Tad when they fell ill. In March, less than a month after arriving in Washington, Willie and Tad both caught the measles, and over the next year they suffered from a variety of colds and other ailments common among young children. Lincoln's cousin, Elizabeth Todd Grimsley observed that "[k]ind little words . . . flowed from his lips constantly to these sick children, the anxious mother, and all others."

Just as it had in Springfield, church attendance for the Lincoln family brought a set of challenges. Lincoln and Mary attended the New York Avenue Presbyterian Church, but they occasionally allowed Willie and Tad to go to Sunday services at Fourth Presbyterian with the Taft family. Julia recalled one Sunday when, "as Tad sat on the floor of the pew, as he usually did amusing himself with whatever he had in his pocket, a young officer, who was with us, gave him his knife, thinking Tad could not open it. But he did and cut his finger and I had to bind it up with my best embroidered handkerchief."

"I will never take you to church again, Thomas Lincoln," Julia hissed softly, using the boy's full name, which she knew he did not like.

To Julia's horror, Tad then blurted out loud in front of the congregation, "Just keep your eyes on Willie, sitting there good as pie."

Soon after that incident, Lincoln was in the sitting room of the White House "sprawled out in his big chair by the window" reading his "worn leathered-covered Bible." It was a familiar scene to Julia, who often saw him reading that book there "in his stocking feet with one long leg crossed over the other, the unshod foot slowly waving back and forth, as if in time to some inaudible music." Mary and the boys, as well as the Taft children, were with him in the room.

"Why do our boys like to go to your church, Julie?" Lincoln inquired.

"Why, I reckon our church is livelier," she replied.

"Do you think it's livelier, Willie?" the president asked his son.

"Oh, yes," the boy replied, "Lots livelier. Only, maybe it won't be so lively any more." Willie then explained that a Union lieutenant had threatened members of the congregation, who tended to have Confederate sympathies, with arrest if they continued to bang on pew doors and leave in the middle of the service whenever the pastor offered prayers for Lincoln. "And Pa," Tad asked, "why do the preachers always pray so long for you, Pa?"

"Well Tad," Lincoln said seriously, "I suppose it's because the preachers think I need it and I guess I do."

Though Lincoln attended Sunday services more regularly than he had in Springfield, he still refused to formally join any church. He did, however, expose Willie and Tad to religion. But he did not push it on them as his own father had with him. Moreover, there is no evidence that he conveyed to them any of his own reservations about organized religion, perhaps sensing that the boys were too young to reconcile a firm belief in God with a skepticism of organized religion. In any case, the results of Lincoln's efforts to expose the boys to religion were mixed, with only Willie taking the experience seriously. "The boys attended the Sabbath School," wrote cousin Elizabeth Todd Grimsley, "Willie, conscientiously, and because he loved it, Tad as a recreation, and to be with Willie." When

Tad had earlier observed Willie sitting in church "good as pie," he was contrasting Willie's proper Sunday behavior with his own display of defiance. The Sunday school was at Fourth Presbyterian. On Saturday mornings, Willie and Tad went to the Taft house to study the lesson for the next day. Using a blue question book, Julia quizzed the boys. One morning, "Willie sighed as he said that there were 'more hard words than ever in it.' He and Bud debated whether their teacher would require them to have it perfect or would 'let them off easy on the names.'" Willie studied "with set, determined looks," while Tad's lack of serious effort left him unprepared for class, where he "wriggled and fidgeted" throughout the lesson. When Willie was later counseled that "no one is without example, and as your father's son, I would remember the Sabbath day to keep it holy," Willie replied, "I will." Thereafter, Willie preferred to stay at home on Sunday afternoons while Tad and his parents went for a carriage drive, though he did not view Sunday playtime with Bud as contrary to keeping the Sabbath holy. "Both the Lincoln boys were here this afternoon looking over pictures with Bud & Holly," Horatio Taft wrote one Sunday evening. "They are evidently not kept on Sundays with puritan strictness. They like to feel quite 'free and easy' with our boys."

On October 20, 1861, Lincoln had a leisurely visit with his old Springfield friend and fellow lawyer, Edward D. Baker, the man after whom Lincoln had named his second son, Eddy. Baker, who was by then a senator from Oregon, had organized a regiment of soldiers from New York as part of the Army of the Potomac. In August, Baker brought his troops to Washington, where Lincoln reviewed them during exercises and later in a parade. Baker's thinning gray hair and receding hairline made him look older than his fifty years, but he was nevertheless "a handsome man, of sturdy, vigorous frame and fine presence," particularly when decked out in his officer's uniform. On that beautiful October afternoon, Lincoln "sat on the ground leaning against a tree; Colonel Baker was lying prone on the ground his head supported by his clasped hands." Willie played nearby, "tossing the fallen leaves about in childish grace and abandon." The two men talked, "low voiced, earnest and serious." When they finished, "Baker arose, took the President's hand and bade him adieu, lifted the child and kissed it, and went to his horse which was held by an orderly near by, mounted and rode away. The President's gaze followed the retiring officer until he disappeared to the West, when he took the child by the hand, and slowly and sadly returned to the house." The next day, Baker was killed at the battle of Ball's Bluff. Lincoln received news of Baker's death by telegram. "Sir, I have to inform you," the telegram read, "that . . . Baker was killed this afternoon at 5 o'clock in an engagement with the enemy near Leesburg. Knowing your great friendship and esteem of . . . Baker I lose no time in apprising you of our loss. He fell while leading on his command saying pleasant & cheering words to the men." When informed of Baker's death, Nicolay later wrote, Lincoln "left headquarters, utterly unheeding to the orderly's salute, both hands pressed to his heart, his features convulsed with grief."

A week after Baker's death, the editor of the *Washington National Republican* newspaper opened an envelope to find a letter from Willie. "Dear Sir: I enclose you my first attempt at poetry. Yours truly, William W. Lincoln." Two months shy of his eleventh birthday, Willie had spent time in the days following Baker's death writing a tribute to the fallen family friend. Willie was aware that his father liked to read and write poetry, and perhaps he had been told about the anonymous poem that appeared in the Springfield paper shortly after Eddy's death, so he decided to try his hand at writing some verse. The editor found the poem "quite creditable, as a first effort, for one so young," and published it a few days later "with pleasure, and [with] hope that Willie's desire, as expressed in the last verse, will meet with a ready response by the whole country."

On the Death of Colonel Edward Baker

There was no patriot like Baker,
So noble and so true;
He fell as a soldier on the field,
His face to the sky of blue.

His voice is silent in the hall,
Which oft his presence grac'd,
No more he'll hear the loud acclaim,
Which rang from place to place.

Robert Todd Lincoln at the dedication of the Lincoln Memorial. Lincoln, right, stands with Chief Justice William Howard Taft, left, and President Warren G. Harding, center.
COURTESY OF THE LIBRARY OF CONGRESS.

Thomas Lincoln
COURTESY OF THE KEYA MORGAN
COLLECTION/LINCOLNIMAGES.COM

The Globe Tavern
COURTESY OF THE LIBRARY OF CONGRESS

Abraham and Mary Lincoln in 1846
COURTESY OF THE KEYA MORGAN COLLECTION/LINCOLNIMAGES.COM

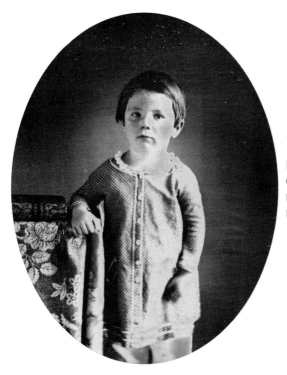

Eddy Lincoln

Lincoln at the time of the Cooper
Union speech

Robert Todd Lincoln at the time he
entered Harvard
COURTESY OF THE KEYA MORGAN
COLLECTION/LINCOLNIMAGES.COM

The Lincoln house at Eighth and Jackson. Lincoln, Willie, and Tad are shown
standing behind the fence.
COURTESY OF THE KEYA MORGAN COLLECTION/LINCOLNIMAGES.COM

Tad Lincoln in uniform
COURTESY OF THE KEYA MORGAN
COLLECTION/LINCOLNIMAGES.COM

The White House ball on the evening that Willie was sick. *Harper's Weekly*, January 25, 1862.
REPRINTED WITH THE PERMISSION OF APPLEWOOD BOOKS, PUBLISHERS OF AMERICA'S LIVING PAST

Willie Lincoln shortly before his death
COURTESY OF THE KEYA MORGAN
COLLECTION/LINCOLNIMAGES.COM

Anderson Cottage at the Soldiers' Home compound where the Lincolns vacationed
COURTESY OF THE LIBRARY OF CONGRESS

The burden of the presidency. At left is Lincoln in the fall of 1860, shortly before his election at the age of fifty-one. At right is Lincoln in February 1865, two months before his death at the age of fifty-six.

COURTESY OF THE KEYA MORGAN COLLECTION/LINCOLNIMAGES.COM

Lincoln and Tad entering the Davis mansion. *Frank Leslie's Illustrated*, 29 April 1865.

COURTESY OF THE LIBRARY OF CONGRESS

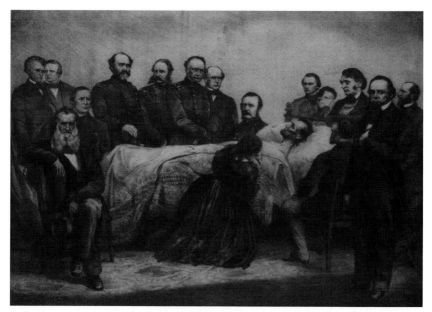

Depiction of the deathbed of Abraham Lincoln. Mary is kneeling beside the bed. Robert, his face partially covered with a handkerchief, can be seen just above Lincoln's head. While all of the people in this depiction were at Lincoln's deathbed at one time or another that evening, they were not all there as the same time as depicted here.

No squeamish notions filled his breast,
The Union was his theme,
"No surrender and no compromise,"
His day thought and night's dream.

His country has *her* part to play,
To'rds those he has left behind,
His widow and his children all—
She must always keep in mind.

If nothing else, the poem affirms that the Lincolns were succeeding in their efforts to educate Willie. Shortly after arriving in Washington, the Lincolns hired a tutor for the boys, Alexander Williamson, who was on the payroll at the Treasury Department. Bud and Holly often attended the sessions with the boys, which were held in the state dining room on the southwest corner of the first floor of the White House. To give it the feel of a classroom, Mary installed a desk and blackboard into the otherwise formal room. As he did with his Sunday school lessons, Willie took his studies seriously. He exhibited a particular interest in current events and carefully assembled a collection of newspaper clippings on matters that interested him, including dates of battles and deaths of distinguished people. Willie also excelled in his grammar and writing, evidenced not only by the Baker poem but by letters he wrote to a friend back in Springfield. Eight-year-old Tad, on the other hand, "was a little unruly," and seemed to have "a very bad opinion of books and no opinion of discipline." Not pushed by his parents, Tad learned little and would not even begin a serious attempt to learn how to read until he was nearly thirteen.

Meanwhile, Robert had settled in for the remainder of his freshman year at Harvard, where he took a room at "Pasco's, corner of Main & Linden Sts." His friend from Springfield and Exeter, George Latham, who had failed the Harvard entrance examination, decided to enroll at rival Yale, which accepted his application. Latham arranged to room with their mutual friend from Springfield, Clinton Conkling, who was now a sophomore. "Bob Lincoln must feel rather out of humor to have you taken his companion from him," Conkling's mother wrote her son. Over the course of the next three years, Conkling's parents wrote their son several letters urging him to keep up his correspondence and contacts with Robert, as they recognized that the son of the president was potentially a valuable friend to have. "Do you write to Bob or hear from him?" wrote James Conkling. "You may as well keep up your correspondence with him. It may favor advantages."

Robert studied Greek, Latin, composition, mathematics, elocution, religion, and history. In May 1861, during a scheduled break in classes, Robert returned to Washington to visit his family. On the same day that the *New York Tribune* reported that Lincoln was limiting his interviews to "matters of urgent importance," Robert joined his father's private secretaries, John Hay and John Nicolay, on a horseback ride into Virginia to see the recently abandoned house of Confederate General Robert E. Lee. Hay and Nicolay were only a few years older than the president's son, and the three soon developed a close friendship. Nicolay later reported that when they reached the Lee house, "in the garden we found an old negro at work, who was born at Mt. Vernon before General Washington's death. We asked him many questions—delighted him with introducing Bob, the President's son, in whom [he] expressed lively interest—and further pleased him with a gift of small change."

By July, Robert was back at Harvard for final exams, but he soon caught the mumps. As his condition abated, he telegraphed his worried father that he was "not sick at all," and informed him that he would return to Washington "in a few days" when school adjourned for the summer. Lincoln invited Robert to a state dinner on August 3 given in honor of Prince Napoleon of France. The monarch's initial introduction at the White House on the morning of the event did not go well. "The Prince, arriving with Baron Mercier, found no one—neither butler nor doorman—at the main entrance to show him in." The first person that the two men ran into was Willie. "One goes right in [the White House] as if entering a café," Mercier later wrote with astonishment. The prince's meeting with Lincoln was "not so gay," and miffed by the informality of his reception, the prince "took cruel pleasure in remaining silent" in the presence of the president. By evening, however, the prince has gotten over his annoyance with his reception earlier in the day, and the dinner was a smashing success. The prince was "in full dress, his breast a flame of decoration, over which was crossed the broad crimson sash of a marshal of the Empire." The Lincolns, Robert, Hay, Nicolay, General Winfield Scott, Lincoln's cabinet, and a few others attended the evening feast. According to Mary's cousin, Elizabeth Todd Grimsley, who also attended, "a beautiful dinner, beautifully served, gay conversation in which the French tongue predominated, led Prince Napoleon to remark gallantly, that after enjoying the elegant hospitality of Washington, and especially of those presiding in the Executive Mansion, he should be forced to confess that 'Paris is not all the world.'" It was at that dinner that the aging General Scott, veteran of the War of 1812 and hero of the Mexican War, who had fast become a great admirer of Lincoln, famously remarked to Lincoln that "I have dined with every President since Jefferson and that in my mind, the last should be first."

A few days after that affair, Robert left for New York City, where Mary, Willie, Tad, and Elizabeth Grimsley soon joined him. Mary planned a short vacation in Long Branch, New Jersey, a cool spot on the Atlantic coast. There, they could all escape the oppressive summer heat and humidity of Washington, as well as the pesky flies and mosquitoes that infiltrated the White House along with the pungent odor of raw sewage that drifted in from the nearby Potomac flats. The family could relax, do some "sea bathing," and walk along the seashore. Mary predicted that the venue would be "perfectly quiet." Lincoln was too busy to make the trip, so he stayed in Washington.

Earlier, Mary had invited Mrs. John Henry Shearer, her neighbor in Springfield, to join her on the vacation. "Bring your boys with you," Mary pleaded. "[I]t will be more pleasant all around. I am going to take my boys, with me, with a servant man, who will take charge, of your children also." Mrs. Shearer agreed to go, and met up with Mary's party in Philadelphia en route to New York City, where Robert was already waiting. After a day of shopping, the entire party traveled to a resort in Long Branch, where they stayed in a suite of rooms at the Mansion House hotel. Mary originally planned to be there for just a week, but when Tad developed a cold she decided to delay the departure until he was fit to travel. A few days later, a family friend also vacationing in New

Jersey reported to Lincoln that "Tad has entirely recovered & is as bright as a lark." So the entire Lincoln party traveled to Saratoga and then to Niagara Falls, where they bid goodbye to Elizabeth Grimsley, who left to return home to Springfield after living in the White House for six months. Mary, Willie, and Tad then headed back to Washington, while Robert left for Cambridge to begin his sophomore year at college.

Residing in Room 22 of the Stoughton dormitory, Robert settled in for another year at Harvard. His course schedule included Greek, Latin, mathematics, rhetoric and themes, chemistry, elocution, and botany. Robert became a member of the Institute of 1770, a social club that promoted public speaking, which he generally shied away from, and served one term as editor of its journal. He also became a member of a "Secret Society," the name of which he never publicly revealed.

In December 1861, Robert returned to Washington to spend Christmas with the family. When he entered the White House, he found that it had undergone a substantial interior renovation. When the Lincolns moved in, "the only elegance of the house was concentrated on the East, Blue and Red rooms, while the family apartments were in a deplorably shabby condition as to furniture (which looked as if it had been brought in by the first President), although succeeding house-keepers had taxed their ingenuity and patience to make it presentable." Recognizing that the house was not up to standards for a president, Congress appropriated $20,000 for new furniture and other interior renovations. Undisciplined in matters of money and budgets, Mary went on a spending spree in Washington and New York, and by the time she was finished she had exceeded the appropriation by nearly $7,000. "You must get me out of this difficulty," Mary said to Benjamin Brown French, the newly appointed commissioner of public buildings, as she choked back tears. She begged him to convince Lincoln to ask Congress for more money to cover her overrun but to do so without revealing that *she* had asked French to make the request. When French approached Lincoln, the president was appalled at Mary's extravagance. After going line by line through the list of expenditures, all the while expressing disbelief as to how certain items could cost so much ("I would like to know where a carpet worth $2,500 can be put!" exclaimed the president), an exasperated Lincoln questioned the entire need for the renovation: "It was all wrong to spend one cent at such a time, and I never ought to have had a cent expended; the house was furnished well enough, better than any one we ever lived in, and if I had not been overwhelmed with other business I would not have had any of the appropriation expended, but what could I do? I could not attend to everything." He was too busy being president to also manage the domestic household, but Mary, too, seemed incapable of exercising proper judgment. "Mrs. Lincoln *must* bear the blame, let her bear it, I swear I won't!" fumed the president. He then vowed to French that he would never approve an increased appropriation bill. Shortly thereafter, however, he relented. Congress eventually passed two bills approving the expenditures, and Lincoln promptly signed them.

Christmas Day found Lincoln trying to resolve an international crisis. Two months earlier, the Union Navy had stopped and searched the British mail ship *Trent* as it left Cuba, removing and imprisoning two Confederate diplomats who were on missions to England and France. In what became known as the Trent Affair, the British government charged that in boarding the ship and seizing the men, the United States had violated international law and insulted the British flag. While the North celebrated the capture of the men, Britain demanded that the prisoners be released immediately. The Trent Affair soon escalated to the point where war with Britain became a real possibility, so on December 25 Lincoln held a cabinet meeting to try to diffuse the situation. The meeting lasted until 2:00 p.m. Meanwhile, Willie and Tad spent the afternoon at the Taft house, where they kept "very busy firing off Crackers and Pistols" with Bud and Holly, and then ate a late lunch. Later that evening, after the boys returned home, the Lincolns hosted a large Christmas dinner at the White House that included cabinet members, Washington friends, and some family members from Kentucky and Illinois. The next day, Lincoln called another cabinet meeting and, against the advice of some of the participants, agreed to release the Confederate prisoners, thus resolving the Trent Affair and averting war with Britain.

As 1861 drew to a close, the Lincoln family celebrated the holidays together at the White House. It had been a difficult year for Lincoln professionally, as he was governing a deeply divided nation in the throes of a civil war that was producing mounting casualties on both sides. But in his home life, he had one son who was doing well in college and maturing into a promising young man and he had two younger boys who were enjoying their youth and providing him with immense satisfaction as a father. Mary later wrote of that time in their lives, "We were having *so much bliss.*" Unfortunately, it was not to last.

CHAPTER 8

We Loved Him So

On January 1, 1862, Lincoln hosted the traditional New Year's reception at the White House. From 11:00 a.m. to noon, cabinet members and their families, the gold-braided diplomatic corps, justices of the Supreme Court, and uniformed army and navy officers filed through the newly decorated mansion to shake hands with the president and his wife. Then, from noon to 2:00 p.m., the doors were opened to the general public. Later in the day, Lincoln spent time in his office dictating correspondence related to the war.

As the New Year began, Willie and Tad took up where they left off, spending as much time as possible with Bud and Holly Taft. On January 7, the Lincolns gave a party at the White House from 8:30 to 10:30 p.m. The overflow crowd included Horatio Taft and his family. Later that night, Taft wrote about the evening in his diary. "Levee at the [President's] tonight, 'Bud' & Holly went. The[y] were with the Lincoln boys all the evening and had a rare time." The next day, Lincoln took Willie, Tad, and the two Taft boys over to visit General George B. Mc-Clellan, commander of the Army of the Potomac, who was recovering from an illness. A week later, Willie and Tad ate dinner with the Tafts and "brought a request from their Mother that our boys 'Bud' and 'Holly' would go home and sleep with them tonight." On Sunday, January 26, Willie and Tad hurried over to the Taft house to invite Bud and Holly to go see the new pony that Willie had received as a belated birthday gift after turning eleven the previous month, but Mr. Taft would not allow such an activity on the Sabbath: "The two Lincoln boys were here after our boys to go up there to see their new pony. Our boys could not go on Sunday," he wrote tersely. Back at the White House, Lincoln met with various members of his cabinet on the effective manufacture of mortars, an unfortunate subject to address on a holy day, while Mary stayed in her bedroom nursing a mild illness.

A few days after the boys invited Bud and Holly to see their pony, both Willie and Tad became sick. At first it appeared that the boys had merely contracted common colds. They had been out riding the pony in the frosty weather, and their symptoms included chills and fevers. Tad recovered fairly quickly, but Willie's illness lingered. On February 5, the Lincolns hosted an elegant ball. They had sent invitations to more than seven hundred people, most of whom were expected to attend. Though Mary had been planning the event for weeks, she considered postponing it due to Willie's condition. Before they made a decision, Lincoln summoned Dr. Robert King Stone, a leading Washington physician, to examine Willie. The doctor reported that Willie was on the mend and that "there was every reason for an early recovery" and that the boy "was in no immediate danger." Relieved at Stone's prognosis, the Lincolns decided to proceed with the ball.

Just before the guests began to arrive, Willie took a turn for the worse. Mary sat by his bedside, "holding his feverish hand in her own, and watching his labored breathing." The Lincolns again summoned the doctor, who once more said there was no cause for alarm. After the couple got dressed, Mary took her husband's arm and they walked down to the party, leaving Willie in the care of Elizabeth Keckley, a former slave who had become Mrs. Lincoln's dressmaker and was fast becoming an important confidante to her. Keckley, a mulatto, was a handsome woman with a somewhat somber appearance highlighted by a soft but perpetual frown, droopy eye sockets, and tightly braided hair. She was, at once, both proud and patient, a successful and independent businesswoman who had the remarkable ability to, in the same sentence, defer to Mary's wishes and then proceed to tell her what to wear. She was described as "the only person in Washington who could get along with Mrs. Lincoln, when she became mad with anybody for talking about her and criticizing her husband." Over the years, Keckley would witness many intimate conversations between Lincoln and Mary. Once, as Mary was dressing for a dinner party with Keckley's assistance, Lincoln entered the room and said, "I declare, you look charming in that dress. Mrs. Keckley has met with success."

Lincoln's secretary, John Nicolay, later wrote that "the East Room was filled with well dressed guests looking very beautiful and the [midnight] supper was magnificent." The press later reported the evening as the "most superb affair of its kind ever seen here." Upstairs, where Willie lay in bed, Keckley recalled that "the rich notes of the Marine Band in the apartments below came to the sick-room in soft, subdued murmurs, like the wild, faint sobbing of far-off spirits." The Lincolns, however, could not enjoy themselves. Throughout the night, Mary left the party several times to check on Willie, leaving her husband to worry alone in the company of his guests. By morning, Willie's condition had worsened further.

For the next several days, Lincoln spent many hours away from the office to be with Willie. The press was now following the boy's condition almost daily, as it was affecting Lincoln's work as chief executive. "The president is not attending to much public business owing to the severe illness of his son," the *New York Tribune* reported. Lincoln's secretary, William O. Stoddard, wrote that "work in all the rooms goes on as usual, but now and then the President rises nervously from his chair by the desk and window, walks hastily out of his office and over to the family side of the building." By February 10, five days after the ball, Willie seemed to improve, but then Tad got sick again. The next day, Lincoln gave "pretty much all his attention" to the boys. Because of their illnesses, Lincoln and Mary canceled a small reception planned for that evening. The press began to report that the boys were suffering from either typhoid fever or bilious fever. On February 14, both boys seemed to rally. "The children we are glad to say are on the mend," reported the *Washington Evening Star*. In Willie's case, however, the improvement was only temporary. The next day, the Lincolns canceled another reception "in consequence of the continued illness in the family."

A few days later, Lincoln and Stoddard walked to General McClellan's house to discuss war strategy. Lincoln had become increasingly frustrated with McClellan, both for the general's seeming unwillingness to take his forces into battle and for his occasional intrusion into matters of politics. Rather than summoning McClellan to the White House, Lincoln decided to go to the general. After the short walk from the White House, they arrived at McClellan's house and rang the bell. A servant ushered them into what Stoddard described as "an elegant reception room" where McClellan joined them along with two members of his senior staff.

After brief introductions, Lincoln and McClellan met alone in another room while Stoddard and the general's aides waited nearby. After the long meeting finally ended, Lincoln and Stoddard walked back to the White House. Stoddard reported that Lincoln was "cheerful" and even chuckled at reports that some of McClellan's men were having trouble pronouncing the names of the French officers that the general had put on his staff. As the two men approached the mansion in the moonlight, Lincoln stopped at the parapet on the eastern end of the front near the portico, "gazing silently southward" toward the Potomac. After a minute of reflection, Lincoln turned and walked toward the entrance, joined again by Stoddard.

Old Edward, who saw them approaching, swung open the door and said in a somber tone, "The doctor has been here, sir."

"What did he say?" Lincoln inquired.

"The Madame would like to see you right away, sir. Soon as you came in," Edward answered softly. Lincoln turned to the right and rushed up the stairway.

"Is Willie really sick, Edward?" Stoddard asked.

"I think he is, indeed," Edward said, "but she told me not to alarm the President. We'll know more in the morning."

Willie's condition had become grave. He begged his parents to call for his best friend, Bud, to come visit him. Lincoln complied. Over the next several days, Bud, who was a year older than Willie, spent countless hours with the sick boy. "The President would come in and stand awhile at the bedside," recalled Bud's sister, Julia, "then go out without speaking. Once he laid his arm across Bud's shoulder and stroked Willie's hair. It was late and he said, 'you ought to go to bed, Bud.'" Not wanting to leave his friend, Bud replied, "If I go he will call for me." Lincoln acceded to

Bud's request and let him stay. Later that night, Lincoln entered the room again and, finding Bud asleep, picked him up and "carried him tenderly to bed."

By February 17, the press reported that Willie was "past all hope of recovery." The next day, Attorney General Edward Bates recorded in his diary that Willie was "*in extremis*" and that Lincoln was "nearly worn out, with grief and watching." Two days later Willie rallied a bit but soon relapsed. The next morning, one newspaper reported that the White House was "overspread with the gloom of the expected death of the President's son." The seesaw nature of Willie's illness suggests that the newspapers finally got it right when they reported that he had bilious fever, a form of typhoid in which the symptoms of fever, vomiting, diarrhea, and gastric pain come and go. Willie likely caught the illness from playing in a swampy canal near the White House. On February 20, Willie once again summoned Bud, who came to his room and held his hand. At five o'clock that evening, as the sun set over Washington, Willie Lincoln died.

In a daze, Lincoln walked down to his office, where his secretary, John Nicolay, stood outside of the door. "Well Nicolay, my boy is gone—he is actually gone," Lincoln said, barely getting out the words. Lincoln then burst into tears and went into his office and shut the door. Later that night, after Elizabeth Keckley helped wash and dress the body, Lincoln came into Willie's room. Walking softly over to the bed where Willie lay, Lincoln "lifted the cover from the face of his child, gazed at it long and earnestly, murmuring 'My poor boy, he was too good for this earth. God has called him home. I know that he is much better off in heaven, but then we loved him so. It is hard, hard to have him die.'"

As with Eddy's death in the month of February twelve years earlier, Lincoln was devastated by the loss of his son. According to some, Willie had become Lincoln's "favorite." Julia described Willie as "the most loveable boy I ever knew, bright, sensible, sweet-tempered and gentle-mannered." Mary said that he combined a "great amiability and cheerfulness of character," and his love of books and poetry was characteristic of his father. Elizabeth Grimsley, Mary's cousin who lived with the Lincolns during their first six months in the White House, described Willie as a boy "of great mental activity, unusual intelligence, wonderful memory, methodical, frank and loving, a counterpart of his father, save that he was handsome." William Florville, Lincoln's barber in Springfield, said Willie was "a smart boy for his age, so considerate, so manly; his knowledge and good sense, far exceeding most boys more advanced in age." Willie, like his father but through no fault of his own, was also careless in dress. One visitor to the White House described Willie's dress as "homely" and "a style . . . altogether different from that of the curled darlings of fashionable mothers, but there was a glow of intelligence and feeling on his face which made him particularly interesting and caused strangers to speak of him as a fine little fellow."

In contrast to the bright but standoffish Robert and the gregarious but unlearned Tad, Willie seemed to combine the best traits of his father: natural intelligence, a love of learning, a talent for prose, and a homespun demeanor. Willie was, according to Edward Bates, "a fine boy of 11 yrs., too much idolized by his parents." If Willie was Lincoln's favorite, it was not because he loved the boy any more than he did Robert or Tad. Rather, it was because Willie was very much like himself. In much the same way, Lincoln's father, Thomas, had seemed partial to his stepson John Johnston who, unlike Lincoln, was drawn to the frontier life that defined Thomas's very existence.

After Lincoln emerged from his office, he summoned his good friend, Senator Orville Browning, who immediately came to the White House in a carriage sent by Lincoln. Browning and Lincoln had known each other for nearly thirty years, having met when they served together in the Illinois legislature in the 1830s. Carl Sandburg described Browning as "wearing a serenity somewhat blank and colorless, almost empty of humor, precise in form and manners, scrupulous and overly vain about his scruples." He typically wore his hair in such an unkempt state that it called attention away from his receding hairline. After Nicolay informed Browning of the details of Willie's death, Browning sent for his wife, Elizabeth, who soon joined her husband at the White House. They were just the right friends that the Lincolns needed at the time—patient, caring, and helpful. In an old custom of "sharing the burden," the Brownings stayed up all night with the grieving parents, taking turns sitting next to the body. Over the next three nights, the couple took turns staying up and nursing Tad, who was still both physically sick and emotionally grieving over the loss of his brother. The Lincolns also brought in a nurse, Rebecca Pomroy, to help with Tad's care. Pomroy later reported that Tad was "weeping for his dear brother Willie, who would never speak to him any more."

For the second time in his life, Lincoln faced the unenviable task of planning a funeral for one of his young sons. When Eddy died, Lincoln was a private citizen, and all the people who crowded into the small Lincoln home to attend the funeral were close friends, family, and neighbors. When Willie died, Lincoln was the president of the United States, and his son's lingering illness and untimely death were widely reported in the newspapers. *Harper's Weekly* reported, "The President's son, William, ten [sic] was relieved of his painful illness, this after a delirium of 90 hours, by death at five o'clock on 20th ... Mr. Lincoln feels his loss very deeply." Lincoln also received many written condolences, including a heartwarming note from General McClellan. "I have not felt authorized to intrude upon you personally in the midst of the deep distress I know you feel in the sad calamity that had befallen you & your family," wrote McClellan two days after Willie's death, "yet I cannot refrain from expressing the sincere & deep sympathy I feel for you." Lincoln realized that this time his son's funeral needed to be a somewhat more public affair, open to not only friends and family, but members of his cabinet and other government officials. On the evening of Willie's death, Nicolay went to see Lincoln, who had "lain down to quiet T[ad]." He asked the president "if I should charge Browning with the direction of the funeral. 'Consult with Browning' said he." Browning promptly enlisted the help of Benjamin Brown French, the commissioner of public buildings. The two men soon scheduled the funeral for February 24.

The day after Willie's death, Lincoln's cabinet met without him and requested that Congress cancel the planned illumination of public buildings in celebration of George Washington's birthday. Congress granted the request, and then adjourned out of respect for the Lincoln family. Later in the day, Dr. Charles D. Brown embalmed Willie's body using a new technique called "Sucquet" that promised better preservation. Willie was then dressed and placed in a small metal casket decorated as faux rosewood, which was taken to the Green Room where the lid was kept open for viewing. Greenish-yellow flowers were placed on his left breast. That evening, cabinet members and their wives visited Lincoln and Mary to express their condolences. Later, Lincoln went downstairs and alone sat quietly with the boy.

In the wake of Willie's death, Mary was inconsolable, and in her grief she made a decision that deeply hurt Willie's two best friends. Once the funeral date was set, Mary wrote a letter to Bud's and Holly's mother: "Please keep the boys home the day of the funeral; it makes me feel worse to see them." When Lincoln found out about this, he tried to figure out a way to include the boys, or at least Bud, in the family's mourning without crossing Mary. Respecting Mary's wish that the Taft boys not attend the funeral, Lincoln decided to ask Bud to come to the White House for a private viewing of Willie. After Bud gazed at Willie's lifeless body, the little boy who had so faithfully stayed with his dying friend in those last difficult days "had to be carried from the room and was ill for some days later." Mary's desire not to see the Taft boys extended beyond the funeral. "My mother naturally waited for some word from Mrs. Lincoln before allowing us to go to the White House," Julia Taft later wrote. "But the word never came." Shortly after the funeral, when Mr. Taft's tenure in the Patent Office ended, the Taft family quietly moved away from Washington. Bud and Holly never saw Tad or his parents again.

As a violent rainstorm with damaging winds raged outside, the funeral began at 2:00 p.m. on February 24 in the East Room, a place normally reserved for festive balls and diplomatic receptions. More than a hundred people attended, including Lincoln's cabinet, congressmen and senators, Vice President Hannibal Hamlin and his wife, and General McClellan. The mourners sat in a semicircle of chairs arranged by French. Willie's casket, covered with a white crepe, lay on a bier in the adjacent Green Room, visible though the open doors. On the lid, which was now closed, was a silver plate bearing Willie's name and the dates of his birth and death.

Mary, who had excluded the Taft boys from the services because it would have made her "feel worse to see them," was too grief-stricken to attend the funeral herself. Two hours before the services started, Lincoln,

Mary, and Robert viewed the body together for a half hour, then Mary returned to her room upstairs where she stayed secluded for the remainder of the day. Tad was still sick, so he stayed in his room with the new nurse, Rebecca Pomroy. Robert, who had returned to Harvard after the ball but came back to Washington when he got word of Willie's death, sat with his father during the "solemn affair." Dr. Phineas D. Gurley, pastor of the New York Avenue Presbyterian Church that the Lincolns attended with some regularity, officiated and delivered the principal eulogy. Gurley at once recognized the burden that Lincoln carried in both presiding over the nation's affairs and grieving the loss of his beloved son: "To the unprecedented weight of civil care which presses upon him is added the burden of this great domestic sorrow; and the prayer of the Nation ascends to Heaven on his behalf, and on behalf of the weeping family, that God's grace may be sufficient for them." As Lincoln listened, Gurley then spoke of Willie:

> *The beloved youth, whose death we now and here lament, was a child of bright intelligence and of peculiar promise. He possessed many excellent qualities of mind and heart, which greatly endeared him, not only to the family circle of which he was a member, but to his youthful companions, and to all his acquaintances and friends.*
>
> *His mind was active, inquisitive, and conscientious; his disposition was amiable and affectionate; his impulses were kind and generous; and his words and manners were gentle and attractive. It is easy to see how a child, thus endowed, would, in the course of eleven years, entwine himself round the hearts of those who knew him best . . .*

After the service came the slow, somber journey to the cemetery. Twelve years earlier Lincoln had to make a solemn trip through downtown Springfield to bury Eddy on the outskirts of town. Now, it was the streets of Washington that he needed to traverse with his late son. As Willie's casket was removed from the Green Room, "the funeral procession was preceded by twelve pall bearers, wearing a yard of white silk, with long ends tied around their hats, and wreaths of flowers on their arms." A group of children from Willie's Sunday school class followed behind the casket, which was then placed "in a hearse, drawn by two white horses." Lincoln, Robert, Orville Browning, and Lincoln's old Whig rival from Illinois, Senator Lyman Trumbull, trailed the hearse in a carriage pulled by two black horses. Following Lincoln's carriage, wrote one observer, were "the secretaries and their families, a large number of private carriages, and last of all, the colored help. I never saw anything so imposing." The procession stretched for a half mile.

The cortege of mourners slowly made their way to Oak Hill Cemetery in Georgetown, about two miles from the White House. On arrival, the casket was placed in the Gothic Chapel, and several scripture verses were read. When that brief service ended, the mourners slowly left. Lincoln's friend, William Thomas Carroll, the clerk of the Supreme Court, kindly offered Lincoln the use of his family's large concrete vault at the cemetery as a temporary resting place for Willie until the Lincolns were able to bring him home to Illinois at the end of his presidency. After Lincoln and the other mourners left the chapel, Willie's casket was placed in the vault.

In the years ahead, the Lincolns saw to it that their son's tomb was well taken care of. "All around the tomb were beautiful greens and choice flowers which the servants of Mrs. Lincoln carry twice a week," wrote a friend from Springfield, who visited the cemetery on a trip to Washington. "The beauty and fragrance robs death and the grave of half its gloom."

After Eddy's death twelve years earlier, Lincoln had become increasingly interested in religion. He regularly read the Bible, frequently invoked God's name in his speeches and letters, and attended church more often than he had in the past. Nevertheless, he neither joined a particular church nor expressed a conversion to Christianity. Though Willie's death intensified Lincoln's faith in God, he still neither joined a church nor expressly accepted Christ, leaving historians to argue over whether Lincoln was a Christian or merely a Deist. In any case, following Willie's death, Lincoln continued to make references to God in his speeches and writings, including the Gettysburg Address, and now often acknowledged the importance of prayer in his life. "If I were not sustained by the prayers of God's people," Lincoln told Reverend Noyes W. Miner, an old friend from Springfield, "I could not endure this constant pressure. It has pleased Almighty God to place me in my present position, and looking up to Him for wisdom and divine guidance I must work my destiny as best I can."

In April of 1864, Lincoln was presented a petition signed by nearly two hundred schoolchildren in Concord, Massachusetts, asking him to free all slave children. In his reply to their teacher, Lincoln asked that she "tell these little people I am very glad their young hearts are so full of just and generous sympathy, and that, while I have not the power to grant all they ask, I trust they will remember that God has, and that, as it seems, He wills to do it." Nearly a year later, in his second inaugural address, Lincoln said that both North and South "read the same Bible and pray to the same God, and each invokes his aid against the other. It may seem strange that any men should dare to ask a just God's assistance in wringing their bread from the sweat of other men's faces, but let us judge not that we not be judged." Reverend Miner, who did not attempt to claim that Lincoln had expressed a conversion, probably best summed up the relationship between Lincoln and Christianity when he wrote, "If Mr. Lincoln was not a Christian, he was acting like one." In 1863, Lincoln issued a proclamation calling for a day of fasting and prayer in November in order to give "Thanksgiving and Praise to our beneficent Father who dwelleth in the Heavens." Though some of Lincoln's predecessors declared days of thanksgiving, most did not. Starting with Lincoln's proclamation, Thanksgiving Day has been celebrated in the United States every year since.

When Eddy died, Lincoln turned to God for comfort and to work in order to bring a sense of normalcy back to his life. Lincoln did the same following Willie's death. There were pressing obligations at the office that needed his attention shortly after his son's funeral. He was, after all, the president of the United States, and the country was at war with itself. Though his grief was real and deep, he needed to get back to work. And he did.

CHAPTER 9

It's All Right Now

JUST AS LINCOLN HAD TURNED TO WORK IN THE WAKE OF EDDY'S DEATH twelve years earlier, he did so after Willie's passing. The day after Willie's funeral, as an inconsolable Mary remained secluded in her room, Lincoln held a cabinet meeting in the White House that featured a lively debate over how the military should handle prisoners of war. On March 3, 1862, less than two weeks after Willie died, Stoddard wrote in the *New York Examiner*, "The President is looking somewhat better, the all-absorbing interest of this hour of action serving to draw his thoughts away from his bereavement." But Stoddard's assessment was too sanguine. Lincoln's gloom, if occasionally masked by his ability to work, was deep, and he alternated between work and mourning much more frequently than he had following Eddy's death. Willie died on a Thursday, and as Attorney General Edward Bates observed, on each of the first two Thursdays following his death, Lincoln "gave way to his feelings, and shut himself from all society. . . . [H]e would see no one, and seemed prey to the deepest melancholy." Twice in the week after the funeral, Lincoln visited the vault where Willie's body had been placed. Each time, he opened Willie's casket and stared sadly at his son. Willie's "face was white and cold and his hands were folded across his breast, and he was dressed just as if he was alive and well."

Tad, who had been too sick to attend Willie's funeral, remained largely confined to his bed for two weeks following his brother's death. Mary's sister, Elizabeth Todd Edwards, whom Robert had summoned to Washington to help console his grieving mother, wrote to her daughter Julia back in Springfield that Tad was "very prostrated with his illness, and subdued with the loss he evidently suffers from, yet permits no allusion to. His mother has been but little with him, being utterly unable to control her feelings. We consider Tad quite out [of] dangerous convalescent, but still unable to sit up. Mary has confined herself to her room." While Tad lay in bed, Lincoln often "took his writing into the sick room to sit beside him, placing his table where the boy could watch every pen stroke."

On March 10, John Hay, one of Lincoln's two secretaries, interrupted a cabinet meeting and whispered to the president that Tad's nurse, Rebecca Pomroy, needed to see him. Lincoln excused himself from the room and met Pomroy in the hall. "Mrs. Lincoln insists that I see you, sir," she said apologetically. "Tad won't take his medicine and the doctor left strict orders for me to give it to him regularly." Lincoln and Pomroy then walked down to Tad's room.

"You stay here and I'll see what I can do," Lincoln said softly as he went in to see his son. After a few minutes, Lincoln emerged with a smile and said to Pomroy, "It's all right now. Tad and I have fixed things up." Lincoln then returned to the cabinet meeting as Pomroy went back into Tad's room. She found the boy holding a bank check reading, "*Pay to* 'Tad' (when he is well enough to present) *or bearer* Five *Dollars* $5/00—A. Lincoln." Lincoln's sweet bribe promptly persuaded Tad to take his medicine, and although he remained sick for a few more days, he eventually shook off the illness and regained his health.

Though now well physically, Tad continued to grieve over the loss of his brother. A few weeks later, he gave Willie's train set to his aunt Elizabeth, requesting that she send it home to her grandson, Lewis. "Tad insisted upon sending [the train cars] to Lewis," Elizabeth wrote to her daughter, "saying he could not play with them again."

With Robert back at Harvard and the Taft boys banished by Mary from the White House, Tad now had no young friends with whom to play. In the years ahead, Lincoln would become Tad's principal playmate and companion. Tad "seemed never to want his father out of his sight," wrote Lincoln's other secretary, John Nicolay. "The bond that had always been uncommonly close between them grew stronger after [Willie's] death." The indulgence that the father previously showed both Tad and Willie now multiplied and was focused exclusively on Tad. "I want to give him all the toys I did not have and all of the toys that I would have given the boy who went away," Lincoln once told a White House visitor.

Sensing Lincoln's and Tad's grief over losing Willie, some of the president's advisors, who had been privately critical of the president's lack of parental control and greatly annoyed at Tad's antics, now began to warm up to the boy. Edwin M. Stanton, Lincoln's gruff and humorless secretary of war, described by contemporaries as "gloomy and peculiar" and "rude and offensive," playfully commissioned Tad as a lieutenant in the Army and allowed him to order a batch of muskets for the White House. One evening Tad "discharge[d] the [White House] guard, and he then mustered all the gardeners and servants, gave them guns, drilled them, and put them on duty in their place." These were the same people who, before Willie's death, often looked with displeasure at the boy's games. Lincoln found the entire episode exceedingly humorous. On another occasion, Stanton promptly forgave Tad after the boy squirted him with a garden hose as he crossed the White House lawn, drenching both the secretary and some important papers that he was holding.

Not all of those around Lincoln were willing to give Tad a pass, however. Lincoln occasionally took Tad to the telegraph office at the War Department, where the president received the latest updates from the battlefield. Madison Buell, an employee in the office, recalled how during one such visit "in pure mischief Tad thrust his fingers into an ink-well and wiped them across several of the white [marble counter] tops, making a horrible mess." Buell then "seized the boy by the collar" and took him in the other room, where Lincoln was reading the latest dispatches. "Tad held up his inky fingers," while Buell, "with a look of disgust," pointed to the mess in the other room. Lincoln, "without asking for further explanation, lifted his boy in his arms and left the office, saying in a pleasant tone, 'Come, Tad; Buell is abusing you.'"

Tad continued to interrupt cabinet meetings, just as he and Willie had done together. Lincoln's close friend, journalist Noah Brooks, wrote, "It sometimes happened that, while the President and his Cabinet were anxiously discussing affairs of state, and were in the midst of questions of great moment, Tad would burst into the room, bubbling with excitement, and insist that his complaint or request should be attended to at once." Lincoln, according to Tad's nurse Rebecca Pomroy, "rarely denied a hearing, no matter how closely pressed in other directions." Hay described how Tad would "perch upon his father's knee, and sometimes even on his shoulder, while the most weighty conferences were going on. Sometimes escaping from the domestic authorities, he would take refuge in that sanctuary for the whole evening, dropping to sleep at last on the floor, when the President would pick him up and carry him tenderly to bed." While some cabinet officers and members of Lincoln's inner circle now tolerated Tad's interruptions with better humor, others continued to be silently annoyed. Nicolay's daughter later wrote that her father "had a bachelor's opinion of obstreperous children," and "ignored Tad and his escapades as much as possible, and never ceased to marvel at the President's patience with this youngest son of his. Even when Tad, beating his drum and demanding attention, broke vociferously into the room where his father was holding an important conference, Mr. Lincoln did not seem to mind. He would only ask, 'My son, can't you manage to make a little less noise?' and go on with the matter in hand. Others perforce kept silence, reflecting meanwhile upon what they would do to that boy, if they had half a chance."

With Fido back in Springfield, the White House became home to a variety of pets. In addition to Willie's pony, at various times the Lincoln family hosted dogs, kittens, rabbits, and goats. The Lincolns likely felt that the expansive living quarters and surrounding grounds could better accommodate a host of critters compared to their home back in Springfield. A caring citizen sent two rabbits to Tad as a gift shortly after Willie's death. "Allow me to thank you in behalf of my little son for your present of White Rabbits," Lincoln wrote to the donor. "He is very much pleased with them." Lincoln also bought two goats for Tad, one of which the boy named Nanny. Though the goats boarded in the White House stables, one day while Mary and Tad were out of town, Lincoln wrote his wife that "Nanny was found resting herself, and chewing her little cud, on the middle of Tad's bed. But now she's gone! The gardener kept complaining that she destroyed the flowers, till it was concluded to bring her down to the White House. This was done, and the second day she had disappeared, and has not been heard of since. This is the last we know of poor 'Nanny.'" Lincoln, who probably suspected that an annoyed staff member was behind Nanny's mysterious disappearance and possible demise, then asked Mary to "tell dear Tad, poor 'Nanny Goat,' is lost." Soon after, though, Tad acquired more pet goats. When Mary and Tad were away from Washington, Lincoln telegraphed his wife and instructed her to "[t]ell Tad the goats and father are very well especially the goats."

Just before Christmas 1863, a family friend sent the Lincolns "a fine live turkey . . . with the request that it should be served on the President's Christmas table." Tad soon took a liking to the turkey and named him Jack. When Tad realized that Jack was destined for the dinner table, he "burst into the [Cabinet] room like a bomb-shell, sobbing and crying with rage and indignation." Tad pleaded with the president to spare the plump fowl. "The President of the United States, pausing in the midst of his business, took a card and wrote on it an order of reprieve. The turkey's life was spared, and Tad, seizing the precious bit of paper, fled to set him at liberty."

The Lincolns also had a dog named Jip. Lincoln often brought Jip to lunch, where he sat on the president's lap "to claim his portion first, and was caressed and petted by him through the whole meal." Though Tad undoubtedly missed Fido, he was pleased to receive a report on the dog's well-being from William Florville, Lincoln's barber back in Springfield, who wrote to Lincoln in late 1862: "Tell Tad that his (and Willys) Dog is alive and Kicking doing well he stays mostly at John E. Roll with his Boys Who are about the size now that Tad and Willy were when they left for Washington."

While Tad had the run of the White House, Robert continued his studies at Harvard. After Willie's death in February 1862, Robert returned to Cambridge to finish his sophomore year. The Lincolns looked forward to having Robert home for the summer. "Robert will be home from Cambridge in about 6 weeks and will spend his vacation with us," a clearly proud Mary wrote to a friend in May. "He has grown & improved more than any one you ever saw."

The Lincolns decided to spend the summer in the Soldiers' Home, which Mary described as "a very charming place 2½ miles from the city, several hundred feet, above, our present situation." The Soldiers' Home was a compound of buildings and cottages constructed in the 1850s to house disabled army veterans who were unable to support themselves. In order to assure continued financial support from the government, the Army began inviting presidents and secretaries of war for visits. President Buchanan was the first chief executive to stay there, and he may have recommended it to Lincoln. Located on cool, shady hills northeast of downtown Washington, the place provided a refuge from the hot summer weather that stagnated around the crowded city. From there, Lincoln, who had endured long commutes during his lawyering days on the circuit, could easily make the daily carriage or horseback ride to and from his White House office in about thirty minutes.

During the second week in June, Lincoln, Mary, and Tad moved to the Anderson Cottage on the grounds of the Soldiers' Home compound. A still-grieving Mary looked forward to a respite from the White House. "[I]t will be a greater resort than [the White House]," she wrote to a friend. "[W]hen we are in sorrow, quiet is very necessary to us." Early on, though, it was apparent that this vacation would not be a relaxing time for the president. By the end of the month, Union troops were engaged in fierce fighting with Confederate forces on several fronts. As the death toll on both sides mounted, Lincoln became increasingly frustrated with McClellan, who was unable to make the progress Lincoln expected and kept demanding that the president send reinforcements. Mary reported that her husband was having trouble sleeping at night. Shortly after the July Fourth holiday, with her husband distracted by matters of state, Mary decided to take Tad and go on a shopping trip to New York. There she met up with Robert, who had just completed his final exams.

Separated from his family, Lincoln worked tirelessly. On July 13, he attended the funeral of Secretary of War Stanton's infant son in Washington. Two days later, Orville Browning visited Lincoln at the White House and found him "weary, care-worn and troubled." Browning reported that Lincoln spoke with "a cadence of deep sadness in his voice." In addition to developing and prosecuting war strategy, Lincoln during this time was drafting the Emancipation Proclamation.

Mary and her two sons returned to the Soldiers' Home on July 17. Robert stayed there for nearly a month, and his parents cherished every moment that they had with him. "We are truly delighted, with this retreat, the drives & walks around here are delightful, & each day brings its visitors," Mary wrote to a friend back in Washington. "Then, too, our boy Robert, is with us, whom you may remember. We consider it a 'pleasant time' for us, when his vacations roll around, he is very companionable, and I shall dread when he has to return to Cambridge." In her letter, Mary also revealed her continuing grief over the death of Willie. "In the loss of our idolized boy, we naturally have suffered intense grief, that a removal from the scene of our misery was found very necessary. Yet, in this sweet spot, that his bright nature, would have so well loved, he is not with us, and the anguish of the thought, oftentimes, for days overcomes me." Then, Mary showed her struggle to reconcile Willie's death with her faith: "How often, I feel rebellious, and almost believe that our Heavenly Father, has forsaken us, in removing, so lovely a child from us! Yet I know, a great sin, is committed when we feel this."

In mid-August, after a brief trip to New York City with Mary, Robert returned to Cambridge to begin his junior year. Allowed one elective, he chose French, a language that his mother spoke fluently. His required courses included Greek, Latin, physics, chemistry, declamations, themes, and rhetoric. In January 1863, Robert returned to the White House during a school break. The Lincolns were planning a reception for Charles Sherwood Stratton, widely known as Tom Thumb, the famous midget who toured with the P.T. Barnum circus, and his new bride, Lavinia Warren, who was also a midget. Thumb had earlier been feted in England, where he had an audience with Queen Victoria, and some of Mary's friends suggested that she invite the celebrity newlyweds to the White House during their visit to Washington. Robert, who by then had fully adopted his eastern manners and attitudes in contrast to his father's homespun persona, was appalled that the president of the United States would stoop to participating in such a spectacle. When Mary invited Robert to attend, he tersely replied with air of condescension: "No, mother, I do not propose to assist in entertaining Tom Thumb. My notions of duty, perhaps, are somewhat different from yours." Robert remained in his room while his parents and Tad entertained their guests. Lavinia Stratton, who had a round face and plump figure, later described how "Tad, the favorite son, stood beside his mother and gazing at me . . . whispered to his mother, 'Mother if you were a little woman like Mrs. Stratton you would look just like her.'"

As the summer of 1863 approached, the Lincolns again planned to retreat to the Soldiers' Home. On July 2, as Robert prepared for his final exams, Mary was injured in a carriage accident while on her way to the Anderson Cottage. Lincoln immediately wired the news to his son. "Don't be uneasy. Your mother very slightly hurt by her fall." Robert did not respond. Eight days later, as Mary's condition worsened, Lincoln wired his son again, this time bluntly saying only, "Come to Washington." Perhaps busy with exams, Robert again failed to reply. Three days later, a frustrated Lincoln wired his son a third time. "Why do I hear no more of you?" By the time that telegram reached Cambridge, however, Robert had already left for Washington. While waiting to change trains in Jersey City, as he stood on the elevated platform next to a parked train, the crowd pushed him up against a car just as the train began to move. Robert slipped and fell feet-first into the gap between the train car and the edge of the platform. Almost immediately, Robert later recalled, "my coat collar was vigorously seized and I was quickly pulled up and out to a secure footing on the platform." As Robert looked at his rescuer to express his gratitude, he immediately recognized the man as the well-known actor Edwin Booth. It was Booth's brother, John Wilkes Booth, also a famous actor, who would later assassinate Robert's father.

When Robert finally arrived at the Soldiers' Home, he found his mother on the mend but his father was once again experiencing tremendous stress over the status of the war. Union forces had forced Lee's army to retreat from Gettysburg, and the flooded Potomac prevented them from retreating into Virginia. Sensing that Lee's defeat could finally end the war, Lincoln ordered General George Meade to attack the trapped army. But Meade hesitated, and when the river receded Lee's army crossed into safe territory. Robert entered Lincoln's room and found him "in tears with head bowed upon his arms resting on the table at which he sat." When Robert asked what was wrong, Lincoln said, "My boy, I have just learned at a council of war, of Meade and his Generals, it has been determined not to pursue Lee, and now the opportune chance of ending this bitter struggle is lost." Robert later told John Hay that Lincoln was "grieved silently but deeply about the escape of Lee," and apparently said that "if I had gone up there, I could have whipped them myself." This was not the last time that Lincoln confided his feelings about ill-performing generals to his eldest son. Robert once described a meeting in which his father "was exceedingly urgent or strong in his condemnation" of General Fitz John Porter for failing to support General John Pope at the second Battle of Bull Run. Porter was later court-martialed.

That summer, Lincoln arranged for Robert to get a close-up look at the management of the war. Robert accompanied his father at a demonstration near the Washington Monument of a newly developed repeating rifle invented by Charles M. Spencer. In late July, Robert joined Secretary of State William Seward on a gunboat that traveled to Fortress Monroe in Virginia. Robert returned to Washington after the three-day trip, then immediately left for New York. Mary, who had recovered enough to make a journey outside of Washington, had taken Tad there en route to the mountains in New Hampshire, where they could find cooler weather. Once again, Lincoln was too busy to leave the capital. Robert, Tad, and Mary spent time in the mountains before traveling around New Hampshire and Vermont.

Robert returned to Harvard in the fall for his senior year. This time he chose Italian as an elective, and his required courses included history, physics, forensics, philosophy, and political economy. Back in Washington, Lincoln's disappointment over Meade's failure to pursue Lee after Gettysburg eventually gave way to his decision to travel to the battle site to deliver an address for the dedication of a new cemetery there for the fallen soldiers. On the morning of his departure, November 18, Tad had a sore throat and fever and was too sick to eat breakfast. Mary was hysterical. After losing two children to illnesses, she now overreacted to every cough and sneeze coming from Tad. Nevertheless, Lincoln had an important commitment that he needed to keep, and so he boarded the train to Gettysburg at about noon, leaving Tad in the care of Mary and a nurse.

The next day in Gettysburg, Lincoln delivered the short address that would endure for the ages. That evening he returned to Washington, having contracted a case of varioloid, a mild form of smallpox. For the next two weeks, Lincoln remained partially quarantined. During that time, Tad also remained sick with what had finally been diagnosed as scarlatina, a form of scarlet fever that develops from a strep infection. By the first week in December, however, Tad was well enough that Mary felt comfortable leaving him behind while she took a trip to New York. Mary demanded that her husband wire daily updates of his and Tad's conditions, and Lincoln faithfully complied.

In early January of 1864, after he returned to Cambridge following the Christmas holidays, Robert asked his father for some money, a typical request by a college student. "I send your draft to-day," Lincoln wrote back. "How are you now? Answer by telegraph at once." No response by Robert survives. According to Robert, Lincoln's fulfillment of his requests for money constituted the bulk of the father's correspondence to his son during the Harvard years: "I did not leave home until my father became so busy in public affairs that it was next to impossible for him to write to me. Accordingly the few letters I have, ranging over a period of five years, are with one or two exceptions letters enclosing money—I was much too young for him to write to me on general matters—at least he never did so." Besides money, however, Lincoln did write his son on matters of the boy's health. "Your letter makes us a little uneasy about your health," Lincoln wired his son in late 1864. "Telegraph us how you are. If you think it would help you make us a visit."

When Robert later said that Lincoln never wrote him on general matters, he was once again minimizing his interactions with his father. Though some of the correspondence was indirect, Lincoln did involve Robert in some war-related matters, evidencing a growing and deep respect that he had for his eldest son. On one occasion, Robert wrote his father recommending a military appointment for his Harvard friend and classmate, Henry M. Rogers. Rather than responding to Robert, Lincoln forwarded the letter to Secretary of the Navy Gideon Welles without taking a position on the request: "Mr. Rogers wishes to be an Asst. Paymaster in the Navy. I know not whether there is a vacancy. The within shows that my son 'Bob' has a high opinion of him." Welles soon arranged the appointment. On another occasion, Robert sent a letter to his father requesting the release of a seventeen-year-old boy from military service. Lincoln wrote in the blank space on Robert's letter, "Let this boy be discharged on refunding any bounty received," and then forwarded the letter to the military authorities. In addition to involving Robert in those matters, in early January, 1865, Lincoln had Robert join Secretary of State's Seward's delegation that attended the funerals of former Vice President George M. Dallas and former Ambassador to France and New Jersey Senator William L. Dayton, the man who had beaten Lincoln for the Republican vice-presidential nomination in 1856.

On July 20, 1864, Robert graduated from Harvard along with ninety-eight other men. During his senior year, he ranked thirtieth in his class with a cumulative merit ranking of 79 out of 100. For his entire four years at Harvard, he tied for thirty-second in his class with a cumulative merit ranking of 69. He was basically an average student, though in the ensuing decades Robert achieved more career success than most of his peers. Just as Lincoln had been too busy to attend Robert's graduation from Exeter four years earlier, he passed on the opportunity to see his son graduate from Harvard. "The President will not be at Commencement," Robert curtly wrote to H. P. Sprague, who had inquired about Lincoln's plans. The young man was clearly disappointed that his father did not attend, as any son would be. Mary, however, did attend. The ceremony was held on the campus, outside in the summer heat. Edward Everett of Massachusetts, the noted orator who had preceded Lincoln with a lengthy but forgotten speech at the Gettysburg dedication the previous year, gave the commencement address. As the ceremony went on, Lincoln was back at the White House managing the war, including responding to General Grant's request for 300,000 more troops.

Though Robert's four-year-long education at Harvard was a singular accomplishment, it generated some controversy. Throughout Lincoln's presidency, calls went out for young men to serve in the Union forces. Men from all walks of life volunteered. In May of 1861, as Robert was finishing his freshman year, the *Boston Herald* reported that sixteen undergraduates from Harvard left school to join the army. Robert, of course, was not one of them. In the years ahead, Lincoln received reports, both directly and indirectly, that people were asking why the president's son was not serving in the military when so many sons of ordinary citizens were putting themselves in harm's way. An editorial in *The Crisis*, a partisan critic of Lincoln, asked why "Mr. Lincoln's sons should be kept from the dangers of the field, while the sons of the laboring men are to be hurried into the harvest of death at the front. Are the sons of the rail-splitter, porcelain, and these other common clay?"

In 1863, New York Senator Ira Harris and General Daniel Sickles visited the White House. After losing a leg at the battle of Gettysburg, Sickles, nicknamed "Devil Dan," arranged for the detached limb to be put on display at the Army Medical Museum, and in later years he frequently visited the display. During the White House visit, Harris and Sickles confronted Mary. "Why isn't Robert in the Army?" Sickles asked bluntly. "He is old enough and strong enough to serve his country. He should have gone to the front some time ago."

Mary defended her son and took the blame. "Robert is making his preparations now to enter the Army, Senator Harris," Mary responded defensively and not truthfully. "He is not a shirker as you seem to imply for he has been anxious to go for a long time. If fault be there, it is mine. I have insisted that he should stay in college a little longer as I think an educated man can serve his country with more intelligent purpose than an ignoramus."

Although Robert had discussed with his parents the possibility of leaving school and entering the Army, when Mary met with Sickles and Harris, Robert was not making "preparations" to enter the Army, and Mary knew it. After losing two sons to early deaths, one since moving to the White House, she simply did not want to risk losing yet another. "She is frightened about Robert going into the Army," Mary's half-sister, Emilie Todd Helm, wrote in her diary. Lincoln, fully cognizant of the public-relations aspect of Robert's situation, brought the matter up with his wife, but did so only tepidly. Elizabeth Keckley, Mary's dressmaker, described their conversations. "We have lost one son, and his loss is as much as I can bear," Mary said. "But many a poor mother has given up all her sons," Lincoln mildly suggested, "and our son is not more dear to us than the sons of other people are to their mothers." Of course, the Lincolns had by then already lost *two* sons. Mary was clearly referring to Willie, the one son they had lost since arriving in Washington.

Five days before Robert graduated from Harvard, the *Chicago Journal* reported, "It is rumored that Mr. Robert Todd Lincoln, the President's son, on graduation from Harvard College, will immediately enter the army as a private." The rumors proved to be unfounded. Following his graduation, Robert went on a brief vacation with his mother and Tad to Long Branch, New Jersey, on the Atlantic coast, then up to Vermont and New York. When Robert returned to Washington, he had a conversation with his father about his future. Two versions of the conversation survive and are consistent with each other except in one important respect. In the first version, Robert allegedly said, "I returned from college in 1864 and one day I saw my father for a few minutes. He said 'Son, what are you going to do now?' I said, 'As long as you object to my joining the army, I am going back to Harvard, to study law.' 'If you do,' said my father, 'you should learn more than I ever did but you will never have so good a time.' That is the only advice I had from my father as to my career." In the second version, Robert leaves out the rather derisive remark about his father's limited career advice: "At the end of the vacation after my graduation from Harvard, I said to him that as he did not wish me to go into the Army (his reason having been that something might happen to me that would cause him more official embarrassment than could be offset by any possible value of my military service), I was going back to Cambridge and enter Law School. He said he thought I was right." The second version is probably more accurate, as it can be traced to Robert's own hand. The first version, which appears in Sandburg's biography of Lincoln, fails to cite a source and certainly plays to those wishing to find emotional distance between father and son.

In any case, it is not clear whether the "official embarrassment" that Lincoln supposedly feared was the prospect of Robert being taken prisoner of war or the possibility that Robert might cause some blunder in the act of duty that would give Lincoln's political opponents an issue to use against him in the 1864 presidential election. In both versions of the story, Robert suggested that it was Lincoln (and not just Mary) who was standing in the way of Robert's entry into the military. In carrying out his dual roles as president and as father, Lincoln was clearly conflicted. On the one hand, he saw both the political implications of Robert not serving and the basic matter of fairness that the president's son was safely away at college while the sons of ordinary Americans were fighting and dying for their country. On the other hand, Lincoln had already lost two sons to premature death, and he knew that if Robert was allowed to join the Army in an ordinary capacity, he would be entering a very bloody conflict and experiencing a far more dangerous battlefield than what Lincoln encountered during his service in the Blackhawk War thirty years earlier.

Just a few days before Robert graduated, Lincoln issued a request for an additional 500,000 volunteers (200,000 more than Grant requested). Despite this call for a massive number of fresh troops, when Robert approached his father with his future plans, Lincoln made no effort to loosen his or Mary's opposition to their son's enlistment. So in September, Robert quietly returned to Cambridge and began law school.

Back in Washington, in November Lincoln once again faced the voters, and was comfortably reelected against his Democratic opponent, former General George B. McClellan, whom Lincoln had relieved as commander of Union forces in 1862. Just months before the election, as the war seemed to drag on without an end in sight, Lincoln considered himself so unpopular that he convinced himself that he was going to lose. "You think I don't know I am going to be beaten," Lincoln told a friend, "*but I do* and unless some great change takes place *badly beaten.*" Only a series of Union victories over the summer redeemed his hopes, and in the end the people stood with the president. On election day, after Tad informed his father that the soldiers guarding the White House had left their posts to go vote, the two of them looked out the window to see Tad's pet turkey Jack following the men as they walked to the polling place. When Lincoln asked Tad if the turkey was going to vote, to his father's amusement Tad quickly replied: "Oh, no; he isn't of age yet."

Robert did not like law school. At that time, Harvard Law School boasted only three professors, whose long, daily lectures often left the students bored and unchallenged. Robert once sat in uncomfortable silence as Professor Joel Parker, known as a strict constructionist on matters of the Constitution, strongly denounced Robert's father and his expansive use of presidential power in prosecuting the war, including his attempt to suspend the writ of habeas corpus.

Over the Christmas holiday, Lincoln and his son had a heart-to-heart talk about Robert joining the Army. Perhaps Robert's dissatisfaction with his law studies was the catalyst for the discussion. In any case, Lincoln was finally ready to let Robert serve. With the election now behind him, Lincoln may have felt that Robert could now join without it appearing that he had been pressured into service by political considerations. Moreover, with the end of the war in sight, Lincoln saw a way to get his son into uniform without placing him in too much danger, thus addressing Mary's principal objection to Robert going off to war. On January 19, 1865, almost six months to the day after Robert graduated from Harvard, Lincoln wrote the following letter to General Ulysses S. Grant, general-in-chief of Union forces.

> *Lieut. General Grant:*
> *Please read and answer this letter as though I was not President, but only a friend. My son, now in his twenty second year, having graduated at Harvard, wishes to see something of the war before it ends. I do not wish to put him in the ranks, nor yet to give him a commission, to which those who have already served long, are better entitled, and better qualified to hold. Could he, without embarrassment to you, or detriment to the service, go into your Military family with some nominal rank, I, and not the public, furnishing his necessary means? If so, say so without the least hesitation, because I am anxious, and as deeply interested, that you shall not be encumbered as you can be yourself.*

This remarkable letter revealed a man torn between his duties as a father and his duties as president. Lincoln began by asking Grant to forget that he was president and instead treat him as any ordinary citizen and father making a request, something that he must have known would be impossible for Grant to actually do. He then told Grant that Robert "wishes to see something of the war before it ends," a rather understated description of his son's interest in joining the military that risked leaving Grant with the impression that Robert simply wanted to be a spectator in a conflict that was just about over rather than be an active participant in a cause that in fact appealed to the young man's sense of patriotic duty.

While Lincoln's request that Robert not be put "in the ranks" would have exposed Lincoln to heavy criticism that he was using his power as president to keep his son out of harm's way at the front lines of the battlefield, he was likely making efforts to address Mary's (and perhaps his own) concern about the possibility of tragically losing a third child, as well as his own previously expressed concern that something might happen to Robert that would cause embarrassment, such as being taken captive by Confederate forces or making a costly tactical blunder. At the same time, Lincoln's instruction that Robert not be given a commission was likely designed to avoid criticism that the president's intervention amounted to special treatment for his son by advancing him ahead of more deserving soldiers. Two days later, Grant replied from his headquarters at City Point:

> *Your favor of this date in relation to your son serving in some Military capacity is received. I will be most happy to have him in my Military family in the manner you propose. The nominal rank given him is immaterial but I would suggest that of Capt. as I have three staff officers now, of considerable service, in no higher grade. Indeed I have one officer with only the rank of Lieut. who has been in the service from the beginning of the war. This however will make no difference and I would still say give the rank of Capt.*

Unable for all practical purposes to deny the president's request, Grant commissioned Robert as captain and assistant adjunct general of volunteers, a rank on par with or above Grant's other staff officers. Immediately after Lincoln informed Robert of Grant's decision, an overjoyed Robert wrote Grant to express his appreciation and request a favor. "I have been informed by my father this morning, of your kindness in allowing me to become one of your Staff, and I desire to express to you both his and my hearty thanks for it. As I have been living in Cambridge for nearly five years, and left there with the expectation of returning, it will be necessary for me to go back and arrange my affairs before going to City Point; and as I also very much desire to be present at the Inauguration, unless I can be useful before, I would request your kind indulgence until after that time, when I will have the honor to report to you in person."

Though he did not address the issue in his initial letter to Lincoln, Grant later decided to reject Lincoln's offer to pay Robert's salary and instead put him on the regular Army payroll. On February 20, 1865, after leaving Harvard Law School, Robert took the oath of office and sent a letter to the Army accepting the appointment. As Robert prepared to embark on his service, he prevailed upon his father to buy him a horse. As they stood together on the front portico of the White House, "an orderly was in the act of riding a stylish-looking animal up and down one of the driveways in front of the mansion." The seller wanted $200, but Lincoln thought that it was only worth $150. After some discussion, the seller accepted Lincoln's price, and "much to Robert's delight, the horse was or-dered to be delivered to the White House stables." Riding his new steed, Robert left Washington on February 22 and headed for City Point, Vir-ginia, to join Grant at his headquarters. A concerned Lincoln telegraphed Grant on February 24, "I have not heard of my son's reaching you." Grant promptly replied, "Capt. Lincoln reported on the 22nd and was assigned to duty at my headquarters." Though Robert had previously asked Grant if he could delay first reporting for duty until after his father's second inauguration on March 4, either Grant rejected that request or Robert later changed his mind and decided to report before then. In any case, after Robert joined Grant at headquarters, the general subsequently gave Robert leave to attend the inauguration festivities.

On March 4, 1865, Lincoln took the oath of office and began his second term. The capture by Union forces of Savannah and Atlanta at the end of 1864 marked the beginning of the end of the war. In his inaugural address, which Walt Whitman likely found to be in perfect harmony with his view that Lincoln represented a perfect blend of manliness and tenderness, the president made his memorable plea for reconciliation: "With malice toward none; with charity for all; with firmness in the right, as God gives us to see the right, let us strive on to finish the work we are in; to bind up the nation's wounds; to care for him who shall have borne the battle, and for his widow, and his orphan—to do all which may achieve and cherish a just, and a lasting peace, among ourselves, and with all nations." For the first time since he became president, Lincoln could see that a time of peace was almost at hand.

During his first term, Lincoln had borne the burdens of his office and suffered the tragic loss of his beloved son Willie. He had entered the presidency in 1861 looking relatively youthful at age fifty-two. As he began his second term, the fifty-six-year-old Lincoln looked considerably older than his age. Despite those difficult times, he still thrived as a father and grew closer to his surviving sons. In Tad, he had a constant companion, a source of amusement, and a welcome distraction from the serious and often somber duties of his office. Lincoln needed Tad as much as Tad needed Lincoln. In Robert, Lincoln was able to observe with great satisfaction the fruits of his efforts as a father for the past two decades. Robert had developed into a handsome and poised young man, educated at Harvard and eager to serve his country in uniform. Though Robert had put his law studies on hold to join the army, Lincoln likely knew that Robert would one day resume those studies and follow in his father's footsteps as a lawyer. And now, looking ahead to the end of his presidency in just a few short and hopefully peaceful years, Lincoln anticipated that he and his family would finally return to Springfield, where he could resume the practice of law that he loved so much.

CHAPTER 10

Richmond

SHORTLY AFTER LINCOLN'S SECOND TERM BEGAN, GENERAL GRANT'S wife, Julia, who was staying with her husband at his headquarters at City Point, read reports that Lincoln was looking physically worn out due to the burdens of his office and the long work hours that he was keeping. Julia thought that it would do Lincoln some good to get out of the White House and spend time observing firsthand the progress being made by the Union army, so she advised her husband to invite the president and his family for a visit. At first, Grant demurred, telling her, "If President Lincoln wishes to come down, he will not wait to be asked. It is not my place to invite him."

"Yes, it is," Julia persisted. "You know all that has been said about his interference with army movements, and he will never come for the fear of appearing to meddle with army affairs." Grant remained unconvinced until a few days later when Julia asked Robert, who was on Grant's staff, if he thought his parents would come if invited. Robert's answer demonstrated that both he and Julia knew Lincoln better than Grant did.

"I suppose they would, if they were sure they were not intruding," Robert said respectfully.

On March 20, Grant relented and telegraphed the president, inviting him and Mary to join the general at the front. Lincoln accepted, and on March 23, Lincoln, Mary, and Tad left Washington on the steamer *River Queen*, en route to City Point, Virginia. The *River Queen* was a large floating hotel, on which the family could relax as it lay anchored in the bay. From Grant's headquarters just onshore at City Point, Lincoln could receive frequent updates on several critical battles that held the prospect of finally bringing to an end the bloody civil war. With Grant's permission, Robert would occasionally be able to join the family for meals on the ship. It was a typical working vacation for Lincoln. Admiral David D. Porter, who supervised Lincoln's arrangements on the *River Queen*, later reported that Lincoln "came, in the first place, for rest; he looked much worn out with his responsibilities since I had last seen him, and needed the repose he sought. He was also very much interested that the army should move upon the enemy, and, though I am quite sure that he had the most unbounded confidence in General Grant and his judgment, yet I am of opinion that he considered himself a good judge of the time when operations should commence."

As March drew to a close, Union forces were within reach of capturing both Petersburg and Richmond. On March 30, Lincoln wrote Stanton from the *River Queen* that "last night at 10:15, when it was dark as a rainy night without a moon could be, a furious cannonade, soon joined by heavy musketry-fire, opened near Petersburg and lasted about two hours. The sound was very distinct here, as also were the flashes of the guns upon the clouds." On April 1, as bloody battles raged around Petersburg and Richmond, Mary returned to Washington, leaving Tad with his father. Early the next morning, Lincoln telegraphed his anxious wife with updated news from the front and added, "Robert yesterday wrote a little cheerful note to Capt. Penrose, which is all I have heard from him since you left." Later that day, after receiving a telegram from Mary indicating that she soon planned to return to the family on the *River Queen*, Lincoln wired back, informing her of Grant's report that Union forces had surrounded Petersburg and taken a large number of Confederate prisoners. "Gen. Grant telegraphs that he has Petersburg completely enveloped. . . . [S]uggests that I shall go out and see him . . . which I think I will do." He added, "Tad and I are both well, and will be glad to see you and your party at the time you name."

The next morning, April 3, Lincoln wired Stanton. "This morning General Grant reports Petersburg evacuated, and he is confident Richmond also is. He is pushing forward to cut off, if possible, the retreating army. I start to him [in Petersburg] in a few minutes." Upon receiving

Lincoln's telegram, Stanton immediately wired back expressing concern for the president's safety: "Allow me respectfully to ask you to consider whether you ought to expose the nation to the consequence of any disaster to yourself in the pursuit of a treacherous and dangerous enemy like the rebel army. If it was a question concerning yourself only I should not presume to say a word. Commanding generals are in the line of their duty in running such risks; but is the political head of a nation in the same condition?"

Stanton's cautionary telegram reached City Point after Lincoln had already left. Without ever informing Mary that he was bringing Tad, perhaps to keep her from worrying over the boy's safety, the father and his son traveled by train to Petersburg, accompanied by Admiral Porter. It was not the first time that Lincoln had brought Tad with him on a venture into military territory. Lincoln often let the boy accompany him to various exercises and parades around Washington and occasionally took his son with him to installations away from the city. On those occasions, Tad was his usual irrepressible self. Prior to a planned visit to Fort Monroe on Chesapeake Bay in Virginia, Lincoln had anticipated that Tad would be disruptive. "Tad, if you will be a good boy and not disturb me any more till we get to Fortress Monroe, I will give you a dollar," the president offered. Tad accepted the proposal but soon forgot his promise and engaged in his typical unruly behavior. When they reached their destination, Tad said, "Father, I want my dollar."

Lincoln replied by asking, "Tad, do you think you have earned it!"

"Yes," replied the boy.

According to one witness, "Lincoln looked at him reproachfully for an instant, and then taking from his pocket-book a dollar note, he said: 'Well, my son, at any rate, I will keep *my* part of the bargain.'"

While en route, Lincoln received a message that Robert was waiting for him at Hancock Station in Petersburg. Once they arrived, the men mounted horses that Robert had brought to the station and rode to a small house where Grant waited. The president's escort was small, consisting only of Robert, a sergeant, and three or four privates. "It was all in keeping with the President's retinue since he first started on this expedition," Porter later recalled of the president's security arrangements, "but it never seemed to strike him as wanting in any way." After meeting with Grant for about an hour and a half, the party began their journey back to the *River Queen*. As Lincoln left the city, he stopped at a tobacco store, where the proprietor presented him with four bales of the weed weighing about three pounds each. Ever anxious to make his presence known and to participate in the goings-on, Tad begged his father for four tobacco bales of his own, which Lincoln promptly bought for him.

After he returned to the *River Queen* later that day, Lincoln received news that rebel forces had evacuated Richmond ahead of Major General Godfrey Weitzel's advancing troops. Lincoln knew that the evacuation of the Confederate capital meant that the end of the war was at hand. "Thank God," Lincoln told Porter, "that I have lived to see this! It seems to me that I have been dreaming a horrid dream for four years, and now the nightmare is gone. I want to see Richmond." By then Lincoln had been given Stanton's earlier telegram suggesting that he not go to Petersburg. "Thank you for your caution," Lincoln wired back, "but I have already been to Petersburg. Staid [sic] with General Grant an hour and a half and returned here. It is certain now that Richmond is in our hands, and I think I will go there tomorrow. I will take care of myself." Lincoln also wired Mary to report his safe return from Petersburg and, for the first time, informed her that he had taken Tad with him. "Petersburg and Richmond are both in our hands; and Tad and I have been to the former and been with Bob four or five hours. He is well and in good spirits." Lincoln now decided to take Tad with him to visit Richmond. Once again, not wanting to worry Mary about the boy's safety, Lincoln did not inform her in advance of his decision.

Richmond was located on hills above the James River, accessible by boat from Chesapeake Bay where the *River Queen* was moored. Before the president could depart, however, Union forces needed to clear mines from the river. Once that project was completed to Porter's satisfaction, the party began the journey at 9:00 a.m. on April 4. Porter was aboard the *Malvern*, a small blockade-runner captured from Confederate forces and given to him as a flagship. "I retained her because she was small and drew but little water," Porter wrote, "and I could run about in her at night and day, enter shoal harbors and inlets, and altogether she suited me."

Lincoln's party, which included the president, Tad, and telegraph opera-
tor Samuel Beckwith, followed the *Malvern* aboard the *River Queen*. On
the advice of his military escort, Lincoln and Tad rode on the upper deck,
where they would be in less danger if the ship hit a floating mine. It was
Tad's twelfth birthday, and he was now a year older than Willie had been
when he died.

Several other military vessels made the trip, some racing ahead trying to be the first to dock in Richmond. Porter later recalled that, as the
boats slowly navigated the waters, he remained concerned about Lincoln's
safety with "a heavy feeling of responsibility on my mind, notwithstand-
ing the great care that had been taken to clear the river." Many of the
vessels in the flotilla fell behind as they ran aground in the shallow water.
When both the *River Queen* and the *Malvern* also got stuck, Porter and
Lincoln's party boarded a barge, which was then towed by the tug *Glance*,
operated by a small group of marines. As those two vessels approached a
large bridge across the James River about a mile below Richmond, they
came across a small steamer that was stuck in a current. Porter ordered
the tug and some of the marines to stay and help the steamer, while the
rest of the crew slowly rowed the barge carrying Porter and the Lincoln
party toward Richmond.

Porter later recalled his initial disappointment over their lonely arrival in the captured city: "Here we were in a solitary boat, after having
set out with a number of vessels flying flags at every mast-head, hoping
to enter the conquered capital in a manner befitting the rank of the President of the United States, with a further intention of firing a national
salute in honor of the happy result." Lincoln, however, found amusement
in the circumstances: "Admiral, this brings to my mind a fellow who once
came to me to ask for an appointment as minister abroad. Finding he
could not get that, he came down to some more modest position. Finally,
he asked to be made a tide-waiter [a seaport customs collector]. When
he saw he could not get that, he asked me for an old pair of trousers. But
it is well to be humble."

Lincoln's landing not only lacked a supporting flotilla, but was also
devoid of a welcoming party. Porter, who had never landed in Richmond
before, was unsure where he should dock the barge. "We pulled on, hop-

ing to see some one of whom we could inquire," Porter wrote, "but no one was in sight. The street along the river-front was as deserted as if this had been a city of the dead. The troops had been in possession some hours, but not a soldier was to be seen." After battling some currents, Porter finally docked at about 11:00 a.m. at Rocketts landing at the east end of the city, the nearest acceptable landing site he could find. Lincoln and Tad watched as the crew secured the barge to the dock. Looking rather formal, Lincoln wore a white shirt with a bow tie, black trousers, a black frock coat, and a black stovepipe hat that made him seem much taller than his already long six-foot-four height. Tad sported his favorite outfit, a dark blue soldier's uniform with a regulation cap.

Porter described the scene as Lincoln and Tad disembarked: "There was a small house on this landing, and behind it were some twelve negroes digging with spades. The leader of them was an old man of sixty years of age. He raised himself up to an upright position as we landed, and put his hands up to his eyes. Then he dropped his spade and sprang forward. 'Bress de Lord,' he said, 'dere is de great Messiah! I knowed him as soon as I seed him. He's been in my heart fo' long yeahs, an' he's come at las' to free his chillum from deir bondage! Glory, Hallelujah!' And he fell upon his knees before the President and kissed his feet. The others followed his example." Lincoln looked down, "much embarrassed at his position. 'Don't kneel to me,' he said. 'That is not right. You must kneel to God only, and thank him for the liberty you will hereafter enjoy. I am but God's humble instrument.'"

A couple of minutes after the commotion began, at Porter's urging, those surrounding the president backed away. The crowd sang a brief hymn; then Porter decided that it was time to head into the city. Porter grumbled that none of Weitzel's troops were there with a carriage or horse for the president. "We'll walk," Lincoln said. "It's a long way, Mr. President," Porter replied. "I'm used to long walks, admiral," Lincoln said as they began the two-mile walk toward downtown. As they walked, scores of other former slaves gathered near the party. Porter ordered the marines who had accompanied Lincoln on the barge to fix their bayonets and surround the president as he walked along. Porter did not believe that the former slaves posed a threat to the president's safety, for "it seemed to me that he had an army of supporters there who could and would defend him against all the world." Instead, he thought that it was "likely there were scowling eyes not far off; men were perhaps looking on, with hatred in their hearts, who were even then seeking an opportunity to slay him."

As Lincoln walked along, gently holding Tad's little hand, many of the freed slaves tried to touch the president, but Lincoln's guards kept them at bay. At one point the crowd was so large that the party could not move forward, so the president stopped and made some brief remarks. He exhorted the men and women to value their new freedom and to "learn the laws and obey them; obey God's commandments and thank him for giving you liberty, for to him you owe all things. There, now, let me pass on; I have but little time to spare. I want to see the capital, and must return at once to Washington to secure to you that liberty which you seem to prize so highly."

As they neared the edge of the city, a few white citizens began to join the crowd. The day before, a Union officer had ordered all Richmond citizens to remain in their homes until further notice. Yet the excitement of Lincoln walking the streets caused some to disregard that order. As the party passed Libby Prison, where many Union soldiers had been held as prisoners of war in deplorable conditions, some in the crowd clamored for it to be torn down. "No," Lincoln replied, "leave it as a monument." Lincoln walked on "with his usual long, careless stride, and looking about with an interested air and taking in everything." He continued to hold Tad's hand as the boy nestled closely to his father.

The group eventually reached Main Street, a dusty road leading into the heart of the city. The weather had warmed up. Porter observed that Lincoln looked thirsty, but the president did not ask for any relief. Many residents, who were afraid to leave their houses in violation of the curfew, opened their windows and looked out "with eager, peering faces." Thomas Morris Chester, a black newspaper correspondent, described the scene:

> *The colored population was wild with enthusiasm. Old men thanked God in a very boisterous manner, and old women shouted upon the pavement as high as they had ever done at a religious revival. . . . Every one declares that Richmond never before presented such a*

spectacle of jubilee. It must be confessed that those who participated in this informal reception of the President were mainly negroes. There were many whites in the crowd, but they were lost in the great concourse of American citizens of African descent. Those who lived in the finest houses either stood motionless upon their steps or merely peeped through the window blinds.

Judith McGuire, a white resident of Richmond, offered a different perspective, writing in her diary:

His reception was anything but complimentary. Our people were nothing rude or disrespectful; they only kept themselves away from a scene so painful. There are very few Unionists of the least respectability here; these met them . . . with cringing loyalty, I hear, but the rest of the small collection were of the low, lower, lowest of creation. They drove through several streets, but the greeting was so feeble from the motley crew of vulgar men and women, that the Federal officers themselves, I suppose, were ashamed of it.

A *New York Times* reporter, knowing that his audience was largely in the North, described Lincoln's walk through the city this way:

The colored population turned out in great force, and for a time blockaded the quarters of the President, cheering vociferously. It was to be expected that, a population that three days since were in slavery, should evince a strong desire to look upon the man whose edict had struck forever the manacles from their limbs. A considerable number of the white population cheered the President heartily, and but for the order of the Provost-Marshall yesterday, ordering them to remain within their homes quietly for a few days, without a doubt there would have been a large addition to the numbers present.

Perhaps it was Charles C. Coffin of the *Boston Journal* who best summed up the inability of writers and artists to truly capture the majesty of the moment, at least from a northerner's perspective, when he wrote,

"[N]o written page or illuminated canvas can give the reality of the event—the enthusiastic bearing of the people—the blacks and poor whites who have suffered untold horrors during the war, their demonstrations of pleasure, the shouting, dancing, the thanksgiving to God, the mention of the name of Jesus—as if President Lincoln were next to the son of God in their affections—the jubilant cries, the countenances beaming with unspeakable joy, the tossing of caps, the swinging of arms of a motley crowd—some in rags, some bare-foot, some wearing pants of Union blue, and coats of Confederate gray, ragamuffins in dress, through the hardships of war, but yet of stately bearing."

At one point, a girl of about seventeen made her way through the crowd carrying a bundle of roses and "gracefully presented her bouquet to the President." Lincoln accepted the gift and made some brief remarks as he held her hand, temporarily releasing his grip on Tad. "There was no cheering at this, nor yet any disapprobation shown," Porter recorded. When Lincoln finished his talk, two of the soldiers in Lincoln's escort walked the girl back through the crowd and onto the sidewalk. By this time, Porter had become more concerned about Lincoln's safety. When he spotted a Union cavalryman attached to the occupying force, Porter ordered him to go to General Weitzel "and tell him to send a military escort here to guard the President and get him through this crowd." About twenty minutes later, a troop of cavalry galloped up and cleared the street by firmly but politely ordering the bystanders to congregate on the sidewalks. This allowed Lincoln's party to "walk along uninterruptedly."

Soon Lincoln reached the mansion that Jefferson Davis had lived in and occupied as his headquarters, located at the corner of Twelfth and Clay. Porter described the house as "a quite small affair compared with the White House, and modest in all its appointments, showing that while President Davis was engaged heart and soul in endeavoring to effect the division of the States, he was not, at least, surrounding himself with regal style, but was living in a modest, comfortable way, like any other citizen." Generals Weitzel and George F. Shepley, who were now using the house as their headquarters, greeted the president on the steps. Before going in, Lincoln removed his hat and wiped his brow, then looked at Tad, whose face was flushed from the heat that he, too, had to endure during the long walk.

After the group entered the parlor, a high-ceilinged room at the front of the house, Lincoln promptly plopped down in a chair, looking "pale and haggard, utterly worn out." A black servant, who had stayed behind after Davis had evacuated, brought everybody some much-needed glasses of water. He also offered whiskey to the men, which Lincoln politely declined but the others accepted. After a few minutes, Lincoln asked to see the rest of the house. After they entered Davis's office, Lincoln walked immediately to the modest working desk and sat down behind it. Tad stood right next to him. "This must have been President Davis's chair," Lincoln said softly as he crossed his legs and "looked far off with a serious, dreamy expression." As Shepley and Weitzel described an earlier meeting with several prominent Confederate citizens in Richmond, Lincoln "listened patiently, and indicated the magnitude of the proposition submitted for his consideration by great nervousness of manner, running his hands frequently through his hair, moving to and fro in [Davis's] official chair." Though Lincoln exuded a deep sense of satisfaction, he did not gloat and spoke no unkind words about his adversary. Navy Captain John S. Barnes, who had commanded one of the ships in the flotilla that brought Lincoln to Richmond and who had been at Lincoln's side since their arrival, reported that "there was no triumph in his gesture or attitude. He lay back in the chair like a tired man whose nerves had carried him beyond his strength."

Soon the servant called the group for lunch. One Richmond citizen who later learned the details of Lincoln's visit to the house wrote, "It is said that they took collation at . . . Our President's house!! Ah! It is a bitter pill. I [wished] that dear old house, with all its associations, so sacred to the Southerners, so sweet to us as a family, had shared in the general conflagration. Then its history would have been unsullied, though sad. Oh, how gladly I would have seen it burn!"

After the meal, two Confederate representatives, John A. Campbell and General Joseph Reid Anderson, called on the president to discuss peace terms. Campbell was a former justice of the United States Supreme Court who had resigned his seat and sided with the Confederacy.

Anderson owned Tredegar Iron Company in Richmond, which supplied ordnance and munitions for the Confederate army throughout the war. "I spoke to him particularly for Virginia," Campbell later wrote, "and urged him to consult with her public men . . . as to the restoration of peace." He also told Lincoln that "when leniency and cruelty play for conquest of a kingdom the gentlest player will be the soonest winner." Lincoln listened carefully and then asked Campbell to visit him the next day aboard the *Malvern* for further discussions. Campbell accepted the invitation, and the three men ended their meeting. Fearful for their own safety, Campbell and Anderson asked the reporters following Lincoln not to publish their names. "It is asserted that two or three of the most prominent citizens sought and obtained an interview with Mr. Lincoln during his short stay here," wrote a *New York Times* reporter. "I have been requested not to mention their names."

After some brief conferences with his military officers, Lincoln, Tad, Admiral Porter, and Generals Weitzel and Shepley left the Davis house and boarded an open carriage that had been brought for the president so that he could tour the city. Because the carriage was designed to hold only four people, Tad had to sit on his father's lap. As a large crowd cheered around them, the carriage slowly pulled away, driven by a black coachman and followed by a cavalry escort. The procession soon reached the state capitol building, which had been designed by Thomas Jefferson. The carriage stopped for a moment, and Lincoln stood up and waved to the crowd. After studying the elegant building for a moment, he sat down and whispered something into Tad's ear. Tad then looked carefully at the building.

When Lincoln heard shouts from the crowd that they needed food, Lincoln ordered Weitzel to see that their needs were met in the beleaguered city. Lincoln then stood again and waved to the crowd. After he sat back down, the carriage left the capitol grounds and headed back to Rocketts landing. Along the way, Lincoln is said to have stopped at the house of Confederate General George Pickett, whose division suffered devastating losses at the Battle of Gettysburg. According to Mrs. Pickett, she answered the knock at the door while holding her baby. She immediately told the caller that her husband was not home. Lincoln introduced himself and told her that he had known young Pickett way back when his old law partner, John T. Stuart, recommended him for an appointment to West Point. After a brief conversation, Lincoln kissed the baby and said goodbye.

Soon the carriage reached Rocketts landing, and Lincoln, Tad, and the other men got out and walked toward the waiting barge. Before boarding, Weitzel asked Lincoln what should be done with captured Confederate soldiers. Lincoln thought for a moment, then replied, "If I were in your place, I'd let 'em up easy. Let 'em up easy." With that, the father and son boarded the barge, which took them to the *Malvern* and eventually back to the *River Queen*.

In remembering Lincoln's visit to Richmond, historians have typically focused on the memorable images of Lincoln walking the streets of the battle-scarred city as liberated slaves bowed in reverence, and of him visiting Jefferson Davis's abandoned office where he sat at his rival's desk. In doing so, they have traditionally characterized Lincoln's time in Richmond as the quiet triumph of an American president over both the scourge of slavery and a vanquished opponent. Yet Lincoln's day in Richmond was also a revealing moment in his father-son relationship with Tad. The Richmond journey represented much that was good about Lincoln the father. He was, at once, physically and emotionally close to Tad, their bond enhanced as they quietly walked hand in hand through the dusty, rubble-strewn streets of the fallen capital. Since entering the presidency, Lincoln often allowed Tad to observe up close his daily toils at the White House. But the young boy was usually fooling around, and in reality he understood little about what Lincoln was actually trying to achieve as he governed the divided nation. In Richmond, however, Tad saw firsthand the lasting significance of his father's work over both the past four years and the decade preceding his ascension to the presidency. On that day, Lincoln also taught Tad some important lessons. He let Tad see that, despite the incantations of the freed slaves toward him, he was just a man and that it was God to whom they should offer their devotions. He also showed the boy that in victory, even following a hard-fought war, one should be both dignified in celebration and gracious toward the defeated enemy. In a way, Lincoln was living out the words of his second inaugural address, when he spoke of binding up the nation's wounds. Tad was so mesmerized by the experience that, for once, he remained on his best behavior throughout the entire day.

It had been quite a memorable day for the two—indeed, a day that Tad would never forget. Just ten days later, however, tragedy would once again strike the Lincoln family.

CHAPTER 11

They Have Killed Papa Dead

ON THE MORNING OF APRIL 14, 1865, ROBERT LINCOLN JOINED HIS parents for breakfast at the White House. Now carrying the physique of a mature young man, Robert was both handsome in appearance and confident in manner. He had accompanied Grant to Washington, where the general was to attend a cabinet meeting later in the day. Lincoln had arranged Robert's entry into the military back in January because the young man "wishe[d] to see something of the war before it ends." Much to the relief of his parents, Robert never engaged in any combat or even came close to being in harm's way. He generally stayed with Grant at headquarters and left only to escort visitors back and forth on secure roads. Nevertheless, Robert made a positive impression on those around him. Robert "soon became exceedingly popular," wrote one fellow officer. "He inherited many of the genial traits of his father, and entered heartily into all the social pastimes at headquarters. He was always ready to perform his share of hard work and never expected to be treated differently from any other officer on account of being the son of the Chief Executive of the nation."

Perhaps the most satisfying and memorable part of Robert's service, however, came on April 9, 1865, when he traveled with Grant and the rest of the general's staff to the village of Appomattox Court House to accept General Robert E. Lee's surrender of the army of Northern Virginia, which effectively ended the war. While at the home of Wilmer McLean, where the somber meeting took place, Grant introduced the president's son to General Lee. With Tad's visit to Richmond and Robert's presence at Appomattox, both surviving Lincoln boys witnessed significant events in the waning days of the bloody civil war that had consumed so much of their father's time and energy over the past four years.

During breakfast, the conversation turned to Robert's future. "Well, my son," Lincoln said, "you have returned safely from the front. The war is now closed and we will soon live in peace with the brave men who have been fighting against us. I trust, that an era of good feeling has returned and that henceforth we shall live in harmony together." Lincoln then offered some fatherly advice. "You must lay aside your uniform and return to college. I wish you to read law for three years, and at the end of that time I hope that we will be able to tell whether you will make a lawyer or not." Before breakfast ended, Mary asked Robert if he wanted to join her and her husband that evening at Ford's Theatre for a performance of *Our American Cousin*. The young man declined, preferring to stay home for a quiet evening in the White House with his friend, John Hay. Throughout the day, at least eleven other people that Lincoln or Mary asked to the theater, including General Grant, would decline the invitation.

In the late afternoon, Lincoln and Mary went for a carriage ride in the country on the outskirts of Washington. "I never saw him so supremely cheerful—his manner was even playful," Mary later fondly recalled. "We must *both* be more cheerful in the future," Lincoln said to his wife as they rode along. "Between the war & the loss of our darling Willie—we have both been very miserable." Recalling his fond memories of riding the circuit, Lincoln told Mary that after his term was over he would like to practice law again, perhaps in Springfield or even Chicago. He also wanted to travel, perhaps to Europe and California.

After eating dinner at the White House with Robert and Tad, the Lincolns left for Ford's Theatre a little after 8:00 p.m. Along the way they picked up Major Henry R. Rathbone and his fiancée, Clara Harris, the couple who finally accepted the Lincolns' theater invitation. Clara, whom Mary described as "a dear friend," was the daughter of New York Senator Ira Harris, who had once criticized Lincoln for not allowing Robert to join the Army. Clara had accompanied Mary to another play the previous month and was excited to join the Lincolns at Ford's Theatre. Meanwhile,

Tad went to the National Theatre with Alphonso Donn, a White House doorman, to see *Aladdin, or the Wonderful Lamp*, while Robert remained at home studying Spanish with John Hay.

At 10:13 p.m., John Wilkes Booth shot Lincoln as Mary watched in horror. There are varying accounts as to how Robert first heard the news of the shooting. According to the most probable account, sometime after ten o'clock, Robert fell ill, so he and Hay retired to their rooms. Just as Robert picked up a spoon and a vial of medicine, White House guard Thomas F. Pendel knocked on the bedroom door and entered. "Captain, . . . something happened to the President; you had better go down to the theatre and see what it is." Robert immediately asked Pendel to fetch Hay, and the two friends rushed to the theater.

By the time they arrived, Lincoln, who had been shot in the back of the head by John Wilkes Booth, was removed from the theater and taken across the street to a small room at a boardinghouse owned by William Peterson. When guards tried to stop Robert and Hay from entering the house, Robert pleaded, "It's my father! My father! I'm Robert Lincoln."

Once the guards recognized Robert, they immediately allowed him into the room. His father, unconscious and breathing slowly and deliberately, lay diagonally across the small bed that was too short to correctly accommodate his tall frame. Many government officials and friends were already present. Robert stood in shock at the headboard, occasionally turning to New York Senator Charles Sumner for comfort. Dr. Charles Sabin Taft, the older brother of Bud and Holly Taft, Willie's and Tad's former playmates, had been in the audience at the theater and now attended the wounded president along with several other physicians. Taft later recalled that "at first [Robert's] grief overpowered him but soon recovering himself he leaned his head on the shoulder of Senator Charles Sumner, and remained in silent grief during the long, terrible night." Navy Secretary Gideon Welles observed Robert crying on Sumner's shoulder. "He bore himself well, but on two occasions gave way to overpowering grief and sobbed aloud, turning his head and leaning on the shoulder of Senator Sumner."

Robert, who later described his own feeling of being "utterly desperate, hardly able to realize the truth," bore the additional burden of trying to comfort Mary. At one point, Mary asked that Tad be brought to the room from the White House, saying that Lincoln "would speak to him because he loved him so." If Robert saw this as a slight, he never spoke of it. Mary eventually became so hysterical that Secretary of War Edwin Stanton ordered that she be taken out of the room to wait elsewhere in the house.

Tad soon returned from the National Theater with his chaperone, Alphonso Donn. Upon hearing the news that his father had been shot, he remained at the White House the entire evening. Pendel, the White House guard who had earlier informed Robert of the shooting, tried to comfort the boy, who kept repeating, "[T]hey have killed papa dead! They have killed papa dead!" At midnight, as Lincoln faded toward death at the Peterson house, Pendel took Tad into Lincoln's White House bedroom, dressed him in his pajamas, and put him in the bed. Pendel then lay down next to Tad until the broken-hearted boy fell asleep. At 7:22 a.m. on April 15, as Tad slept at the White House and Robert waited anxiously with Mary in another room at the Peterson house, Abraham Lincoln died.

Shortly after Lincoln died, Dr. Phineas D. Gurley, who had delivered the eulogy at Willie's funeral, escorted the grieving Mary back to the White House. Dr. Gurley had rushed to Lincoln's bedside when he heard the news of the shooting. As they exited the carriage under the North Portico, Tad came outside and repeatedly cried, "Where is my Pa? Where is my Pa?"

"Taddy, your Pa is dead," Gurley said somberly.

It was too much for the boy. "O what shall I do? What shall I do?" Tad wailed. "My Brother is dead. My Father is dead. O what shall I do?" Tad instantly realized what the loss of his father meant. "What will become of me? O what shall I do? O mother you will not die will you. O don't you die Ma. You won[']t die will you Mother? If you die I shall be all alone. O don[']t die Ma."

At that point, even Dr. Gurley broke down. The next morning he told a friend that "up to that time [I] had not shed a tear, but [I] could not witness Tad[']s grief unmoved and the Tears flowed freely. . . . I felt as though I had been engaged all night in a terrible Battle and had but just strength enough left to drag myself off the field."

The next morning, when Tad saw Navy Secretary Gideon Welles and Attorney General James Speed descending the stairs of the White House while Welles's wife comforted Mary, the boy tearfully asked, "Oh, Welles, who killed my father?"

"Neither Speed nor myself could restrain our tears," Welles later confided to his diary, "nor give the poor boy a satisfactory answer." In the coming days and years, Tad had to deal with his own sense of loss as well as that of Mary, whom he tried to comfort. "Tad's grief at his father's death was as great as the grief of his mother," wrote Elizabeth Keckley, "but her terrible outbursts awed the boy into silence. Sometimes he would throw his arms around her neck, and exclaim, between his broken sobs, 'Don't cry so, Mamma! don't cry, or you will make me cry, too. You will make me cry, too.'" Keckley also wrote of how Tad, when he would hear his mother sobbing at night, "would get up, and go to her bed in his white sleeping-clothes: 'Don't cry, Mamma; I cannot sleep if you cry! Papa was good, and he has gone to heaven. He is happy there. He is with God and brother Willie. Don't cry, Mamma, or I will cry too.'"

At first, Mary did not want to bury Lincoln in Springfield, but she soon changed her mind. The family then arranged for Willie's casket to be removed from the Carroll vault at Oak Hill Cemetery and be placed on the train that took Lincoln's body and the family back home to Illinois. For thirteen days, with the grief-stricken family on board, the Lincoln funeral train meandered its way back to Springfield on a route that was almost the reverse of the path that had brought the Lincolns to Washington four years earlier. Following the local funeral service, the caskets of Lincoln and Willie were placed in a temporary vault at Oak Ridge Cemetery until a larger family tomb was completed in 1874.

Lincoln's assassination was not the last tragedy to befall the family. Tad, who finally learned to read and write, became a constant companion and source of comfort to his mother. But in July 1871, at the age of eighteen, he died after suffering for several weeks with what was thought to be a severe cold that eventually caused his lungs to fill with fluid.

Robert thus became Lincoln's only son to survive into adulthood. He became a prominent Chicago lawyer and served as secretary of war in the administrations of Presidents James A. Garfield and Chester A. Arthur.

Friends encouraged him to seek the Republican presidential nomination in 1884, but he quickly dismissed the notion and in fact never sought high elective office. President Benjamin Harrison appointed him minister to Great Britain in 1889. Less than a decade later, the board of directors of the Pullman Railroad Company named Robert president pro tempore of the company following the death of its founder, George Pullman. Robert had been the company's legal counsel for many years and had gained the confidence of the board in the years preceding Pullman's death. The board made Robert the company's permanent president four years later. During his tenure at Pullman, the company experienced substantial growth and profitability, which made Robert a very wealthy man.

Robert later told a family friend that the seat at Ford's Theatre that he would have occupied on the fateful night in April 1865 would have placed him between the door that Booth entered and his father, and that had he accepted his father's invitation to attend the play, he may have thwarted the assassination.

In a strange twist of fate, Robert was present at the scenes of two more presidential assassinations. On July 2, 1881, while serving as secretary of war, Robert entered the Sixth Street station in Washington just seconds after President Garfield had been shot in the lobby while waiting for his train. Twenty years later, on September 6, 1901, as Robert disembarked a train in Buffalo, New York, where he had gone to visit the Pan American Exposition, he heard the news that President William McKinley had just been shot while inside the Temple of Music building on the exposition grounds. Robert later visited the wounded McKinley at a house in Buffalo where the president had been taken following the shooting. McKinley died there a few days later.

In the years following Lincoln's death, Mary suffered public humiliation as her spendthrift ways and large debts became public. Though the administrator of her late husband's estate established an annual stipend to cover her living expenses, Mary determined that it was insufficient and successfully lobbied Congress to enact a modest pension for widows of presidents. To raise additional money, she sold her White House wardrobe, which caused Robert much embarrassment. In order to preserve some measure of Mary's dignity, Robert "systematically bought up any books that reflected [poorly] on Mrs. Lincoln." In 1875, after months of watching his mother's behavior grow more and more erratic, Robert initiated proceedings to have Mary declared legally insane. A jury agreed with his petition, whereupon the court ordered her confined to a state hospital for the insane. She remained there for nearly a year until a second jury declared that she was "restored to reason." Mary died in 1882, having survived her husband by seventeen years.

Lincoln, Mary, Eddy, Willie, and Tad are all interred in the large family tomb in Springfield. When Robert's son, Abraham Lincoln II, died in 1890 at the age of sixteen, Robert placed the boy's casket in the family tomb, and expected that he himself would later be buried there as well. However, when Robert died in 1926 at the age of eighty-three, his widow had him buried at Arlington National Cemetery outside of Washington. She also moved the body of Abraham Lincoln II from Springfield for reinterment at Arlington. While those proffering the view that Lincoln and Robert were permanently estranged might be tempted to point to this physical separation in death as being symbolic of the distance between the two in life, such a conclusion would overlook the fact that Robert's widow selected the venue of his grave and in fact overrode Robert's own intentions to be buried in the family tomb in Springfield. In any case, it is worth noting that Robert, who was present in the aftermath of the assassinations of Presidents Lincoln, Garfield, and McKinley, lies entombed at Arlington not far from the burial site of President John F. Kennedy, the fourth chief executive to be struck down by an assassin's bullet, thus completing Robert's physical proximity to all four of America's assassinated presidents.

EPILOGUE

MARK TWAIN ONCE SAID, "IT IS A WISE CHILD THAT KNOWS ITS OWN father, and an unusual one that unreservedly approves of him." In his youth, Abraham Lincoln knew his father, but did not unreservedly approve of him. In that way, young Lincoln was, accordingly to Twain, both wise and ordinary. Twain's insight, however, speaks as much to fathers as it does to their children. Fathers are charged with responsibilities relating to discipline, education, career guidance, moral example, and religious training, as well as fostering emotional bonds that link the family together as a single unit. For a son to unreservedly embrace all that his father is or does essentially requires that the two see the same future. Thomas Lincoln, who grew up with frontier colonial-era values in the early post-colonial era, became a father during a period of transition in fatherhood roles. Unable to see beyond the frontier, Thomas believed that he would largely satisfy his patriarchal duty if he trained his son to succeed in a life of subsistence farming. He de-emphasized education and rarely thought about getting ahead or bettering himself financially. Thus, he did not expect anything different from his son. Thomas also saw much value in rigid discipline and placed no value on establishing any degree of emotional attachment with his son.

Lincoln, who by early manhood managed to see opportunities in urban America that extended well beyond the life that Thomas offered, desired not only a different way of life for himself, but he also wanted to be a different kind of father to his own children. Along with other men of his generation, Lincoln embraced a form of fatherhood that moved away from the rigid patriarchy of the colonial era and instead emphasized a middle-class lifestyle that valued education for children, upward mobility, and financial security for both the present household and future generations. This new conception of fatherhood came with some degree of diminished paternal influence within the household, as more domestic power was ceded to mothers who stayed home while their husbands were increasingly absent as they developed careers outside the home. But it also brought an increased desire for emotional attachment with children. By not seeing their children constantly throughout the day as they would in a rural setting, and by being occasionally absent as they traveled away from home on business, these nineteenth-century middle-class fathers placed increasing importance on developing emotional ties with their children, often through greater physical affection.

Just as Thomas raised his family during a period of transition in fatherhood roles, unable to fully understand the greater paternal changes that were taking place around him, Lincoln, too, came of age as a father during the early stages of that transition. Lacking a role model, Lincoln struggled with the new conception of fatherhood. On occasion, he parented on the opposite extreme from Thomas, as in the case of failing to impose any meaningful degree of discipline on his sons when they misbehaved. At other times, he struggled to break free from Thomas's influence, as he seemed to value education for Robert and Willie but failed to push it for Tad. Though partially explained by his perception that Tad had a learning disability, Lincoln's disregard for the boy's education likely had some roots in his own experience of succeeding despite a lack of education countenanced by Thomas.

It is tempting to focus on the tragedies that befell the Lincoln family. The premature deaths of Eddy and Willie, together with Lincoln's assassination and the untimely death of Tad, are heart-wrenching to any observer. To focus on these tragedies, however, diminishes the value of the lessons of Lincoln's life. If the manner and timing of Lincoln's death call out for a greater meaning, it is that Lincoln was, in a sense, the last casualty of the bloody Civil War that divided the nation and then forever changed the way that America sees itself. In the same way, the deaths of Eddy and Willie represented more than the tragic losses of two young boys—those losses reveal much about Lincoln as a father and about nineteenth-century fatherhood in general. At a time when the mortality rate among infants and children was high, parents were expected to bear their losses with a silent resignation to God's will. Lincoln, however, was among an increasingly defiant generation of parents who deeply felt their losses and were not afraid to show their emotion. Like many others, he did so, not by turning away from God or by silently accepting the loss as His will, but rather by turning to God for comfort and hope in the midst of an outward grief.

Perhaps Lincoln's greatest success as a father came when he commingled his career with his parenting. Thomas forced young Lincoln into hard physical labor without showing him the larger value of the work. As a result, the boy came to resent both Thomas and the work itself. Rather than seeing his father's daily toils as a source of pride and dignity, Lincoln looked for ways to distance himself from his roots. In his early years as a lawyer, as he struggled to find his own way as a father, Lincoln did little to show his sons the greater meaning of his chosen profession. Yet once he became president and was able to work close to his boys, he let them see his daily efforts in a manner that did not drive them away. Even Robert, who was off at college during most of Lincoln's presidency, was often able to see his father at work. That Robert chose to follow in his father's footsteps with a career in law and public service suggests that Lincoln succeeded where Thomas failed.

For a century and a half, Lincoln's life and public career have been dissected, examined, analyzed, and interpreted. In the decades immediately following his death, Lincoln was elevated to near mythical proportions. In the twentieth century, however, historians and biographers produced more balanced reviews of his presidency. As with most great historical figures, there is much to praise and some to criticize. In 1936, historian James G. Randall rhetorically asked, "Has the Lincoln theme been exhausted?" Thousands of books and articles had already been written about the man. So, what more could be said? The answer, of course, was that a lot more could be said. Old letters and documents continued to be discovered, and new interpretations of existing information abounded. Randall himself went on to produce a three-volume study called *Lincoln the President.*

In addition to examining and reexamining Lincoln's presidency, modern scholars have researched and written about his marriage, physical health, mental health, faith, and other aspects of his personal life. Lincoln's relationship with his children, however, has remained largely ignored, often reduced to simple conclusions that he was an overindulgent parent and not very close to Robert. Yet the story of Lincoln the father reveals a side of him that helps complete the picture of the sixteenth president and demonstrates what most people instinctively suspect but find difficult to reconcile with the larger than life image that has been created around him: that Lincoln was, in many ways, just an ordinary man. He loved his career and found meaning in his work, but he also knew that he had to fulfill his obligations as a father. His frequent absences from home, especially early in his career, often brought work and family into conflict. Yet he persisted in carrying out his fatherhood roles. Along the way, he experienced the typical joys and challenges of fatherhood: playing with his children, mediating sibling disputes, seeing a son off to college, giving career guidance, forging emotional bonds, worrying about family finances, offering religious training, and leading by example.

As Robert stood at the Lincoln Memorial on that beautiful May afternoon in 1922, he and the thousands of other guests and spectators paid tribute to Lincoln the president. Robert was a private man who craved privacy for his family. Throughout his life he spoke little about his and his brothers' relationship with Lincoln. Robert believed that such matters were not the business of the public. Robert feared that those writing about his father's personal life would focus on gossip and innuendo, with an emphasis on matters that would have been hurtful to his mother while she was alive and damaging to the growing historical reputation of his late father. Yet even as Robert watched the dedication ceremony from the main level of the memorial in 1922, the story of Lincoln the father was already written, preserved in the letters, diaries, and recollections of Lincoln and his contemporaries, waiting to be pieced together and told. Despite his fears, Robert had little to worry about because the appeal of the story lies in the inescapable conclusion that Abraham Lincoln was, as a father, quite ordinary. He was ordinary in the sense that he did things that most fathers do, felt things that most fathers feel, and made mistakes like most fathers make. For this very reason, we can more fully appreciate the man that he was.

Notes on Sources and Acknowledgments

One of the advantages that a historian has when writing about Abraham Lincoln is the vast quantity of primary and secondary sources available for research. Whenever possible and practicable, I used primary sources to tell this story. In many cases, however, I relied on the excellent work of writers who came before me, both recently and long ago. As my manuscript progressed, I gained an increased appreciation for the hard work that they did in uncovering some oftentimes very obscure sources. I believe that every Lincoln biographer owes a debt of gratitude to these previous writers, not only for their diligent research but also for their unique perspectives and interpretations. Occasionally, these writers quoted someone or made some important factual assertion without citing an underlying source. While many times I was able to track down these sources on my own, other times I was not. So, in the cases in which I could not find the underlying source myself, unless I had some concern about the credibility of the writer or his or her work, I used the information anyway, and then cited their work as the source.

In doing my research, I often came across conflicting versions of the same event. This occurred in both primary sources and secondary sources. When I believed that the conflict was material, I noted the conflict in an endnote. Similarly, I occasionally found what appeared to be inaccurate memories by people who were apparent eyewitnesses to various events. This is not unusual when, for example, someone was recollecting an event or precise words supposedly spoken many months or years before. Thus, whenever I believed that there might have been a faulty recollection regarding something material, I noted that possibility either in the text or in an endnote. In their invaluable volume *Herndon's Informants*, Professors

Wilson and Davis acknowledged the "precarious qualities of memories" of some important Lincoln witnesses and correspondents. However, they also offered a compelling argument against too easily dismissing these witnesses and correspondents as being unreliable. Their analysis of how we should assess and value these sources is a must read, not only for Lincoln scholars but for all historians.

In addition to my gratitude to the many writers who came before me, I also owe a debt to the many librarians and archivists across the country who helped me locate all types of documents that made this book possible. I offer a special thanks to the staff at the Abraham Lincoln Library and Museum. They were instrumental in helping me locate several important unpublished letters, diaries, and other materials, as well as old and often difficult to find newspapers. It was a pleasure to spend time there. I also wish to acknowledge the staff at the Lincoln Home National Historic Site in Springfield, Illinois, for their courtesy in showing me some of the more unique characteristics of the Lincoln home. Finally, the staff at the Library of Congress was always extremely efficient, helpful, and courteous.

Being able to see photographs of Lincoln and his family helps humanize the story of his life. I want to thank Keya Morgan of Keya Morgan Collection/Lincolnimages.com for graciously allowing me to use his Lincoln images in this book. Keya has assembled the largest collection of original Lincoln photographs in the world by purchasing and preserving, among other things, the original daguerreotype plates of Lincoln and his family that were made by Matthew Brady and his associates, as well as plates made by other photographers of Lincoln's time. These plates contain extraordinary detail that truly brings the subjects to life. By digitizing these images with high-quality equipment, Keya has not only made it possible to include some of them in this book, he has preserved for the ages these precious and invaluable glimpses into our past. Keya is himself publishing a remarkable book that contains every known photograph of Lincoln, Mary, and the boys, as well as other photographs related to Lincoln. Keya's collection is truly a national treasure.

I must also thank those who read drafts of this manuscript and offered suggestions on how to improve it, including Professor Kenneth

J. Winkle of the University of Nebraska-Lincoln, himself an eminent Lincoln scholar, Professors Matthew Clavin and Steve Belko of the University of West Florida, and Dr. Stephen M. Frank, who authored one of the definitive works on nineteenth-century fatherhood. My good friend Professor Jay Clune of the University of West Florida has also been a constant source of support and encouragement. Others who read portions of the manuscript and provided helpful comments include Jesse Rigby and Will Dunaway. My wife and best friend, Karen Manning, also deserves my thanks, not only for her critical editing eye but also for her unfailing support of my work on this book. Karen, I love you with all my heart.

I am also grateful for the support and encouragement of the faculty and administration at both Pensacola Catholic High and the University of West Florida, as well as for the support and encouragement of my former law partners and colleagues at Clark, Partington, Hart, Larry, Bond & Stackhouse, in Pensacola, Florida.

My literary agent, Mike Hoogland of Dystel & Goderich Literary Management, shared my unwavering belief that this book contains an important story that needs to be told. His wise counsel made publication of this book possible. I was also truly blessed to have had Keith Wallman as my editor. I have long admired Keith's work on other narrative non-fiction books, especially books on presidents, and I was honored that he was willing to edit this one. Keith is great editor because he loves books, has deep knowledge of and passion for the subject matter of the books that he edits, and champions his projects throughout the publication process.

Finally, I owe a debt of gratitude to the poet Clayton Eshleman. When I was fourteen, he was a special guest teacher in my English class at Washington Irving Junior High School in Los Angeles. Over the course of several lessons and assignments, Eshleman inspired me to love words and to love writing. After gently critiquing what was surely an awful poem that I had written about the assassination of Robert F. Kennedy, he was perceptive enough to see that I loved presidential history. When I told him that I wanted to write a book someday, he encouraged me to do it, and to pursue it with a passion. He advised me first to read how others wrote about history, and then to write it myself. For many years, reading presidential history was my passion, but it was also just a hobby—a relaxing diversion from my busy law practice that paid the bills. After a successful twenty-five-year career in law, I decided to take a road less traveled and make teaching, researching, and writing presidential history my full-time passion and profession. And, as Robert Frost once said, that has made all the difference. Thank you, Clayton Eshleman. I will never forget you.

NOTES

x. and descendants of slaves.: "Greatest Throng in City's History Takes Part in Honoring Heroes," *Washington Post*, May 31, 1922, 3; "Harding Dedicates Lincoln Memorial; Blue and Gray Join," *New York Times*, May 31, 1922, 1; Edward F. Concklin, *The Lincoln Memorial* (Washington, DC: United States Government Printing Office, 1927), 73–91; Christopher A. Thomas, *The Lincoln Memorial & American Life* (Princeton: Princeton University Press, 2002), 152–58.

x. in the eyes of most Americans.: Concklin, *The Lincoln Memorial*, 44, 73.

xi. tribute to his lofty character and his immortal deed.": For the full text of Moton's speech, see Concklin, *The Lincoln Memorial*, 73–81. Moton may have been oblivious to the rather poignant irony that, as he spoke about Lincoln's ideals of freedom, military ushers were confining blacks to a segregated listening area at the back of the crowd in the grass and weeds, where those lucky enough to find a seat were relegated to "rough hewn benches without backs or supports." Thomas, *The Lincoln Memorial & American Life*, 156; Scott A. Sandage, "A Marble House Divided: The Lincoln Memorial, the Civil Rights Movement, and the Politics of Memory, 1939–1963," *The Journal of American History* 80, No. 1 (June 1993), 141–42; Albert Boime, *Unveiling of the National Icons: A Place for Patriotic Iconoclasm in a Nationalist Era* (Cambridge: Cambridge University Press, 1997), 295–96; "Lincoln, Harding, James Crow, and Taft," *Crisis* 24 (July 24, 1922), 122.

xi. A man to match the mountains and the sea.: For the full text of Markham's poem, see Concklin, *The Lincoln Memorial*, 82–83.

xii. proved its quality in the heroic preservation.: For the full text of the Taft and Harding speeches, see Concklin, *The Lincoln Memorial*, 83–86 and 86–91, respectively. See also, "Harding Lauds Lincoln as Nation's Savior," *Washington Post*, May 31, 1922, 1. One scholar argued that Harding's statement that Lincoln would not have resorted to arms to abolish slavery was meant to "reassure the South," though he did not say exactly what Harding was reassuring the South about. Sandage, "A Marble House Divided," 141. It is unlikely that Harding had such a sinister motive. The South was solidly Democratic in Harding's era, and nothing that he could have said would have resulted in any meaningful political advantage for him. Nevertheless, the black press widely denounced the entire dedication ceremony. See, for example, *Washington Tribune*, June 3, 1922, 1, and June 10, 1922, 1; *Chicago Defender*, June 10, 1922, 1; and "Lincoln, Harding, James Crow, and Taft," *Crisis*, 122.

xii. competed with their own ambitions and career demands.: For scholarly analyses of nineteenth-century fatherhood, see Stephen M. Frank, *Life With Father: Parenthood and Masculinity in the Nineteenth Century American North* (Baltimore: The Johns Hopkins University Press, 1998); Shawn Johansen, *Family Men: Middle-Class Fatherhood in Early Industrializing America* (New York: Routledge, 2001); Robert L. Griswold, *Fatherhood in America: A History* (New York: Basic Books, 1993); and James Marten, "Fatherhood in the Confederacy: Southern Soldiers and their Children," *The Journal of Southern History* 63, No. 2 (May 1997), 269–92.

xvi. guided by his own instincts and experiences.: For excellent and balanced analyses of the Lincoln marriage, see Jean H. Baker, *The Lincoln Marriage: Beyond the Battle of Quotations* (Gettysburg College: Robert Fortenbaugh Memorial Lecture, 1999); and Daniel Mark Epstein, *The Lincolns: Portrait of a Marriage* (New York: Ballantine Books, 2008).

1. father's lack of any meaningful expectations of him.: John Y. Simon, *House Divided: Lincoln and His Father* (Fort Wayne, IN: Louis A. Warren Lincoln Library and Museum, 1987), 18.

2. the 'poor white trash' of the South.": William H. Herndon and Jesse William Weik, *Herndon's Lincoln: The True Story of a Great Life*, vol. I (New York: Belford, Clarke & Company, 1889), 3–4; John T. Morse, Jr., *Abraham Lincoln*, vol. I (New York: Houghton, Mifflin and Company, 1893), 9; Woodrow Wilson, *Division and Reunion 1829–1889* (New York: Longmans, Green and Co., 1893), 216.

2. I don't want to see him sat down on.": Jason Emerson, *Giant in the Shadows: The Life of Robert T. Lincoln* (Carbondale and Edwardsville: Southern Illinois University Press, 2012), 265, 268–69, quoting from Robert T. Lincoln to John Hay, April 17, 1885 and January 10, 1886, reel 8, John Hay Papers, Brown University.

3. the best that he could with what he had: Kenneth J. Winkle, *Young Eagle: The Rise of Abraham Lincoln* (Dallas, Texas: Taylor Trade Publishing, 2001), 132. For earlier attempts to rehabilitate Thomas, see William E. Barton, *The Lineage of Lincoln* (Indianapolis, IN: The Bobbs-Merrill Company, 1929); and Louis A. Warren, *Lincoln's Parentage and Childhood: A History of the Kentucky Lincoln's Supported by Documentary Evidence* (New York: The Century Co., 1926).

3. on the family homestead in the backwoods of Kentucky.: There is some dispute over both Thomas's birthdate and the date of his father's murder. Thus, it is not possible to precisely pinpoint Thomas's age at his father's death. According to Lincoln, family tradition held that Thomas was born in 1778 and that Thomas's father died in 1784. Roy P. Basler, ed., *Collected Works of Abraham Lincoln*, vol. IV (New Brunswick, NJ: Rutgers University Press, 1952–55), 61. However, the best evidence to date suggests that Thomas was actually born in 1776 and that his father died in 1786. See Waldo Lincoln, *History of the Lincoln Family: An Account of the Descendants of Samuel Lincoln of Hingham Massachusetts, 1637–1920* (Worcester, MA: Commonwealth Press, 1923), 193–204, 333–42; Warren, *Lincoln's Parentage and Childhood*, 4–9, 41–42. For alternative conclusions, see Albert J. Beveridge, *Abraham Lincoln 1809–1858*, vol. I (Boston: Houghton Mifflin Company, 1928), 11–12; Barton, *The Lineage of Lincoln*, 57, 77; and John G. Nicolay and John Hay, *Abraham Lincoln: A History*, vol. I (New York: The Century Co., 1890), 21.

3. following her husband's death.: For a description of the land holdings of the Lincoln family, see Warren, *Lincoln's Parentage and Childhood*, 9–10.

3. until all of her children reached adulthood.: Warren, *Lincoln's Parentage and Childhood*, 9; Barton, *The Lineage of Lincoln*, 68–70; Basler, ed., *Collected Works of Abraham Lincoln*, vol. IV, 61; Warren, *Lincoln's Parentage and Childhood*, 14–15.

4. and grew up literally without education.": Basler, ed., *Collected Works of Abraham Lincoln*, vol. IV, 61.

4. in the Fourth Regiment of the Kentucky militia.: Warren, *Lincoln's Parentage and Childhood*, 39–40.

4. and millrace in a neighboring county.: Louis A. Warren, *Lincoln's Youth: Indiana Years Seven to Twenty One, 1816–1830* (Indianapolis, IN: Indiana Historical Society, 1991), 4.

4. short venture into the Missouri territory.: Nicolay and Hay, *Abraham Lincoln*, vol. I, 5; Warren, *Lincoln's Parentage and Childhood*, 43–44.

4. with no thought of getting ahead.: Barton, *The Lineage of Lincoln*, 69–70; Warren, *Lincoln's Parentage and Childhood*, 47–49; Warren, *Lincoln's Youth*, 5.

4. illegitimate daughter of Lucy Hanks and an unknown father.: Lincoln himself even suggested that his mother may have been illegitimate. See John Y. Simon, "Family Relationships," in Brian Lamb and Susan Swain, eds., *Abraham Lincoln—Great American Historians on our Sixteenth President* (New York: Public Affairs, 2010), 18–19.

4. overlapping and crossing in endless perplexity.": Warren, *Lincoln's Youth*, 12; Albert J. Beveridge, *Lincoln* (London: Victor Gollancz Ltd., 1928), 12–20; Samuel Haycraft to William Herndon, June 1865, Douglas L. Wilson and Rodney O. Davis, eds., *Herndon's Informants: Letters, Interviews, and Statements About Abraham Lincoln* (Chicago: University of Illinois Press, 1998), 67–68.

5. difficulty surviving long enough to build for the future.": Stephanie Grauman Wolf, *As Varied as Their Land: The Everyday Lives of Eighteenth-Century Americans* (New York: Harper Perennial, 1993), 53, 60.

5. Lincoln would spend his formative years.: Warren, *Lincoln's Parentage and Childhood*, 110–22; Beveridge, *Lincoln*, 23–28, 51–54.

5. his formal education was less than one year.: Warren, *Lincoln's Parentage and Childhood*, 195–217; M. L. Houser, *Lincoln's Education and Other Essays* (New York: Bookman Associates, 1957), 15–19.

6. I get along far better than if I had.": Henry C. Whitney, *Life of Lincoln: Lincoln the Citizen*, vol. I (New York: The Baker & Taylor Company, 1908), 75.

6. he may make something yet.": Francis Fisher-Browne, *The Every-Day Life of Abraham Lincoln* (Minneapolis, MN: Northwestern Publishing Co., 1886), 88.

6. and on till Abe quit of his own accord.": Paul M. Angle, ed., *Herndon's Lincoln: The History and Personal Recollections of Abraham Lincoln as Originally Written by William H. Herndon and Jesse W. Weik* (Cleveland: World Publishing Company, 1942), 33; Statement of Sarah Bush Lincoln, September 8, 1865, Wilson and Davis, eds., *Herndon's Informants*, 108.

6. destroyed some of Lincoln's books to keep him from reading.: Dennis Hanks to William Herndon, June 13, 1865, Wilson and Davis, eds., *Herndon's Informants*, 41;

C. T. Baker, "How Abe Saved the Farm," *Grandview, Indiana Monitor*, August 26, 1920, reprinted October 14, 1926. See also, C. T. Baker, "The Lincoln Family in Spencer County," unpublished manuscript dated 1928, a copy of which is located in the Southwestern Indiana Historical Society Annals, 977.23, So728a, v. 3 and 4, pages 10–21, in the Indiana Room at Central Library of the Evansville-Vanderburgh Public Library.
6. time spent in school as doubly wasted.": John B. Helm to William Herndon, June 20, 1865, Wilson and Davis, eds., *Herndon's Informants*, 48.
6. few wants and supplied these.": Nathaniel Grigsby interview, September 12, 1865, Wilson and Davis, eds., *Herndon's Informants*, 113.
6. nature of the agricultural world in which [they] lived.": E. Anthony Rotundo, "American Fatherhood: A Historical Perspective," *American Behavioral Scientist* 29, No. 1 (September/October 1985), 8.
7. people just raised what they needed.": Arthur E. Morgan, "New Light on Lincoln's Boyhood," *Atlantic Monthly* 125 (February 1920): 213. For a discussion of the responsibility of colonial-age fathers to assist their sons in finding a career, see Wolf, *As Various as Their Land*, 23.
7. so you will go back to school today.": L. H. Butterfield, ed., *Diary and Autobiography of John Adams*, vol. III (Cambridge, MA: Harvard University Press, 1961), 257.
7. handling that most useful instrument.": Wolf, *As Various as Their Land*, 120–21; Basler, ed., *Collected Works of Abraham Lincoln*, vol. IV, 62.
7. repay a debt that Thomas had incurred.: Leonard Swett, "Mr. Lincoln's Story of His Own Life," in Allen Thorndike Rice, ed., *Reminiscences of Abraham Lincoln by Distinguished Men of His Time* (New York: North American Publishing Company, 1886), 458–59.
7. writing, ciphering, writing poetry, etc.": Dennis Hanks interview, 8 September 1865, Wilson and Davis, eds., *Herndon's Informants*, 104.
8. showed industry in attainment of knowledge.": Statement of A. H. Chapman, 8 September 1865, Wilson and Davis, eds., *Herndon's Informants*, 102.
8. but never learned him to love it.": John Romine interview, 14 September 1865, Wilson and Davis, eds., *Herndon's Informants*, 118.
8. was the exclusive province of males.: Simon, *House Divided*, 7.
8. "he seldom failed of success.": A. H. Chapman statement, September 8, 1865, Wilson and Davis, eds., *Herndon's Informants*, 96; Dennis F. Hanks interview, June 8, 1865, Wilson and Davis, eds., *Herndon's Informants*, 27–28.
8. pulled a trigger on any larger game.": Basler, ed., *Collected Works of Abraham Lincoln*, vol. IV, 62.
8. depended on it for a living—nay, for life.": Dennis F. Hanks interview, June 13, 1865, Wilson and Davis, eds., *Herndon's Informants*, 40.
8. wild turkeys and deer were very abundant.": Dennis F. Hanks interview, June 8, 1865, Wilson and Davis, eds., *Herndon's Informants*, 27–28.
8. which Thomas clearly saw as central to family life.: Some have suggested that it was Lincoln's "tender feelings for animals" that drove his distaste for hunting. See Michael Burlingame, *The Inner World of Abraham Lincoln* (Urbana: University of Illinois Press, 1994), 40.

9. unwelcome tear, as evidence of his sensations.": Dennis Hanks interview, June 13, 1865, Wilson and Davis, eds., *Herndon's Informants*, 39. See also, Morgan, "New Light on Lincoln's Boyhood," 214.

10. farther westward," a description equally applicable to Thomas.: Winkle, *Young Eagle*, 147.

10. appeared to be very proud of him.": A. H. Chapman to William H. Herndon, September 2, 1865, Wilson and Davis, eds., *Herndon's Informants*, 134.

10. for Johnston hurt Lincoln deeply.": Burlingame, *The Inner World of Abraham Lincoln*, 39. See also, Simon, *House Divided*, 18–19. While Lincoln's early writings do not evidence a rivalry with Johnston, their relationship clearly deteriorated in later years. As an adult, Johnston continued to live nearby the aging Thomas while Lincoln found success, financial and otherwise, in the city. Johnston and Thomas occasionally appealed to Lincoln for financial help, which he sometimes provided, if reluctantly, and sometimes refused. In turning down one request for money after Thomas's death, Lincoln scolded Johnston and urged him to "face the truth—which truth is, you are destitute because you have idled away all your time." Basler, ed., *Collected Works of Abraham Lincoln*, vol. II, 111.

10. and spiritual growth of his children.": Rotundo, "American Fatherhood: A Historical Perspective," 8.

11. became active in the leadership of the congregation.: See Dennis Hanks interview, June 8, 1865, Wilson and Davis, eds., *Herndon's Informants*, 28; A. H. Chapman interview, September 8, 1865, Wilson and Davis, eds., *Herndon's Informants*, 95; Charles Friend to William H. Herndon, March 19, 1866, Wilson and Davis, eds., *Herndon's Informants*, 234; John W. Hall interview, 1883–89, Wilson and Davis, eds., *Herndon's Informants*, 693. For a general discussion of the religious activities of Thomas Lincoln and his family, see Warren, *Lincoln's Parentage*, 218–48.

11. important men" in his local church.: Ida M. Tarbell, *In the Footsteps of the Lincolns* (New York: Harper & Brothers, 1924), 143.

11. hold "any views very strong.": Dennis Hanks to William H. Herndon, March 19, 1866, Wilson and Davis, eds., *Herndon's Informants*, 233.

11. any profession while in Indiana that I know of.": Nathaniel Grigsby to William H. Herndon, January 21, 1866, Wilson and Davis, eds., *Herndon's Informants*, 169.

11. but not as much as he said.": Sarah Bush Lincoln interview, September 8, 1865, Wilson and Davis, eds., *Herndon's Informants*, 107.

11. "it was the type found among the pioneers.": Warren, *Lincoln's Parentage*, 227, 231–48.

11. encountered the same struggle (as do modern parents).: Johansen, *Family Men*, 156.

12. emphasized upward mobility and urbanization.: See generally, Rotundo, "American Fatherhood: A Historical Perspective," 8–13; Ralph LaRossa, *The Modernization of Fatherhood: A Social and Political History* (Chicago: The University of Chicago Press, 1997), 24–30; E. Anthony Rotundo, "Learning About Manhood: Gender Ideals and the Middle-Class Family in Nineteenth Century America," in J. A. Mangan and James Walvin, eds., *Manliness and Morality: Middle-Class Masculinity in Britain and America 1800–1940* (New York: St. Martin's Press, 1987), 35–51; E. Anthony Rotundo, "Boy

Culture: Middle-Class Boyhood in Nineteenth-Century America," in Mark C. Carnes and Clyde Griffen, eds., *Meanings for Manhood: Constructions of Masculinity in Victorian America* (Chicago: The University of Chicago Press, 1990), 15–36; and David G. Pugh, *Sons of Liberty: The Masculine Mind in Nineteenth-Century America* (Westport, CT: Greenwood Press, 1983), 3–43.

12. and muscle being sufficient to make the man,": John B. Helm to William Herndon, June 20, 1865, Wilson and Davis, eds., *Herndon's Informants*, 48.

12. "the distinctly male worlds of politics and finance.": Rotundo, "American Fatherhood: A Historical Perspective," 12.

12. "distant, didactic, and condescending,": Mary Beth Norton, *Liberty's Daughters: The Revolutionary Experience of American Women, 1750–1800* (Boston: Little, Brown & Co., 1980), 102.

12. "intense emotional involvement between generations of males.": Rotundo, "American Fatherhood: A Historical Perspective," 12.

13. would not be more painful than pleasant.": Basler, ed., *Collected Works of Abraham Lincoln*, vol. II, 97.

13. I don't think he did.": Dennis Hanks to William H. Herndon, January 26, 1866, Wilson and Davis, eds., *Herndon's Informants*, 176.

13. claim credit for being a self-made man.: George B. Forgie, *Patricide in the House Divided: A Psychological Interpretation of Lincoln and His Age* (New York: W.W. Norton & Company, 1979), 33–36; and John Locke Scripps, *The Life of Abraham Lincoln* (Peoria, IL: Edward J. Jacob, 1860, reprinted 1931), 8; and Kenneth J. Winkle, "Abraham Lincoln: Self-Made Man," *Journal of the Abraham Lincoln Association* 21, no. 2 (Summer 2000): 1–16.

14. stable life in both small towns and larger urban areas.: Harvey J. Graff, *Conflicting Paths: Growing Up in America* (Cambridge, MA: Harvard University Press, 1995), 29–51, 59–122, 173–85. See also Kathleen Neils Conzen, "A Saga of Families," in Clyde A. Milner II, Carol A. O'Connor, and Martha A. Sandweiss, eds., *The Oxford History of the American West* (New York: Oxford University Press, 1994), 315–57; and Stephen Thernstrom and Peter R. Knights, "Men in Motion: Some Data and Speculations About Urban Population Mobility in Nineteenth Century America," in Tamara K. Hareven, ed., *Anonymous Americans: Explorations in Nineteenth Century Social History* (Englewood Cliffs, NJ: Prentice-Hall, Inc., 1971), 17–47.

14. cut himself adrift from his old world.": Eleanor Gridley, *The Story of Abraham Lincoln* (Chicago: M.A. Donohue, 1900), 84.

15. penniless, boy" who "did not know much.": Winkle, *Young Eagle*, 40–41; Lincoln to Martin S. Morris, March 26, 1843, Basler, ed., *Collected Works of Abraham Lincoln*, vol. I, 320, and vol. IV, 63–64.

15. reach the family in the event of an emergency.: Benjamin P. Thomas, *Lincoln's New Salem* (New York: Knopf, 1954), 5–57; Herndon and Weik, *Herndon's Lincoln*, vol. I, 79; Basler, ed., *Collected Works of Abraham Lincoln*, vol. I, 64.

15. naturally attracted any ambitious young man.": Winkle, *Young Eagle*, 77.

16. owed to one of his more impatient creditors.: Benjamin P. Thomas, "Lincoln the Postmaster," *Bulletin of the Abraham Lincoln Association* 31 (June, 1933): 1–9; Nicolay and Hay, *Abraham Lincoln: A History*, vol. 1, 109–12; James Short to William Herndon, July 7, 1865, Wilson and Davis, eds., *Herndon's Informants*, 72–75; Thomas, *Lincoln's New Salem*, 109–110; Winkle, *Young Eagle*, 96–111.

16. I can truly say I was often hungry.": Speech in the House of Representatives on the Presidential Question, July 27, 1848, Basler, ed., *Collected Works of Abraham Lincoln*, vol. I, 510; Winkle, *Young Eagle*, 86–95.

17. votes he actively solicited, Lincoln was elected.: Autobiography written for John L. Scripps, June 1860, Basler, ed., *Collected Works of Abraham Lincoln*, vol. IV, 64; David Herbert Donald, *Lincoln* (London: Jonathan Cape, 1995), 42–46, 52–53.

17. to tell stories and make speeches.: Magali Sarfatti Larson, *The Rise of Professionalism: A Sociological Analysis* (Berkeley: University of California Press, 1977), 125–26.

18. Springfield went right along for the ride.: N. W. Miner, Personal Reminiscences of Abraham Lincoln, N. W. Miner Papers, Abraham Lincoln Presidential Library; United States Census Office, *Eighth Census of the United States, 1860* (Washington, DC: United States Government Printing Office, 1864); Eric H. Monkkonen, *America Becomes Urban: The Development of U.S. Cities & Towns 1780–1980* (Berkeley: University of California Press, 1988), 5.

18. established lawyers tended to control the best business.: Larson, *The Rise of Professionalism*, 126.

18. prairie grass that often stood as high as a horse.: For a vivid description of a typical journey on the circuit, see James C. Conkling to Mercy Ann Conkling, April 19, 1843, James C. Conkling Papers, Abraham Lincoln Presidential Library.

19. socialized with each other at night.: Robert H. Wiebe, "Lincoln's Fraternal Democracy," in John L. Thomas, ed., *Abraham Lincoln and the American Political Tradition* (Amherst, MA: The University of Massachusetts Press, 1986), 11–30.

19. in the Preparation for the small Pox.: John Adams to Abigail Smith, April 12, 1764, L. H. Butterfield, *Adams Family Correspondence*, Vol. 1 (Cambridge, MA: The Belknap Press, 1963), 24–25.

19. contacts that could advance his political ambitions.: David Davis interview, Wilson and Davis, eds., *Herndon's Informants*, 348–49.

19. only end upon his election to the presidency.: Henry C. Whitney, *Life on the Circuit With Lincoln* (Caldwell, IN: Caxton Printers, 1940), 61–88; Donald, *Lincoln*, 104–06; Ruth Painter Randall, *Mary Lincoln: Biography of a Marriage* (Boston: Little, Brown and Company, 1953), 79–80.

19. were married by their mid-twenties.: Winkle, *Young Eagle*, 220.

19. "and should not have been by her, if she could have avoided it.": Lincoln to Mary S. Owens, 7 May 1837, Basler, ed., *Collected Works of Abraham Lincoln*, vol. I, 78.

20. as an angel—full of love—kindness—sympathy.": William G. Greene interview, May 30, 1865, Wilson and Davis, eds., *Herndon's Informants*, 17–21.

20. and did not work for nearly a month.: Donald, *Lincoln*, 55–57. The accuracy of the Ann Rutledge story is controversial among Lincoln scholars. Indeed, it was Herndon's inquiry into this reported romance that turned Robert and Mary against him as he endeavored to gather biographical information about his former law partner. For discussions over this controversy, see Donald, *Lincoln*, 608–09 and the sources cited therein.

20. ; and if you're willin' let it be done straight off.": Carl Sandburg, *Abraham Lincoln: The Prairie Years*, vol. I (New York: Charles Scribner's Sons, 1942), 41.

21. who would be block-headed enough to have me.": Lincoln to Mrs. Orville H. Browning, April 1, 1838, Basler, ed., *Collected Works of Abraham Lincoln*, vol. I, 118–19. In comparing Owens to his aging "mother," Lincoln was undoubtedly referring to his stepmother, Sarah, rather than his biological mother, Nancy. Nancy died at just thirty-four, when Lincoln was a boy, while Sarah was already nearly fifty at the time Lincoln made this comment.

22. forehead ... wrinkled even in his youth.": Joshua Fry Speed, *Reminiscences of Abraham Lincoln and Notes of a Visit to California* (Louisville: 1884), 34.

22. could barely find a woman to speak to him.: Donald, *Lincoln*, 84.

22. one degree or another for the next two decades.: Donald, *Lincoln*, 84–85; Statement of Elizabeth Todd Edwards, Wilson and Davis, eds., *Herndon's Informants*, 443–445; See also, Angle, ed., *Herndon's Lincoln*, 179.

23. by appealing to his sense of financial inadequacy.: See Epstein, *The Lincolns: Portrait of a Marriage*, 7–18; Randall, *Mary Lincoln*, 36–51. For a detailed examination of Lincoln's melancholy and how it impacted both his life and presidency, see Joshua Wolf Shenk, *Lincoln's Melancholy: How Depression Challenged a President and Fueled His Creativity* (New York: Houghton Mifflin Company, 2005).

23. "drown[ing] his cares among the intricacies and perplexities of the law,": J. C. Conkling to Mercy Levering, March 7, 1841, in Carl Sandburg and Paul M. Angle, *Mary Lincoln: Wife and Widow* (New York: Harcourt, Brace & Co., 1932), 180.

23. existed once before became readily apparent again.: Epstein, *The Lincolns*, 34.

23. having to supply her guests with candles.: Randall, *Mary Lincoln*, 78; Donald, *Lincoln*, 95.

24. she soon realized that would not be the case.: Earl Schenk Miers, ed., *Lincoln Day by Day: A Chronology 1809–1865*, part I (Dayton, OH: Morningside, 1991), 193–94.

24. having a namesake at our house, can't say exactly yet.": Lincoln to Speed, March 24, 1843, Basler, ed., *Collected Works of Abraham Lincoln*, vol. I, 319; Randall, *Mary Lincoln*, 78. For the view that Mary was indeed pregnant just before the wedding, see Wayne C. Temple, *Abraham Lincoln: From Skeptic to Prophet* (Mahomet, IL: Mayhaven Publishing, 1995), 27–28. See also, James Matheny interview, May 3, 1866, Wilson and Davis, eds., *Herndon's Informants*, 251.

25. would formally nominate Baker.: Lincoln to Speed, March 24, 1843, Basler, ed., *Collected Works of Abraham Lincoln*, vol. I, 319.

25. as a church-going Presbyterian, felt alone.: Jean H. Baker, *Mary Todd Lincoln: A Biography* (New York: W.W. Norton Company, 1987), 62–63.

25. speech for the Whig congressional candidate.: Miers, ed., *Lincoln Day by Day*, part I, 205–09.

25. "we are but two, as yet," Robert Todd Lincoln was born.: Lincoln to Speed, July 26, 1843, Basler, ed., *Collected Works of Abraham Lincoln*, vol. I, 328.

25. emotional and physical support to his wife.: J. Jill Suitor, "Husbands' Participation in Childbirth: A Nineteenth Century Phenomenon," *Journal of Family History* 6 (Fall 1981): 278–93; Frank, *Life With Father*, 57–62; Johansen, *Family Men*, 101–05.

25. love and tenderness when [Robert] was born.": Mary Lincoln to Rhoda White, December 20, 1869, in Justin G. Turner and Linda Levitt Turner, eds., *Mary Todd Lincoln: Her Life and Letters* (New York: Alfred A. Knopf, 1972), 536. One of Mary's principal biographers, Jean Baker, seems to conclude that Lincoln was not present at Robert's birth, as does Daniel Epstein, who wrote a revealing book about the Lincoln marriage. Baker, *Mary Todd Lincoln*, 101–02; Epstein, *The Lincolns*, 80.

25. five years older than most first-time fathers of his generation.: Winkle, *Young Eagle*, 220.

26. final decision was made by mutual agreement.: Frank, *Life With Father*, 109–111; Johansen, *Family Men*, 68–71.

26. "and not for any connection with any Lincoln bearing the name.": Robert T. Lincoln to Ida Tarbell, August 6, 1920, Ida M. Tarbell Lincoln Collection, Allegheny College Library.

26. "May God bless and protect my little namesake.": Katherine Helm, *The True Story of Mary, Wife of Lincoln, Containing the Recollections of Mary's Sister Emilie (Mrs. Ben Hardin Helm), Extracts from Her War-Time Diary, Numerous Letters and Other Documents Now First Published* (New York: Harper, 1928), 98.

26. no written correspondence to friends or acquaintances.: Miers, ed., *Lincoln Day by Day*, part I, 210; Basler, ed., *Collected Works of Abraham Lincoln*, vol. I, 329.

27. around the block in a baby carriage.: Harry E. Pratt, *The Personal Finances of Abraham Lincoln* (Springfield, IL: Abraham Lincoln Association, 1943), 84; Effie Sparks, "Stories of Abraham Lincoln," unpublished manuscript, 23–24, and memo containing statements of Mrs. John Bradford, Ida M. Tarbell Lincoln Collection, Allegheny College Library; Reminiscence of Judith A. Bradner, in Walter B. Stevens, *A Reporter's Lincoln*, ed. Michael Burlingame (St. Louis, MO: Missouri Historical Society, 1916; Lincoln, NE: University of Nebraska Press, 1998), 94.

27. tend to business at his office in Springfield.: Miers, ed., *Lincoln Day by Day*, part I, 210–14.

27. hired the day maid for about $1.50 per week.: Pratt, *The Personal Finances of Abraham Lincoln*, 85.

28. city-dwellers who owned a home of their own.: Monkkonen, *America Becomes Urban*, 198–200. See also Lee Soltow, *Men and Wealth in the United States 1850–1870* (New Haven: Yale University Press, 1975), 21–61.

28. renting a three-room frame cottage at 214 South Fourth Street,: John E. Vaughn, "A Handful O' Sorts," *Illinois State Journal*, November 12, 1927.

28. a milk cow pastured in an adjacent field.: Thomas J. Dyba and George L. Painter, *Seventeen Years at Eighth and Jackson: The Lincoln Family in Their Springfield Home* (Chicago: IBC Publications, 1985), 7, 10.

28. country had got a middle-class president, at last.": Ralph Waldo Emerson, *The Complete Works of Ralph Waldo Emerson*, Vol. 11, *Miscellanies* (Boston: Houghton Mifflin Company, 1903), 334. For general histories on the rise of the middle class in America, see Stuart M. Blumin, *The Emergence of the Middle Class: Social Experience in the American City, 1760–1900* (New York: Cambridge University Press, 1989); and Burton J. Bledstein, *The Culture of Professionalism: The Middle Class and the*

Development of Higher Education in America (New York: W.W. Norton & Company, Inc., 1976).

29. unpredictable outbursts and often unreasonable demands.: Epstein, *The Lincolns*, 88. For a descriptive history of domestic housework in America, see Jeanne Boydston, *Home and Work: Housework, Wages, and the Ideology of Labor in the Early Republic* (New York: Oxford University Press, 1990).

29. to hide nakedness—ugliness . . . have done it often.": Elizabeth Todd Edwards interview, James Gourley interview, and Frances Todd Wallace interview, Wilson and Davis, eds., *Herndon's Informants*, 445, 452–53, and 485–86, respectively.

29. missed spending Easter Sunday with Mary.: Miers, ed., *Lincoln Day by Day*, part I, 219–33.

30. "was a sweet child but not good looking.": Harriet A. Chapman interview, Wilson and Davis, eds., *Herndon's Informants*, 646. Mary tended to give elaborate birthday parties for the boys. Years later, Mary wrote to a friend about a party she threw for her third son, Willie. "Willie's [ninth] birthday came off on the 21st of Dec. and as I had long promised him a celebration, it duly came off. Some 50 or 60 boys & girls attended the gala, you may believe I have come to the conclusion, that they are nonsensical affairs. However, I wish your boys, had been in their midst." Mary Lincoln to Hanna Shearer, January 1, 1860, Turner and Turner, eds., *Mary Todd Lincoln*, 61–62.

30. ask about Bob she became very indignant.": Harriet Chapman interview with Jesse W. Weik, October 16, 1914, in Michael Burlingame, ed., *The Real Lincoln* (Lincoln, NE: University of Nebraska Press, 2002), 328.

30. playing with the little boy," Harriet Hanks later recalled.: Harriet A. Chapman to William H. Herndon, December 10, 1866, Wilson and Davis, eds., *Herndon's Informants*, 512.

30. bootlegs reaching clear up to his little body.": William Harris Gibson, "My Recollections of Abraham Lincoln." *Woman's Home Companion* 30 (November 1903), 11.

30. the offspring of much animal spirits.": Lincoln to Speed, October 22, 1846, Basler, ed., *Collected Works of Abraham Lincoln*, vol. I, 391.

31. "by now, very likely he is run away again.": Lincoln to Speed, October 22, 1846, Basler, ed., *Collected Works of Abraham Lincoln*, vol. I, 391.

31. covered in mud after falling into a puddle.: Margaret Ryan interview, October 27, 1886, Wilson and Davis, eds., *Herndon's Informants*, 596–97; Frank Edwards, "A Few Facts Along the Lincoln Way," typed manuscript, attached to letter from Mrs. Jacob H. Stoner to William E. Barton, July 21, 1930, William E. Barton Papers, University of Chicago.

31. falsely it turned out, of stealing ten cents.: Josiah P. Kent interview with Jesse W. Weik, November 21, 1916, in Burlingame, ed., *The Real Lincoln*, 363; A. Longfellow Fiske, "A Neighbor of Lincoln," *Commonweal* (March 2, 1932): 494. Shortly after Lincoln's death, Mary denied ever whipping her children. "It is a new story—that in my life I have ever whipped a child—In the first place, *they* never required it, a gentle, loving word, was all sufficient with them—and if *I* have erred, it has been, in being too indulgent." Mary Lincoln to Alexander Williamson, June 15, 1865, Turner and Turner, eds., *Mary Todd Lincoln*, 251. In light of the overwhelming evidence of Mary's short temper and the misbehavior of the boys, Mary's denial of ever whipping her children is not credible.

31. lax disciplinarians and indulging their children.: Steven Mintz and Susan Kellogg, *Domestic Revolution: A Social History of American Family Life* (New York: The Free Press, 1988), 48, 58–59. See also Robert Sunley, "Early Nineteenth Century American Literature on Child Rearing," in Margaret Mead and Martha Wolfenstein, eds., *Childhood in Contemporary Cultures* (Chicago: University of Chicago Press, 1955), 150–67.

31. simply letting them be themselves.: Arthur W. Calhoun, *A Social History of American Family Life From Colonial Times to the Present* (New York: Barnes & Noble, Inc., 1960), 53. Foreign travelers often commented on the informality and permissiveness of the paternal role that was largely absent in Europe. See Mintz and Kellogg, *Domestic Revolution*, 54.

32. or making any reply to his wife.": Harriet A. Chapman to William H. Herndon, November 21, 1866, Wilson and Davis, eds., *Herndon's Informants*, 407.

32. laughs and plays with them until bedtime.: Rotundo, "Boy Culture: Middle-Class Boyhood in Nineteenth-Century America," 33; Griswold, *Fatherhood in America*, 13–14; LaRossa, *The Modernization of Fatherhood*, 28–30; Mintz and Kellogg, *Domestic Revolution*, 48–60.

33. "would say so publicly in any manner.": Lincoln to Henry E. Drummer, November 18, 1845, Basler, ed., *Collected Works of Abraham Lincoln*, vol. I, 350.

33. "Let the pith of the whole argument be 'Turn about is fair play.'": Miers, ed., *Lincoln Day by Day*, part I, 259; Lincoln to Benjamin F. James, December 6, 1845, Basler, ed., *Collected Works of Abraham Lincoln*, vol. I, 351–52.

33. & through the upper counties.": Lincoln to Benjamin F. James, January 14, 1846, Basler, ed., *Collected Works of Abraham Lincoln*, vol. I, 353–54.

33. "I am entirely satisfied with the old system," he wrote.: Lincoln to Hardin, January 19, 1846, Basler, ed., *Collected Works of Abraham Lincoln*, vol. I, 356–57.

33. and think *differently* of this matter.": Lincoln to Hardin, February 7, 1846, Basler, ed., *Collected Works of Abraham Lincoln*, vol. I, 360–65 (italics in original).

34. omitted any references to a father.: Lincoln to Andrew Johnston, February 24, 1846, Basler, ed., *Collected Works of Abraham Lincoln*, vol. I, 366–67.

34. He is quite smart enough.": Lincoln to Speed, October 22, 1846, Basler, ed., *Collected Works of Abraham Lincoln*, vol. I, 391.

35. would never meet his grandson.: Epstein, *The Lincolns*, 96.

35. thinking and talking, to himself.": Volrey Hickox, "Lincoln at Home," *Illinois State Journal*, October 15, 1874.

35. victory over his Democratic opponent in the general election.: Miers, ed., *Lincoln Day by Day*, part I, 269–78. For the official announcement of Lincoln's nomination, see *Sangamo Journal*, May 7, 1846.

36. fearful of having strangers in the house.: James Gourley interview, Wilson and Davis, eds., *Herndon's Informants*, 452–53.

36. and washed out the boy's mouth.: Elizabeth A. Capps, "My Early Recollections of Abraham Lincoln," Manuscript Files, Lincoln Collection, Abraham Lincoln Presidential Library.

36. "North-up-stairs room," where the couple stored their furniture.: Lease Contract Between Abraham Lincoln and Cornelius Ludlum, Basler, ed., *Collected Works of Abraham Lincoln*, vol. I, 406–07.

37. and Mary looked happy.: Information on the Daguerreotype Miniature Gallery was obtained from Jean H. Baker, *Not Much of Me: Abraham Lincoln as a Typical American* (Fort Wayne, IN: Louis A. Warren Lincoln Library and Museum, 1988), 14.

38. son-in-law of State Senator Robert S. Todd had been elected to Congress.": William H. Townsend, *Lincoln and His Wife's Home Town* (Indianapolis, IN: The Bobbs-Merrill Company, 1929), 137.

38. at Frankfort, where they boarded a train to Lexington.: Miers, ed., *Lincoln Day by Day*, part I, 295. One author, John W. Starr Jr., suggested that the Lincolns took a different route and met up with Speed in his hometown of Louisville, where they then took a stage to Lexington. John W. Starr Jr., *Lincoln and the Railroads* (New York: Dodd, Mead & Company, 1927), 47–48. The fact that the St. Louis *Daily Era* places Speed in St. Louis with the Lincoln family on October 28 proves that Starr's account is in error. Starr was also incorrect when he later placed Lincoln and Mary in Philadelphia in July and August 1849, when they were clearly home in Springfield. Thus, Starr's book must be used as a source only with great caution. Compare Starr, *Lincoln and the Railroads*, 54–56, where Starr states that the Lincolns were in Philadelphia in late July and early August 1849, with Miers, ed., *Lincoln Day by Day*, part II, 17–18, which clearly places him in Springfield at that time based on a variety of primary sources.

39. never returned while the Lincolns were there.: Helm, *The True Story of Mary, Wife of Lincoln*, 99–102; Townsend, *Lincoln and His Wife's Home Town*, 101–02.

39. both his own and those of others.: Helm, *The True Story of Mary, Wife of Lincoln*, 99–100.

40. oblivious to the antics of the children around him.: Helm, *The True Story of Mary, Wife of Lincoln*, 101; Townsend, *Lincoln and His Wife's Home Town*, 156.

40. took a room at Brown's Indian Queen Hotel.: Miers, ed., *Lincoln Day by Day*, part I, 295; Randall, *Mary Lincoln*, 106–07; Allen C. Clark, *Abraham Lincoln in the National Capital* (Washington, DC: W.F. Roberts Co., 1925), 3. Townsend states that when the Lincolns left Lexington, they rode "the stage for Maysville, where they would take a steamboat up the Ohio on their journey to Washington." Townsend, *Lincoln and His Wife's Home Town*, 161. While it is possible that the Lincolns took the route that Townsend described, taking the stage to Winchester followed by a series of trains to Washington, as described by Miers, was much more direct and thus was likely the route that the Lincoln family actually followed. Also, Starr's account agrees with this direct route, and although he was incorrect on his account of the journey from Springfield to Lexington and on a later claim that Lincoln was in Philadelphia when he was not, he is probably correct here. Starr Jr., *Lincoln and the Railroads*, 48.

40. Congressional session was forecast to last only until midsummer.: Samuel C. Busey, *Personal Reminiscences and Recollections of Forty-Six Years' Membership in the Medical Society of the District of Columbia and Residence in this City, with Biographical Sketches of Many of the Deceased Members* (Philadelphia: Dornan, 1895), 26.

41. a good job for the people who elected him.: Busey, *Personal Reminiscences and Recollections*, 27.

41. hindered me some in attending to business.": Lincoln to Mary Lincoln, April 16, 1848, Basler, ed., *Collected Works of Abraham Lincoln*, vol. I, 465.

41. stay in Washington while Lincoln was a Congressman.: David C. Mearns, ed., *The Lincoln Papers*, vol. I (Garden City, NY: Doubleday & Company, 1948), 4–5.

41. to some degree at the expense of time with his family.: Busey, *Personal Reminiscences and Recollections*, 27. Busey described Lincoln as "a very awkward bowler." For a summary of Lincoln's time in Washington as a congressman, see Clark, *Abraham Lincoln in the National Capital*, 3–8.

42. caused Lincoln great distress throughout their marriage.: Lincoln to Mary Lincoln, July 2, 1848, Basler, ed., *Collected Works of Abraham Lincoln*, vol. I, 495.

42. "he seemed to have his own way.": Busey, *Personal Reminiscences and Recollections*, 28.

42. send their love to you. The others say nothing.": Lincoln to Mary Lincoln, April 16, 1848, Basler, ed., *Collected Works of Abraham Lincoln*, vol. I, 465.

43. very much outsiders, and treated them accordingly.: Donald, *Lincoln*, 120–21; Epstein, *The Lincolns*, 122–23; David Davis to Sarah Davis, August 15, 1847, David Davis Papers, Chicago History Museum.

44. in search of a pair of socks for his young son.: Lincoln to Mary, April 16, 1848, Basler, ed., *Collected Works of Abraham Lincoln*, vol. I, 465.

44. "Don't let the blessed fellows forget father.": Lincoln to Mary, April 16, 1848, Basler, ed., *Collected Works of Abraham Lincoln*, vol. I, 465.

45. E[ddy's] eyes brighten at the mention of your name.": Mary Lincoln to Lincoln, May 1848, in David Herbert Donald, *Lincoln at Home: Two Glimpses of Abraham Lincoln's Family Life* (New York: Simon & Schuster, 1999), 65–69.

45. "Everybody here wants to see our dear Bobby.": Lincoln to Mary, June 12, 1848, Basler, ed., *Collected Works of Abraham Lincoln*, vol. I, 477–78.

45. Kiss and love the dear rascals.": Lincoln to Mary, July 2, 1848, Basler, ed., *Collected Works of Abraham Lincoln*, vol. I, 495–96.

46. spend more time with his children.: Albert G. Browne to Sarah Browne, December 1838, Browne Family Papers, Box 1, Schlesinger Library, Radcliffe College, cited in Frank, *Life With Father*, 73–74.

46. General Zachary Taylor, the Whig nominee for president.: Miers, ed., *Lincoln Day by Day*, part I, 318.

46. had never heard of this obscure congressman from the west.: While Miers suggests that Mary and the boys joined Lincoln in late July, that timing is unlikely. If Miers is correct, they would have re-joined Lincoln for nearly a month at Mrs. Sprigg's house. Yet there is no evidence of them being present there a second time, and it is unlikely that Mary would have wanted to return there after Lincoln's letter suggesting that some other residents were indifferent to her well-being. Moreover, Busey, who vividly recalled the Lincolns' stay at Mrs. Sprigg's house, makes no mention of a second visit. It is more probable that Mary and the boys caught up with Lincoln in September, somewhere in Massachusetts. Compare entry for September 28, 1848, Miers, ed., *Lincoln Day by Day*, part I, 321, with Epstein, *The Lincolns*, 144; Randall, *Mary Lincoln*, 127–28; and Busey, *Personal Reminiscences and Recollections*, 28; and see Mary Lincoln to Henry C. Deming, December 16, 1867, Turner and Turner, eds., *Mary Todd Lincoln*, 263, in which Mary implies that she and the boys joined Lincoln after Congress adjourned. For an account of Lincoln's probable travel routes, see Starr Jr., *Lincoln and the Railroads*, 48–53, though, as noted earlier, this source must be viewed with great caution.

47. Never dried, never froze, never slept, never rested.": Basler, ed., *Collected Works of Abraham Lincoln*, vol. II, 10–11.

47. the Lincolns were finally home again in Springfield.: Miers, ed., *Lincoln Day by Day*, part I, 322.

47. kept some extra income coming in.: Octavia Roberts, "We All Knew Abr'ham Lincoln," *Abraham Lincoln Quarterly* (March 1946): 25–28; Epstein, *The Lincolns*, 145. Sometime during the initial lease term, Mason Brayman, a prominent Springfield attorney, joined Ludlum in the house. On Lincoln's return from Washington, he and Ludlum and/or Brayman extended the term of the lease for a few more months. Basler, ed., *Collected Works of Abraham Lincoln*, vol. I, 407; Miers, ed., *Lincoln Day by Day*, part I, 324, part II, 12.

48. narrowly lose the seat to the Democratic nominee.: Winkle, *Young Eagle*, 241–44.

49. when he suspended the writ of habeas corpus.: Miers, ed., *Lincoln Day by Day*, part II, 9.

49. Lincoln's prominence on the political stage was just beginning.: Miers, ed., *Lincoln Day by Day*, part II, 9–10.

49. service in Congress took a toll on his time with the boys.: Epstein, *The Lincolns*, 147.

49. only crumb of patronage which Illinois expects," Lincoln lamented.: Busey, *Personal Reminiscences and Recollections*, 28; Lincoln to Duff Green, May 18, 1849, Basler, ed., *Collected Works of Abraham Lincoln*, vol. II, 49; Donald, *Lincoln*, 140.

50. continued involvement would eventually be rewarded.: Thomas Ewing, "Lincoln and the General Land Office, 1849," *Journal of the Illinois State Historical Society* XXV, No. 3 (October 1932): 145, 152–53.

51. That always ended it with Lincoln.": Angle, ed., *Herndon's Lincoln*, 246–47.

51. "sit down & die in Chicago.": Donald, *Lincoln*, 142; David Davis interview, September 20, 1866, Wilson and Davis, eds., *Herndon's Informants*, 348–49.

52. were "private ones.": Lincoln to Thomas Ewing, September 27, 1849, Basler, ed., *Collected Works of Abraham Lincoln*, vol. II, 65; Anson Henry to Thomas Ewing, August 21, 1849, Thomas Ewing Papers, Library of Congress.

54. the most trying period of our lives.": Thomas Butler Carter to Aaron Carter, November 8, 1842, Thomas Butler Carter Papers, Newberry Library, Chicago, IL; George W. Borrowe to John Moore, October 1822, John Moore Collection, Huntington Library, San Marino, CA. For a historical analysis of colonial and nineteenth-century views on infant death, see Johansen, *Family Men*, 78–82; Phillipe Ariés, *Centuries of Childhood: A Social History of Family Life*, translated by Robert Baldick (New York: Vintage, 1962), 38–39; Nancy Schrom Dye and Daniel Blake Smith, "Mother Love and Infant Death, 1750–1820," *The Journal of American History* 73, No. 2 (September

1986): 329–46; Edward Shorter, *The Making of the Modern Family* (New York: Basic Books, 1975), 169–75; Lewis O. Saum, "Death in the Popular Mind of Pre-Civil War America," *American Quarterly* 26 (December 1974): 484–86; Sylvia D. Hoffert, "'A Very Peculiar Sorrow': Attitudes Toward Infant Death in the Urban Northeast, 1800–1860," *American Quarterly* 39, No. 4 (Winter 1987): 601–16; David E. Stannard, *The Puritan Way of Death: A Study in Religion, Culture, and Social Change* (New York: Oxford University Press, 1977), 58–59; Peter G. Slater, "'From the Cradle to the Coffin': Parental Bereavement and the Shadow of Infant Damnation in Puritan Society," in N. Ray Hiner and Joseph N. Hawes, eds., *Growing Up in America: Children in Historical Perspective* (Urbana, IL: University of Illinois Press, 1985), 30; and Phillipe Ariés, *Western Attitudes Toward Death: From the Middle Ages to the Present* (Baltimore: Johns Hopkins University Press, 1974), 67–68.

54. at times, which I can hardly control.": Samuel Longfellow, ed., *Life of Henry Wadsworth Longfellow, With Extracts from His Journals and Correspondence*, vol. 2 (Boston: Ticknor and Company, 1886), 136.

54. middle-class nineteenth-century Americans were changing their view of death.": Johansen, *Family Men*, 81–82.

55. and hundreds of other city residents.: Miers, ed., *Lincoln Day by Day*, part II, 21–25; Townsend, *Lincoln and His Wife's Home Town*, 201–208; Epstein, *The Lincolns*, 155.

55. broke up the monotony of the long voyage.: Miers, ed., *Lincoln Day by Day*, part II, 23.

56. and romped with the dogs.": Townsend, *Lincoln and His Wife's Home Town*, 164; Helm, *The True Story of Mary, Wife of Lincoln*, 103. Helm states that these events occurred during a visit in 1851, but she was probably mistaken. See note "I placed in his hands my book" below.

56. the best dressed members of the Lexington bar.": Townsend, *Lincoln and His Wife's Home Town*, 215, recounting a description Parker made in 1919.

56. political matters that had accumulated while he was gone.: Miers, ed., *Lincoln Day by Day*, part II, 23–25; Basler, ed., *Collected Works of Abraham Lincoln*, vol. II, 67–72.

56. talk and play for hours on end.: There is some disagreement among historians as to exactly when Lincoln finally paid off his New Salem debts, but the best evidence suggests that it was sometime between 1848 and 1850. Compare Angle, ed., *Herndon's Lincoln*, 90; Whitney, *Life of Lincoln*, vol. I, 99; Pratt, *The Personal Finances of Abraham Lincoln*, 14–15; Thomas, *Lincoln's New Salem*, 108–110; Thomas P. Reep, *Lincoln at New Salem* (Chicago: Old Salem Lincoln League, 1927), 103; and Zarel C. Spears and Robert S. Barton, *Berry and Lincoln, Frontier Merchants: The Store that Winked Out* (New York: Stratford House, 1947). Spears and Barton argue that there were no debts from New Salem at all, a conclusion that Professor Winkle says is "unrealistic." Winkle, *Young Eagle*, 335, n. 9.

57. away from Springfield for just over a quarter of his life.: One historian stated that Eddy was away from "home" for 40 percent of his life, but in order to reach that figure he must have counted the six months that Eddy lived at the Globe Tavern after the Lincolns returned from New England, even though that was time spent in Springfield.

Harry E. Pratt, "Little Eddie Lincoln—'We Miss Him Very Much,'" *Journal of the Illinois State Historical Society* XLVII, no. 2 (Summer 1954), 302. With no known travels other than the three visits to Lexington and the Washington and New England trips, at most Eddy was away from Springfield for twelve or thirteen months before his death at forty-seven months.

57. "Vermifuge," which was used to treat worms.: Pratt, *The Personal Finances of Abraham Lincoln*, 151–53. The medicines listed above were actually purchased between 1855 and 1860, after Eddy's death, but are likely representative of what the Lincolns purchased when Eddy and Robert were young.

57. a patent medicine containing cough-suppressing opium.: Milton Shutes, "Mortality of the Five Lincoln Boys," *Lincoln Herald* 57 (Spring 1955), 4.

57. "His sympathy was almost motherly.": Miers, ed., *Lincoln Day by Day*, part II, 26–27; Preston H. Bailhache, "Recollections of a Springfield Doctor," *Journal of the Illinois State Historical Society* (Spring 1954), 59–60.

57. and finally died at her home on a chilly Monday night.: Townsend, *Lincoln and His Wife's Home Town*, 225.

57. pulling out one hair at a time from her head.": Interviews with John S. Ritter and Howard Dyson, Ida M. Tarbell Lincoln Collection, Allegheny College, quoted in Epstein, *The Lincolns*, 159. Despite the best efforts of the author and the staff at Allegheny College, this document could not be located again in the collection.

58. all night beside the form of [Eddy's body] that was so strangely still.": Ruth Painter Randall, *Lincoln's Sons* (Boston: Little, Brown and Company, 1955), 22. The author was unable to locate the primary source of Robert's description as paraphrased by Randall.

58. simply could not overcome this debilitating ailment.: Baker, *Mary Todd Lincoln*, 125; See also, United States Census Office, *Mortality Statistics of the Seventh Census of the United States, 1850* (Washington, DC, 1855), 17–28.

59. in the parlor of the Lincoln home at 11:00 a.m. the next morning.: Helm, *The True Story of Mary, Wife of Lincoln*, 116–17; Robert J. Havlik, "Abraham Lincoln and the Reverend Dr. James Smith: Lincoln's Presbyterian Experience of Springfield," *Journal of the Illinois State Historical Society* (Autumn 1999): 222–23; Statement of Rev. William Bishop, February 12, 1897, quoting Dr. James Smith, in William E. Barton, *The Soul of Abraham Lincoln* (New York: George H. Doran Company, 1920), 162; John T. Stuart to Rev. J.A. Reed, December 17, 1872, John Wesley Hill, *Abraham Lincoln: Man of God* (New York: G.P. Putnam's Sons, 1920), 226–28; Baker, *Mary Todd Lincoln*, 126.

59. "It was not our first, but our second child.": Lincoln Home Chronology Drawings, Abraham Lincoln Cottage 1848–50, Lincoln Home National Historic Site, United States Department of Interior, National Park Service; Lincoln to John D. Johnston, February 23, 1850, Basler, ed., *Collected Works of Abraham Lincoln*, vol. II, 76–77.

59. then lowered into the ground.: Barton, *The Soul of Abraham Lincoln*, 156–57; Lucas E. Morel, "Lincoln Among the Reformers: Tempering the Temperance Movement," *Journal of the Abraham Lincoln Association* 20, No. 1 (Winter 1999): 1–34. Eddy's body was eventually reentombed in the Lincoln family tomb at Oak Ridge Cemetery in Springfield, a few miles from the original burial site. His original tombstone is now on display at the Abraham Lincoln Presidential Museum. Hutchinson's cemetery was eventually closed and the graves relocated. A school now sits on the original cemetery site.

60. and bursting into tears left the room.": Interview with Mrs. John Stuart, Ida M. Tarbell Lincoln Collection, Allegheny College Library.

60. would never cease to sorrow for that one.": Lucy Harmon McPherson, *Life and Letters of Oscar Fitzalan Harmon* (Trenton, NJ: MacCrellish & Quigley, 1914), 11.

60. "lay prostrate, turning away from food urged upon her.": Randall, *Mary Lincoln*, 141, paraphrasing Octavia Roberts, *Lincoln in Illinois* (New York: Houghton Mifflin Company, 1918), 67.

60. I do not feel sufficiently submissive to our loss.": Mary Lincoln to "My Dear Friend," July 23, 1853, Turner and Turner, eds., *Mary Todd Lincoln*, 154.

61. For "of such is the kingdom of Heaven.": *Illinois Daily Journal*, 7 February 1850.

62. friend or family member may have penned the poem.: See Jason Emerson, "'Of Such Is the Kingdom of Heaven,' The Mystery of Little Eddie," *Journal of the Illinois State Historical Society* (Autumn 1999): 207–21; Randall, *Mary Lincoln*, 141; Baker, *Mary Todd Lincoln*, 126–28; and William J. Wolf, *The Religion of Abraham Lincoln* (New York: The Seabury Press, 1963), 81; G. Frederick Owen, *Abraham Lincoln: The Man and His Faith* (Wheaton, IL: Tyndale House Publishers, Inc., 1984), 69. The uncertainty over Lincoln's authorship caused editors of the *Collected Works* not to include the poem in those volumes.

62. Bible is the richest source of pertinent quotations.": John Langdon Kaine, "Lincoln as a Boy Knew Him," *The Century Illustrated Magazine* LXXXV (November 1912 to April 1913): 557.

62. he seemed quite cheerful and happy again.": Conversation with Orville H. Browning, June 17, 1875, in Michael Burlingame, ed. *An Oral History of Abraham Lincoln, John G. Nicolay's Interviews and Essays* (Carbondale, IL: Southern Illinois University Press, 1996) , 4.

62. Spirit of Mortal Be Proud," a favorite of Lincoln's.: Lincoln to Andrew Johnston, February 24, 1846, Basler, ed., *Collected Works of Abraham Lincoln*, vol. I, 366–67.

62. if he was writing it in the days following his son's death.: Emerson, "'Of Such Is the Kingdom of Heaven,' The Mystery of Little Eddie," 210. Emerson suggests exactly the opposite, namely, that "considering that every other poem Lincoln wrote had the same simple scheme, and that Lincoln was quite a novice as a poet, the possibility of such a revolution of style at such a traumatic time seems unlikely."

62. for a man who seemed to eschew matters of religion.: Emerson, "'Of Such Is the Kingdom of Heaven,' The Mystery of Little Eddie," 213–15.

63. for Lincoln to both express and share his grief.: Miers, ed., *Lincoln Day by Day*, part II, 27–28; Basler, ed., *Collected Works* II, 72.

63. undertaken under that very trying time in her life.: Some believe that in 1842 Mary and a coauthor may have written a poem under a pseudonym. See Emerson, "'Of Such Is the Kingdom of Heaven,' The Mystery of Little Eddie," 216–17.

63. (such as referring to Eddy as "pure little bud," "angel child," and "angel boy").: Baker, *Mary Todd Lincoln*, 126–27.

63. "my dear, dear boys" and the "blessed fellows".: Speed, *Reminiscences of Abraham Lincoln and Notes of a Visit to California*, 19; Lincoln to Mary, April 16, 1848, Basler, ed., *Collected Works of Abraham Lincoln*, vol. I, 465.

64. written by the poet Mary E. Chamberlin under the pseudonym Ethel Grey.: Samuel P. Wheeler, "Solving a Lincoln Literary Mystery: 'Little Eddie.'" *Journal of the Abraham Lincoln Association* 33, No. 2 (Summer 2012): 34–46.

64. first book of poems titled *Sunset Gleams from the City of the Mounds*, published in 1852.: Ethel Grey, *Sunset Gleams from the City of the Mounds* (New York: John F. Trow, 1852), 68–69.

64. newspaper that printed the poem spelled it "Eddie.": In her early work, historian Jean Baker suggested that the spelling of Eddy's name points to Mary's authorship. Yet Baker cited no evidence that Mary ever spelled the boy's name "Eddie." Baker, *Mary Todd Lincoln*, 126.

65. the parents who loved him so dearly.: Actually, they shorted themselves by four days, as Eddy lived three years, ten months, and twenty-two days, not three years, ten months, and eighteen days (March 10, 1846–February 1, 1850).

66. and the literal picture of the survivors' emotions.": Carl Lindhal, "Transition Symbolism on Tombstones," *Western Folklore* 45, No. 3 (July 1986): 165-66; Joseph Addison, "Thoughts on Westminster Abbey," *Spectator* 26, 30 March 1711; Ruth Moore, "American Epitaphs and Tombstones," *American Speech* 1, no. 7 (April 1926): 383.

66. "Eat Mary, for we must live," he implored his wife.: Roberts, *Lincoln in Illinois*, 67.

66. sympathize with what the parents of the fallen men were going through.: Miers, ed., *Lincoln Day by Day*, part II, 27–29; Lincoln to John D. Johnston, February 23, 1850, Basler, ed., *Collected Works of Abraham Lincoln*, vol. II, 76–77.

67. or of any denomination of Christians in particular.": Handbill Replying to Charges of Infidelity, July 31, 1846, Basler, ed., *Collected Works of Abraham Lincoln*, vol. I, 382–83.

67. and without the consolation of the gospel.": Statement of Rev. William Bishop, February 12, 1897, quoting Dr. James Smith, in Barton, *The Soul of Abraham Lincoln*, 162.

67. based almost exclusively on having faith in their essential truth.: For a concise summary of Lincoln's thoughts on religion, see Edgar DeWitt Jones, *Lincoln and the Preachers* (New York: Harper & Brothers Publishers, 1948), 134–43.

68. join with all my heart and my soul.": Henry Champion Deming, Eulogy of Abraham Lincoln Before the General Assembly of Connecticut (Hartford, CT: A.N. Clark & Co., 1865), 42.

68. though many more attended services regularly.: Elton Trueblood, *Abraham Lincoln: Theologian of American Anguish* (New York: Harper & Row Publishers, 1973), 96.

68. affirm that Lincoln was a committed Christian.: For a comprehensive summary of the efforts to prove that Lincoln was a Christian, see Franklin Steiner, *Religious Beliefs of Our Presidents: From Washington to F.D.R.* (Amherst, NY: Prometheus Books, 1995), 110–45.

68. "loving and sympathetic ministrations.": McPherson, *Life and Letters of Oscar Fitzalan Harmon*, 11.

68. Starkie's *Practical Treatise on the Law of Evidence*, in analyzing various arguments.: Wolf, *The Religion of Abraham Lincoln*, 83.

68. I placed in his hands my book.": Barton, *The Soul of Abraham Lincoln*, 358; Statement of Rev. William Bishop, February 12, 1897, quoting Dr. James Smith, in Barton, *The Soul of Abraham Lincoln*, 162–63. Townsend reported that the Lincolns visited Lexington shortly after Eddy's death and that it was during that visit that Lincoln first read *The Christian's Defence*, which he had found in the late Mr. Todd's library. Townsend, *Lincoln and His Wife's Home Town*, 226–231. He was mistaken, however, because the record clearly indicates that Lincoln was either in Springfield or on the circuit at all times between Eddy's death and the end of the year, and thus during that time he could not have made a trip to Lexington and back, which would have taken at least two weeks plus whatever time he spent there. Miers, ed., *Lincoln Day by Day*, part II, 27–45. In her book, Randall relied on Townsend's erroneous report to state that the Lincolns took a trip to Lexington following Eddy's death. Randall, *Mary Lincoln*, 142–44. Similarly, Emilie Todd later recalled that Mary, Robert, and Willie (but not Lincoln) visited Lexington in the summer of 1851, when Emilie was thirteen, "little Eddie having died in February." She was mistaken on two counts. As of the summer of 1851, Eddy had died a year ago February not the past February, and Emilie was almost fifteen years old, not thirteen. It is likely that Emilie was thinking of the October/November 1849 visit, when she was indeed thirteen, for Emilie makes no mention in her testimony of that otherwise well-documented 1849 visit. Though Willie had not been born at the time of the 1849 visit, Emilie later spent time in Springfield with Willie, and simply may have been confused about Willie's presence in Lexington at that time. Helm, *The True Story of Mary, Wife of Lincoln*, 102–06. See also Miers, ed., *Lincoln Day by Day*, part II, 46–66, which makes no mention of a trip to Lexington during 1851. It is also worth noting that one historian has suggested that Lincoln began reading *The Christian's Defence* during the October/November 1849 visit to Lexington when he found it in the Todd library, and then later got a copy in Springfield from Dr. Smith following Eddy's death, which was the copy that he carefully studied. Since Robert Todd's descendants in fact owned a copy of this book and claimed that it was in the Todd library when Lincoln visited, this explanation is plausible. Havlik, "Abraham Lincoln and the Reverend Dr. James Smith: Lincoln's Presbyterian Experience of Springfield," 225–26; Helm, *The True Story of Mary, Wife of Lincoln*, 227. There is also some debate as to whether Smith gave the book to Lincoln before or after Eddy's death. See Temple, *Abraham Lincoln: From Skeptic to Prophet*, 39–40.

69. now convinced on the truth of the Christian religion.'": Statement of Rev. William Bishop, February 12, 1897, quoting Dr. James Smith, in Barton, *The Soul of Abraham Lincoln*, 162; Dr. James Smith to William Herndon, January 24, 1867, in Barton, *The Soul of Abraham Lincoln*, 323–24; Ninian W. Edwards to James A. Reed, December 24, 1872, in Barton, *The Soul of Abraham Lincoln*, 324; Robert T. Lincoln to Isaac Markens, November 4, 1917, in Paul M. Angle, ed., *A Portrait of Abraham Lincoln in Letters by His Oldest Son* (Chicago: Chicago Historical Society, 1968).

69. views on the subject as I never heard him speak of it.": Robert Todd Lincoln to William Herndon, December 24, 1866, Wilson and Davis, eds., *Herndon's Informants*, 524.

69. "he was not a technical Christian.": Mary Todd Lincoln interview, September 1866, Wilson and Davis, eds., *Herndon's Informants*, 359–61.

69. "heart, was directed towards religion.": Mary Lincoln to James Smith, June 8, 1870, Turner and Turner, eds., *Mary Todd Lincoln*, 567–68.

70. rather than any overt acceptance of Christianity.: John W. Starr Jr., "Abraham Lincoln's Religion in His Eldest Son's Estimation," privately printed manuscript, 1926, William E. Barton Papers, University of Chicago; Isaac N. Arnold, *The Life of Abraham Lincoln* (Chicago: Jansen, McClurg, & Company, 1885), 446–49.

70. very little faith in ceremonials and forms.": Leonard Swett to William H. Herndon, January 17, 1866, Wilson and Davis, eds., *Herndon's Informants*, 162–68.

70. never formally became a member of any church.: Emerson, *Giant in the Shadows: The Life of Robert T. Lincoln*, 23; N. W. Miner, Personal Reminiscences of Abraham Lincoln, N. W. Miner Papers, Abraham Lincoln Presidential Library; Diary of Elizabeth Black, April 17, 1852, Elizabeth Gundaker Dale Black Papers, Abraham Lincoln Presidential Library; Minutes of First Presbyterian Church, April 13, 1852, Richard Paul Graebel Papers, Abraham Lincoln Presidential Library.

71. and adorned with a black haircloth cushion.: *Illinois State Register*, December 10, 1898; Temple, *Abraham Lincoln: From Skeptic to Prophet*, 43, 47–48. Lewis's recollection nearly fifty years after the event was somewhat flawed. In referring to Governor "Madison," he was likely referring to Governor Joel Matteson. However, Matteson was governor from 1853–1857. Thus, it could not have been Matteson's pew that Lincoln took over when the governor "just left the city," because Matteson did not leave Springfield until 1857, and it is clear that the Lincolns rented the pew no later than 1852. See Mary Lincoln to Mrs. Samuel H. Melvin, April 27, 1861, stating that "I had intended requesting Mr. Melvin [the Chairman of the Pew Committee at the time Lincoln became president] to have given me a promise, that upon our return to S[pringfield] we would be able to secure our particular pew, to which I was very much attached, and which we occupied some ten years, may I hope that he will be able to do so." Turner and Turner, eds., *Mary Lincoln*, 85–86. For evidence of Thomas Lewis's service as treasurer of First Presbyterian Church, see note 2, Footnotes of Diary of Elizabeth Black, Richard Paul Graebel Papers, Abraham Lincoln Presidential Library.

72. Mary was pregnant again.: Winkle, *Young Eagle*, 281.

73. where he remained until the following April.: Miers, ed., *Lincoln Day by Day*, part II, 27–51; Willard King to Ruth Painter Randall, September 21, 1953, James G. Randall Papers, Library of Congress; Eulogy on Zachary Taylor, July 25, 1850, Basler, ed., *Collected Works of Abraham Lincoln*, vol. II, 83–90.

73. to work every day for the remainder of the year.: Miers, ed., *Lincoln Day by Day*, part II, 45.

73. (It is a case of baby-sickness, and I suppose is not dangerous.)": Lincoln to John D. Johnston, January 12, 1851, Basler, ed., *Collected Works of Abraham Lincoln*, vol. II, 96–97.

74. through the help of God, hope ere-long [to join] them.": Lincoln to John D. Johnston, January 12, 1851, Basler, ed., *Collected Works of Abraham Lincoln*, vol. II, 96–97.

74. a cold January day at Johnston's house.: Reminiscences of Thomas Goodwin, in Stevens, *A Reporter's Lincoln*, 166–67.

74. after 1880, long after Lincoln's own death.: Statement of George B. Balch, 1885, and Dennis Hanks interview, March 26, 1888, Wilson and Davis, eds., *Herndon's Informants*, 595–96, 653; Mary Lincoln to Sarah Bush Lincoln, December 19, 1867, in Turner and Turner, eds., *Mary Todd Lincoln*, 464–65.

75. and Thomas's lack of the same.: Basler, ed., *Collected Works of Abraham Lincoln*, vol. II, 124.

75. Lincoln was absent even more.: Miers, ed., *Lincoln Day by Day*, part II, 51–90.

75. he will have been absent six (6) weeks.": David Davis to Sarah Davis, May 8, 1854, in Willard L. King, *Lincoln's Manager, David Davis* (Cambridge: Harvard University Press, 1960), 94.

75. often needed transportation to visit nearby towns.: Obed Lewis Account Books, Abraham Lincoln Presidential Library, cited in Miers, ed., *Lincoln Day by Day*, part II, 77; Joseph P. Kent to J.R.B. Van Cleave, January 23, 1909, J.R.B. Van Cleave Manuscript Collection, Abraham Lincoln Presidential Library; N. W. Miner, Personal Reminiscences of Abraham Lincoln, N. W. Miner Papers, Abraham Lincoln Presidential Library.

76. "I wish I had a little girl like you, Julia.": Julia Taft Bayne, *Tad Lincoln's Father* (Lincoln, NE: University of Nebraska Press, 2001), 14.

76. constant reminders of his now-deceased father.: Mary Lincoln to Francis B. Carpenter, November 15, 1865, in Turner and Turner, eds., *Mary Todd Lincoln*, 283–85. Aside from the humor of Tad's physical description, which led to his nickname, Tad's large head apparently caused some internal damage to Mary's body during birth, from which she never fully recovered. Mary Lincoln to Rhoda White, May 2, 1868, in Turner and Turner, eds., *Mary Todd Lincoln*, 475.

76. never called him by it unless I was angry.": Bayne, *Tad Lincoln's Father*, 12.

77. coming there mornings before court to read or study.": Miers, ed., *Lincoln Day by Day*, part II, 94–101, 105–09, 118–23, and 126–32; Recollection of Luman Burr, July 1, 1908, Lincoln Reminiscences, Abraham Lincoln Centennial Association, Abraham Lincoln Presidential Library.

77. occasionally spoke out on current political issues.: Miers, ed., *Lincoln Day by Day*, part II, 77. For examples of Lincoln's political speeches, see Speech to the Springfield Scott Club, August 14 and 16, 1852, Basler, ed., *Collected Works of Abraham Lincoln*, vol. II, 135–157; and Speech at Peoria, Illinois, September 17, 1852, Basler, ed., *Collected Works of Abraham Lincoln*, vol. II, 157–58.

77. try to be United States senator," he wrote to a friend.: See Speeches and Editorials in Basler, ed., *Collected Works of Abraham Lincoln*, vol. II, at 226–27, 229–84; Lincoln to Joseph Gillespie, December 1, 1854, Basler, ed., *Collected Works of Abraham Lincoln*, vol. II, 290.

78. infuriated some of his local supporters.: Donald, *Lincoln*, 172–79.

78. was finally elected on the tenth ballot.: Donald, *Lincoln*, 183–84.

78. an architect of the Kansas-Nebraska Act, would stand for reelection.: Lincoln to Elihu B. Washburne, February 9, 1855, Basler, ed., *Collected Works of Abraham Lincoln*, vol. II, 304–06; Lincoln to William Henderson, February 21, 1855, Basler, ed., *Collected Works of Abraham Lincoln*, vol. II, 306–07.

78. "Having since been beaten out, I have gone to work again.": Lincoln to James S. Sanford, Mortimer Porter, and Ambrose K. Striker, March 10, 1855, Basler, ed., *Collected Works of Abraham Lincoln*, vol. II, 308.

78. chose to do more frequently than in past years.: Randall, *Mary Lincoln*, 150.

79. it continued sending him legal work.: Herndon gave conflicting accounts of this episode. In one case, he said that it was a clerk at the railroad who objected to the bill, and in another case said that it was railroad executive and future Civil War general George B. McClellan, whom Lincoln later defeated for the presidency in the 1864 election, who declined to pay. According to Herndon, upon receipt of the bill, McClellan exclaimed, "Why sir, this is as much as Daniel Webster would have charged. We cannot allow such a claim." While Herndon's account makes a fascinating story given their future confrontation, it is untrue, as McClellan was not employed by the railroad at the time the billing event arose. See Angle, ed., *Herndon's Lincoln*, 284; and Mark E. Steiner, *An Honest Calling: The Law Practice of Abraham Lincoln* (DeKalb, IL: Northern Illinois University Press, 2008), 171.

79. Explain things Carefully—particularly," one neighbor later said.: James Gourley interview, 1865–66, Wilson and Davis, eds., *Herndon's Informants*, 451–453.

79. and so much correspondence occupied his time.": Jeriah Bonham, *Fifty Years' Recollections: With Observations and Reflections on Historical Events* (Peoria, IL: J.W. Franks & Sons, 1883), 183.

79. family story that always brought a laugh when told.: Randall, *Lincoln's Sons*, 31.

79. in deep abstraction, neither heeded nor heard.": Angle, ed., *Herndon's Lincoln*, 474. This description is likely taken from the writings of Ward Lamon, a fellow lawyer and circuit rider, who wrote: "On a winter's morning, he could be seen wending his way to the market, with a basket on his arm and a little boy at his side, whose small feet rattled and pattered over the ice-bound pavement, attempting to make up by the number of his short steps for the long strides of his father. The little fellow jerked at the bony hand which held his, and prattled and questioned, begged and grew petulant, in a vain effort to make his father talk to him. But the latter was probably unconscious of the other's existence, and stalked on, absorbed in his own reflection." Fisher-Browne, *The Every-Day Life of Abraham Lincoln*, 204–05. See also Philip W. Ayers, "Lincoln as a Neighbor," *The American Review of Reviews* (January–June 1918): 183.

80. before his father could put out a hand to detain him.": Noah Brooks, *Washington in Lincoln's Time* (New York: Century Co., 1895), 281.

80. times at each visit when the boys were with him.": Recollection of Joseph Roper, January 27, 1909, Lincoln Reminiscences, Abraham Lincoln Centennial Association, Abraham Lincoln Presidential Library.

80. "come and put this child to bed!": Interview of Mrs. Sina Wilbourn by Bond P. Geddes, *Omaha Daily News*, January 24, 1909; *Macon Daily Telegraph*, August 27, 1860.

80. show any substantial evidence of parental disapproval.": Angle, ed., *Herndon's Lincoln*, 344.

80. filled with law books and newspapers.": Bailhache, "Recollections of a Springfield Doctor," 59.

81. finish this game some other time,' and passed out.": Samuel H. Treat interview, 1883, Wilson and Davis, eds., *Herndon's Informants*, 725–26. In another version of this story, Treat urged the immediate "infliction of summary punishment upon the miscreant, but Lincoln merely picked-up his hat and said, "Considering the position of your pieces, Judge, at the time of the upheaval, I think you had not reason to complain." Fisher-Browne, *The Every-Day Life of Abraham Lincoln*, 206.

81. Love is the chain whereby to lock a child to his parent.'": Mary Todd Lincoln interview, September 1866, Wilson and Davis, eds., *Herndon's Informants*, 357.

81. now run home and have your faces and hands washed.": Randall, *Lincoln's Sons*, 57.

82. Mr. Lincoln released the long-suffering animals.": Randall, *Lincoln's Sons*, 34–35, 37; Carlos W. Goltz, *Incidents in the Life of Mary Todd Lincoln: Containing an Unpublished Letter* (Sioux City, IA: Press of Deitch & Lamar Company, 1928), 55; "Lincoln the Idol of All Children," *New York Herald*, February 10, 1929.

82. likely found amusement in the whole affair.: Recollection of Fred T. DuBois, in Rufus Rockwell Wilson, ed., *Intimate Memories of Lincoln* (Elmira, NY: Primavera Press, 1945), 99.

83. kicked around so I had to withdraw him.": Randall, *Lincoln's Sons*, 32.

84. on his shoulders for the triumphant return home.: Reminiscences of Henry Guest Pike, in Stevens, *A Reporter's Lincoln*, 193; Randall, *Lincoln's Sons*, 32–33.

84. housed—petted—fed—fondled &c &c.": Randall, *Lincoln's Sons*, 35; Ward Hill Lamon interview, 1865–66, Wilson and Davis, eds., *Herndon's Informants*, 466.

85. get your candy back for you," Tad said joyfully, as the boys headed for the store.: George T. M. Davis, *Autobiography of the Late Col. Geo. T.M. Davis, Captain and Aide-de-Camp Scott's Army of Invasion (Mexico)* (New York: Jenkins & McCowan), 362–64.

85. only president to have secured a patent on an invention.: *Report of the Commissioner of Patents, for the Year 1849*, part 1, Arts and Manufactures (Washington, DC: Office of Printers to House of Representatives, 1850), 262; Application for Patent on an Improved Method of Lifting Vessels Over Shoals, March 10, 1849, Basler, ed., *Collected Works of Abraham Lincoln*, vol. II, 32–36; Wayne C. Temple, *Lincoln's Connections With the Illinois & Michigan Canal, His Return from Congress in '48, and His Invention* (Springfield, IL: Illinois Bell, 1986), 35–36, 54–58. Lincoln delivered at least two lectures on the importance of innovation. See "Second Lecture on Discoveries and Inventions," February 11, 1859, Basler, ed., *Collected Works of Abraham Lincoln*, vol. III, 356–63, and n. 1 therein.

85. so turnabout was fair play.: Noah Brooks, "Personal Reminiscences of Lincoln," *Scribner's Monthly* XV, no. 4 (February 1878), 565. This episode regarding the clock is reported in an exhibit at the Abraham Lincoln Presidential Museum in Springfield, but without citation to its source. It is not clear whether this is the same incident, or a different version of the incident, described by Mrs. Benjamin Edwards, in Stevens, *A Reporter's Lincoln*, 162, in which "a new clock was brought home. Mrs. Lincoln told the boys they must not touch it. A short time afterward she went into the room and found that the two of them had taken the clock to pieces. She whipped them."

86. neither freely given nor spent frivolously.: John S. Bliss to William Herndon, January 27, 1867, Wilson and Davis, eds., *Herndon's Informants*, 552–53.

86. "the same love of precision" as his father.: Sandburg, *Abraham Lincoln: The Prairie Years*, vol. II, 249; Willard King to John S. Goff, June 6, 1948, cited in John S. Goff, *Robert Todd Lincoln: A Man in His Own Right* (Norman, OK: University of Oklahoma Press, 1969), 13.

86. and even participation in a junior military company.: Ayers, "Lincoln as a Neighbor," 183; Elizabeth Edwards interview with Jesse W. Weik, undated, in Burlingame, ed., *The Real Lincoln*, 355.

86. he did well," Miner later recalled.: N. W. Miner, Personal Reminiscences of Abraham Lincoln, N. W. Miner Papers, Abraham Lincoln Presidential Library.

87. the official dress of the United States Army.: Randall, *Lincoln's Sons*, 47.

87. never as playmates of Robert and the younger boys.": W.A. Evans, *Mrs. Abraham Lincoln: A Study of Her Personality and Her Influence on Lincoln* (New York: Alfred A. Knopf, 1932), 138.

88. declining Latin nouns as he did the chores of paterfamilias.": Robert Todd Lincoln, Autobiographical Sketch written on his graduation from Harvard, 1864, Harvard University Archives; "Recollections of Howard M. Powell," *Semi Weekly Breeze*, February 12, 1909; Harry Evjen, "Illinois State University, 1852–1868," *Journal of the Illinois State Historical Society* XXXI, No. 1 (March 1938): 58–62; *Catalogue of the Officers and Students of Illinois State University, 1858–59*, Archives of the University of Illinois, Springfield.

88. the Todd disposition rather than that of his father.: John T. Stuart to Elizabeth J. Stuart, January 13, 1856, quoted in Pratt, *The Personal Finances of Abraham Lincoln*, 97; Helm, *The True Story of Mary, Wife of Lincoln*, 108; Recollections of Fred T. Dubois, in Rufus Rockwell Wilson, ed., *Lincoln Among His Friends: A Sheaf of Intimate Memories* (Caldwell, ID: Caxton Printers, 1942), 96–101.

88. would not notice & never heard anything from it.": Josiah P. Kent interview with Jesse W. Weik, November 21, 1916, in Burlingame, ed., *The Real Lincoln*, 362–63.

88. should so mark itself, . . . on a child of seven years.": David Davis to Sarah Walker Davis, August 31, 1850, David Davis Papers, Chicago History Museum.

89. problems of the day with the other boys.": Recollection of Fret T. DuBois, in Wilson, ed., *Lincoln Among His Friends*, 97.

89. so I must bring my letter to an end.": Randall, *Lincoln's Sons*, 42; Willie Lincoln to Henry Remann, June 6, 1859, University of Chicago Library, cited in Randall, *Mary Lincoln*, 177.

90. other students would make fun of him.: Brooks, *Washington in Lincoln's Time*, 281; Evans, *Mrs. Abraham Lincoln*, 59; Randall, *Lincoln's Sons*, 44.

91. His political ambitions still had life.: *Proceedings of the First Three Republican National Conventions, 1856, 1860 and 1864* (Minneapolis, MN: Charles W. Johnson, 1893), 61–66; Whitney, *Life on the Circuit With Lincoln*, 96.

91. spoke to a crowd of about ten thousand.: Miers, ed., *Lincoln Day by Day*, part II, 171–72.

91. "and he was in the fullness of health and vigor.": Miers, ed., *Lincoln Day by Day*, part II, 174–83; Brooks, "Personal Reminiscences of Lincoln," 562.

91. convincing in logic," wrote one Republican newspaper.: *Illinois State Journal*, September 26, 1856.

92. it made no impression whatsoever.": *Illinois Register*, July 24, 1856.

92. Trumbull to the senate instead of Lincoln.": *Peoria Press*, October 15, 1856.

93. "but around the polls, everything was quiet and decorous.": *Illinois State Journal*, 5 November 1856.

93. "A house divided against itself cannot stand.": Edwin E. Sparks, ed., *The Lincoln-Douglas Debates of 1858* (Springfield, Illinois: Illinois State Historical Library, 1908), 461–69.

93. accepting his proposal for the seven-city tour.: Lincoln to Stephen A. Douglas, July 25, 1858, and July 31, 1858, Basler, ed., *Collected Works of Abraham Lincoln*, vol. II, 522, 531; Sparks, ed., *The Lincoln-Douglas Debates of 1858*, 68.

93. my husband towers above Douglas just as he does physically.": Helm, *The True Story of Mary, Wife of Lincoln*, 160.

94. to march in the festivities surrounding the event.: Sparks, ed., *The Lincoln-Douglas Debates of 1858*, 449–50. It is not clear whether Mary attended the Alton debate. Compare Sparks, ed., *The Lincoln-Douglas Debates*, 449–50, and Saul Sigelschiffer, *The American Conscience: The Drama of the Lincoln-Douglas Debates* (New York: Horizon Press, 1973), 353, with Robert T. Lincoln to Horace White, December 31, 1910, Horace White Papers, Abraham Lincoln Presidential Library, and Horace White to Jesse W. Weik, February 24, 1913, in Burlingame, ed., *The Real Lincoln*, 379.

94. and the streets were in a horrid condition.": *Illinois State Journal*, November 5, 1856.

94. are fresh upon me," a disappointed Lincoln wrote to a friend.: Lincoln to John J. Crittenden, November 4, 1856, Basler, ed., *Collected Works of Abraham Lincoln*, vol. III, 335–36. When the General Assembly met on January 5, 1859, Douglas defeated Lincoln fifty-four to forty-six. Don E. Fehrenbacher, *Prelude to Greatness: Lincoln in the 1850s* (Stanford, CA: Stanford University Press, 1962), 118–20.

95. "our own Sangamon circuit court will be in session at that time.": Lincoln to Henry E. Drummer, July 29, 1858, Basler, ed., *Collected Works of Abraham Lincoln*, vol. II, 521; Lincoln to Norman B. Judd, November 16, 1858, Basler, ed., *Collected Works of Abraham Lincoln*, vol. III, 337; Miers, ed., *Lincoln Day by Day*, part II, 235–36; Lincoln to Nathan B. Dodson, July 29, 1859, Basler, ed., *Collected Works of Abraham Lincoln*, vol. III, 396.

95. for the cause of civil liberty long after I am gone.": Lincoln to Anson G. Henry, November 19, 1858, Basler, ed., *Collected Works of Abraham Lincoln*, vol. III, 339.

95. and we shall have fun again.": Lincoln to Charles H. Ray, November 20, 1856, Basler, ed., *Collected Works of Abraham Lincoln*, vol. III, 341–42.

95. Can't we make him President or *vice*.": G. W. Rives to O. M. Hatch, November 11, 1858, O. M. Hatch Manuscript Collection, Abraham Lincoln Presidential Library.

95. Iowa, Ohio, Indiana, Wisconsin, and Kansas.: See, generally, Basler, ed., *Collected Works of Abraham Lincoln*, vol. III, 344–513.

96. and was once fined for his lack of attendance.: Robert Todd Lincoln, Autobiographical Sketch. On Robert's grades, participation, and attendance at Illinois State, see Evjen, "Illinois State University, 1852–1868," 62; and Mrs. K. T. Anderson, "Some

Reminiscences of Pioneer Rock Island Women," *Transactions of the Illinois State Historical Society* (1912): 75. The Philomathean Society was a literary society that promoted learning, discourse, and debate.

96. to take the entrance examination at Harvard.: Robert Todd Lincoln, Autobiographical Sketch. For information on Conkling, see John M. Palmer, ed., *The Bench and Bar of Illinois: Historical and Reminiscent*, vol. 1 (Chicago: The Lewis Publishing Company, 1899), 200; for information on Hay, see William Roscoe Thayer, *The Life and Letters of John Hay*, vol. I (Boston: Houghton Mifflin Company, 1908), 20–51; and for information on Latham, see *Catalogue of the Officers and Students of Illinois State University, 1858–59*, Archives of the University of Illinois, Springfield.

97. "resolved to enter Harvard College.": Robert Todd Lincoln, Autobiographical Sketch.

97. "decided to send Bob to Harvard.": Elwin L. Page, *Abraham Lincoln in New Hampshire* (Boston: Houghton Mifflin Company, 1929), 5–6; Stevens, *A Reporter's Lincoln*, 109.

97. "didn't set no store by them things.": Recollection of Dennis Hanks, January 1889, in Wilson, ed., *Lincoln Among His Friends*, 27–28; Laurence M. Crosbie, *The Phillips Exeter Academy: A History* (Norwood, MA: The Plimpton Press, 1924), 256; Sandburg, *Abraham Lincoln: The Prairie Years*, vol. I, 84–85.

98. on account of his constant devotion to business.": Robert Todd Lincoln to Dr. J. G. Holland, June 6, 1865, in Wilson, ed., *Intimate Memories of Lincoln*, 498–99.

98. loading his saddlebags in preparation for going out on the circuit.": Donald, *Lincoln*, 109.

98. to accompany the judge on the circuit.": Frederick Trevor Hill, *Lincoln the Lawyer* (New York: The Century Co., 1906), 164, n. 1. See also, Frederick Trevor Hill, "Lincoln the Lawyer," *The Century Magazine* LXXI (March 1906): 751, n.1.

98. with saddlebags and a horse to follow the circuit.": Wayne C. Temple, "Lincoln Rides the Circuit," *Lincoln Herald* 62 (Winter 1960), 140.

99. —& the rest is but secondary.": Robert Todd Lincoln to William Herndon, January 8, 1866, Wilson and Davis, eds., *Herndon's Informants*, 155.

99. which I am sure you do not wish to do.": Robert Todd Lincoln to William Herndon, December 13, 1866, Wilson and Davis, eds., *Herndon's Informants*, 516.

100. —especially while they are alive.": Robert Todd Lincoln to William Herndon, December 24, 1866, Wilson and Davis, eds., *Herndon's Informants*, 524.

100. a recent Harvard graduate and clerk in Lincoln's law office.: Many historians have claimed that Robert carried with him a letter of introduction written by Lincoln's former senate opponent Senator Stephen A. Douglas, in which Douglas supposedly introduced Robert to Harvard President James Walker as the son of Abraham Lincoln, "with whom I have lately been canvassing the state of Illinois." The origin of this claim lies in Edward Everett Hale, *James Russell Lowell and His Friends* (Boston: Houghton, Mifflin and Company, 1899), 200. This claim, however, is not true, having been effectively disproven in Emerson, *Giant in the Shadows: The Life of Robert T. Lincoln*, 38–39.

100. "For what do you remember the year 218 BC?": Goff, *Robert Todd Lincoln*, 24–25.

101. and in the end you are sure to succeed.: Lincoln to George C. Latham, July 22, 1860, Basler, ed., *Collected Works of Abraham Lincoln*, vol. IV, 87.

101. offered to George Latham the following year.: Robert Todd Lincoln, Autobiographical Sketch.

101. enrolled at Phillips Exeter along with 133 other students.: Myron R. Williams, *The Story of Phillips Exeter* (Exeter, NH: The Phillips Exeter Academy, 1957), 49, 202.

102. and I was obliged to enter the Subfreshman Class.": Robert Todd Lincoln, Autobiographical Sketch.

103. with a mixture of disappointment and amusement.: Pratt, *The Personal Finances of Abraham Lincoln*, 122, 179; Miers, ed., *Lincoln Day by Day*, part II, 268; Crosbie, *The Phillips Exeter Academy*, 201–02; Mearns, ed., *The Lincoln Papers*, vol. I, 6–7; Frank H. Cunningham, *Familiar Sketches of the Phillips Exeter Academy and Surroundings* (Boston: James R. Osgood and Company, 1883), 149; Robert Todd Lincoln, Autobiographical Sketch. See also *New York Tribune*, June 10, 1878, which suggests that the boys were actually brought before a justice of the peace rather than Dr. Soule.

103. "be allowed to speak on a topic of his own choosing.": James A. Briggs to Lincoln, November 1, 1859, John Nicolay Papers, Library of Congress, cited in Basler, ed., *Collected Works of Abraham Lincoln*, vol. III, 494, n. 1; Lincoln to James A. Briggs, November 13, 1859, Basler, ed., *Collected Works of Abraham Lincoln*, vol. III, 494.

103. just a modest train trip away from the big city.: Page, *Abraham Lincoln in New Hampshire*, 7.

103. Lincoln was away while riding the circuit.: Recollections of George Haven Putnam, in Wilson, ed., *Intimate Memories of Lincoln*, 257.

104. boarded a train in Springfield and headed for New York.: Miers, ed., *Lincoln Day by Day*, part II, 271, 273.

104. touring the city, and worked on his speech.: Ralph Gary, *Following in Lincoln's Footsteps* (New York: Carroll & Graf Publishers, 2001), 266–68.

104. lines from his face and correct a roving eye.: Miers, ed., *Lincoln Day by Day*, part II, 274; Reminiscence of Richard C. McCormick, *New York Evening Post*, May 3, 1865; James Mellon, *The Face of Lincoln* (New York, Viking Press, 1979), 51; Charles Hamilton and Lloyd Ostendorf, *Lincoln in Photographs: An Album of Every Known Pose* (Dayton, OH: Morningside, 1985), 36–37; Roy Meredith, *Mr. Lincoln's Camera Man, Matthew B. Brady* (New York: Scribner's, 1946), 59.

105. then winning the general election in November.: George Haven Putnam, "The Speech that Won the East for Lincoln," *Outlook* 130 (8 February 1922): 220–22.

105. with your kind invitation should his time permit.": Page, *Abraham Lincoln in New Hampshire*, 26–27. Robert later wrote, "After the [Cooper Union] address in February, father came to me at Exeter. The news of his speech had preceded him, and he was obliged to speak eleven times before leaving New England." Recollections of George Haven Putnam, in Wilson, ed., *Intimate Memories of Lincoln*, 259.

106. Lincoln had accepted Benn's invitation to speak at Dover.: Page, *Abraham Lincoln in New Hampshire*, 28–92, 97–98.

106. I treat you no worse than I do others.": Lincoln to Isaac Pomeroy, March 3, 1860, Basler, ed., *Collected Works of Abraham Lincoln*, vol. III, 554.

107. our friend Bob; we were proud of his father.": Recollection of Marshall S. Snow, quoted in Crosbie, *The Phillips Exeter Academy*, 257–58.

107. High and Pleasant Streets, where they continued to talk.: Page, *Abraham Lincoln in New Hampshire*, 111–12; Lincoln to James A. Briggs, March 4, 1860, Basler, ed., *Collected Works of Abraham Lincoln*, vol. IV, 554; Lincoln to Mary Lincoln, March 4, 1860, Abraham Lincoln Papers, Library of Congress.

107. "Robert, you ought to have one.": Page, *Abraham Lincoln in New Hampshire*, 113.

108. a combination of politics, family, and school.: Page, *Abraham Lincoln in New Hampshire*, 114; Miers, ed., *Lincoln Day by Day*, part II, 275–76; Randall, *Lincoln's Sons*, 52.

108. and thus may not have been elected president.: William E. Barton, *The Life of Abraham Lincoln*, vol. I (Indianapolis, IN: The Bobbs Merrill Company, 1925), 409–10.

108. before he spends all of his money in the campaign.": Page, *Abraham Lincoln in New Hampshire*, 133–34.

109. "Lincoln & Hamlin" banner in town.: Randall, *Lincoln's Sons*, 70.

109. "entered into the spirit of the occasion with all the fervor of youth.": "Utah's War Governor Talks of Many Famous Men," *New York Times*, October 1, 1911. For a slightly different version of Lincoln's reply to Fuller, see Frank Fuller, *A Day With the Lincoln Family*, booklet, Abraham Lincoln Presidential Library.

109. brilliant and promising young man.": Amos Tuck to David Davis, August 24, 1860, David Davis Papers, Chicago History Museum.

109. quite a change from the previous year.": Robert Todd Lincoln to William Lincoln Shearer, September 2, 1860, in Charles V. Darrin, "Robert Todd Lincoln and a Family Friendship," *Journal of the Illinois State Historical Society* XLIV, no. 3 (Spring 1951): 216–17; Robert Todd Lincoln, Autobiographical Sketch.

110. considering we never controlled him much.": Lincoln to Anson G. Henry, July 4, 1860, Basler, ed., *Collected Works of Abraham Lincoln*, vol. IV, 81–82.

110. necessary to make the introductions worth arranging.: Mintz and Kellogg, *Domestic Revolution*, 54.

113. great public embarrassment to her and her children.: Betty L. Mitchell, "Out of the Glass House: Robert Todd Lincoln's Crucial Decade," *Timeline* 5, no. 1 (February–March 1988): 2–8.

113. "good health and excellent spirits.": Henry Villard, *Lincoln on the Eve of '61: A Journalist's Story* (New York: A.A. Knopf, 1941), 54. The *Springfield Register* reported, "Robert Lincoln, the oldest son, came home from college to accompany the family to Washington." *Springfield Register*, no date, in Burlingame, ed., *The Real Lincoln*, 307.

114. Lincoln "gave him a gentle slap in the face.": Mercy Conkling to Clinton Conkling, February 12, 1861, James C. Conkling Papers, Abraham Lincoln Presidential Library; Miers, ed., *Lincoln Day by Day*, part III, 9. For a history of the Lincoln home, see, Katherine B. Menz, *The Lincoln Home: Historic Furnishings Report*, United States Department of Interior, National Park Service, 1983.

114. I bid you affectionate farewell.: Farewell Address at Springfield, Illinois, February 11, 1861, Basler, ed., *Collected Works of Abraham Lincoln*, vol. IV, 190–91.

115. a number of other friends and political supporters.: Burlingame, ed., *The Real Lincoln*, 309.

115. Lincoln reluctantly agreed to the arrangements.: Anonymous telegram to Lincoln, November 8, 1860, Abraham Lincoln Papers, Library of Congress; *New York Tribune*, November 10, 1860; *Richmond Times Dispatch*, January 11 and 14, 1861; Villard, *Lincoln on the Eve of '61*, 52–53, 74; Mercy Conkling to Clinton Conkling, February 12, 1861, James C. Conkling Papers, Abraham Lincoln Presidential Library; Winfield Scott, *Memoirs of Lieutenant General Scott*, vol. II (New York: Freeport Press, 1864, reprinted 1970), 611–12; John S. D. Eisenhower, *Agent of Destiny: The Life and Times of General Winfield Scott* (New York: The Free Press, 1997), 350–55.

115. visit the President-elect, and none are desired here.": *New York Tribune*, January 29, 1861.

116. might have treated the bag with a more appropriate level of care.: Ward Hill Lamon, *Recollections of Abraham Lincoln, 1847–1865*, Dorothy Lamon Teillard, ed. (Chicago: A. C. McClurg and Company, 1895), 35–37. There exist somewhat different versions of this incident. In a biography of Lincoln's secretary, Robert is quoted as saying in connection with the gripsack incident, "Father did not scold." Helen Nicolay, *Lincoln's Secretary: A Biography of John G. Nicolay* (New York: Longmans, Green and Co., 1949), 63–65. See also, Miers, ed., *Lincoln Day by Day*, part III, 7–8. See also, James T. Sterling, "How Lincoln 'Lost' His Inaugural Address," Address Before Michigan Commandery of Military Order of the Loyal Legion, November 3, 1898, reprinted in *Lincoln Herald* XLV (February 1944): 23–25. For another comprehensive account of this incident, see Harold Holzer, *Lincoln President-Elect* (New York: Simon & Schuster, 2008), 310–11.

116. and it was to be continued in the White House.": *New York Herald*, February 13, 1861; Randall, *Lincoln's Sons*, 69; Villard, *Lincoln on the Eve of '61*, 74. The privilege of meeting Lincoln was a source of pride for many. Shortly after settling in at the White House, Lincoln received a letter from a boy in Springfield who asked the president to write a letter confirming that the two had in fact met the year before, apparently because friends of the boy did not believe his story. Lincoln obliged, with a short note, lawyerly written nearly in the form of an affidavit that could be entered into evidence at a trial: "To whom it may concern: I did see and talk with Master George Evans Patten, last May, at Springfield, Illinois." Lincoln to George Evans Patten, March 19, 1861, Basler, ed., *Collected Works of Abraham Lincoln*, vol. IV, 294.

117. when they all checked into Willard's Hotel.: Miers, ed., *Lincoln Day by Day*, part III, 24–25; George C. Latham to Jesse W. Weik, January 23, 1918, in Burlingame, ed., *The Real Lincoln*, 340–42.

117. invention that lifted boats over shoals and obstructions.: *Washington Evening Star*, February 26, 1861; and *Philadelphia Inquirer*, February 27, 1861.

117. the once-misplaced document had been found, obliged.: *New York Times*, March 5, 1861.

117. just to the right of the canopy, not far from his father.: *New York Times*, March 5, 1861; Elizabeth Todd Grimsley, "Six Months in the White House," *Journal of the Illinois State Historical Society* XIX (October 1926–January 1927): 45. The original manuscript of this article can be found in the Manuscript Division of the Abraham Lincoln Presidential Library. Elizabeth Todd Grimsley Papers, Abraham Lincoln Presidential Library.

118. I can at least be his hat-bearer," Douglas joked.: *The Diary of a Public Man And a Page of Political Correspondence: Stanton to Buchanan,* foreword by Carl Sandburg (New Brunswick, NJ: Rutgers University Press, 1946), 84–85; George S. Bryan, *The Great American Myth* (New York: Carrick & Evans, Inc., 1940), 54; Grimsley, "Six Months in the White House," 46. One of Lincoln's most credible biographers questioned the authenticity of the story about Douglas taking Lincoln's hat. James G. Randall, *Lincoln the President,* vol. I (New York: Dodd, Mead, 1945–55), 295–96.

118. "reminded me of a galvanized corpse.": Angle, ed., *Herndon's Lincoln,* 401.

118. awkward rigging of his Presidential father.": Villard, *Lincoln on the Eve of '61,* 54.

118. Robert was the son of a possible future president.: Mercy Levering Conkling to Clinton Conkling, October 6, 1860, James Conkling Papers, Abraham Lincoln Presidential Library.

118. and glad to get back to his college.": *New York Herald,* March 5, 1861; Villard, *Lincoln on the Eve of '61,* 78.

118. the messenger, to the maids and scullions.": Grimsley, "Six Months in the White House," 47.

119. the President's unpredictable young son Tad.": Nicolay, *Lincoln's Secretary,* 121.

119. the boys "kept the house in an uproar.": John Hay, "Life in the White House in the Time of Lincoln," *Century Magazine* XLI (November 1890 to April 1891): 35.

119. and a blue sash who flies instead of walking.": Bayne, *Tad Lincoln's Father,* 1–5.

120. or both boys with him when he reviewed military exercises.: Bayne, *Tad Lincoln's Father,* 28, 55–56; Miers, ed., *Lincoln Day by Day,* part III, 40.

120. and Holly to be outfitted in marching uniforms.: Entry of August 7, 1861, Diary of Horatio Nelson Taft, Manuscript Division, Library of Congress.

120. their old mammy, who was washing some clothes in a tub.": Bayne, *Tad Lincoln's Father,* 32; Entry of August 6, 1861, Diary of Horatio Nelson Taft, Manuscript Division, Library of Congress.

120. "but Ma was dressed up, you bet.": Bayne, *Tad Lincoln's Father,* 15, 70.

121. became legendary during Lincoln's presidency.: Bayne, *Tad Lincoln's Father,* 42–43.

121. and I heard their wild whoops below.": Bayne, *Tad Lincoln's Father,* 67.

122. snarled back, "The Madam's wildcat.": Bayne, *Tad Lincoln's Father,* 48–49.

122. "was often short-tempered and bitter-tongued.": Frazier Hunt, "The Little Girl Who Sat on Lincoln's Lap," *Good Housekeeping* (February 1921), 17.

122. they uttered some choice words about the offending rascals.: William O. Stoddard, *Inside the White House in War Times* (New York: C.L. Webster & Co., 1890), 50–51.

122. Lincoln then proceeded upstairs to attend the circus.: Bayne, *Tad Lincoln's Father,* 43–44.

123. Tad said he was proven to be a spy.": Bayne, *Tad Lincoln's Father,* 57–59.

123. 'Pa don't have time to play with us now.'": Bayne, *Tad Lincoln's Father,* 48.

124. and emotionally aloof Victorian patriarchs.": Frank, *Life With Father,* 113–38.

125. and papers to read to the boys and their friends.: Bayne, *Tad Lincoln's Father,* 47.

125. as he could not readily forgive ridicule.": Grimsley, "Six Months in the White House," 53.

125. the anxious mother, and all others.": Grimsley, "Six Months in the White House," 54.

126. "I suppose it's because the preachers think I need it and I guess I do.": Bayne, *Tad Lincoln's Father*, 12–14.

127. They like to feel quite 'free and easy' with our boys.": Grimsley, "Six Months in the White House," 49, 77–78; Entries of December 15 and 25, 1861, and January 12, 1862, Diary of Horatio Nelson Taft, Manuscript Division, Library of Congress.

128. and slowly and sadly returned to the house.": Miers, ed., *Lincoln Day by Day*, part III, 58, 62; Benjamin Rush Cowan, *Abraham Lincoln: An Appreciation by One Who Knew Him* (Cincinnati, OH: The Robert Clarke Co., 1909), 29–30.

128. pleasant & cheering words to the men.": Francis G. Young to Abraham Lincoln, October 21, 1861, Abraham Lincoln Papers, Library of Congress.

128. hands pressed to his heart, his features convulsed with grief.": Nicolay, *Lincoln's Secretary*, 101. Despite Lincoln's grief, he insisted on learning the details of the battle in which Baker had been killed. See Charles P. Stone to Lincoln, October 21, 1861, and second telegram from Francis G. Young to Lincoln, October 21, 1861, Abraham Lincoln Papers, Library of Congress.

129. She must always keep in mind.: *Washington National Republican*, November 4, 1861.

129. to learn how to read until he was nearly thirteen.: Bayne, *Tad Lincoln's Father*, 67, Theodore Calvin Pease and James G. Randall, eds., *The Diary of Orville Hickman Browning*, vol. I (Springfield, IL: Illinois State Historical Society, 1925), 553; Brooks, *Washington in Lincoln's Time*, 281; Wayne C. Temple, "Sketch of 'Tad' Lincoln," *Lincoln Herald* 60, no. 3 (Fall 1958): 79–81, which was a reprint of John Hay, "Tad Lincoln," *Illinois State Journal* (July 21, 1871); Anna L. Boyden, *Echoes from Hospital and White House: A Record of Mrs. Rebecca R. Pomroy's Experience in War Times* (Boston: D. Lathrop and Company, 1884), 85.

129. "Pasco's, corner of Main & Linden Sts.": Robert Todd Lincoln, Autobiographical Sketch.

129. taken his companion from him," Conkling's mother wrote her son.: Mercy Conkling to Clinton Conkling, September 20, 1860, James C. Conkling Papers, Abraham Lincoln Presidential Library.

130. your correspondence with him. It may favor advantages.": James Conkling to Clinton Conkling, February 12, 1861, James C. Conkling Papers, Abraham Lincoln Presidential Library. See also Mercy Conkling to Clinton Conkling, November 19, 1861, and April 14, 1863, James C. Conkling Papers, Abraham Lincoln Presidential Library.

130. composition, mathematics, elocution, religion, and history.: Goff, *Robert Todd Lincoln*, 46.

130. and further pleased him with a gift of small change.": *New York Tribune*, June 1, 1861; John G. Nicolay to Therene Bates, May 31, 1863, quoted in Nicolay, *Lincoln's Secretary*, 106.

130. as if entering a café," Mercier later wrote with astonishment.: Camille Ferri Pisani, *Prince Napoleon in America, 1861: Letters From His Aide-de-Camp*, trans. Georges J. Joyaux (London: The Galley Press, 1959), 94; Daniel Carroll, "Abraham Lincoln and the Minister of France," *Lincoln Herald* 70, no. 3 (Fall 1968): 146–47.

130. pleasure in remaining silent" in the presence of the president.: Pisani, *Prince Napoleon in America*, 100.

131. and that in my mind, the last should be first.": Grimsley, "Six Months in the White House," 70. For an interesting, if not amusing, description of the dinner from the perspective of a Frenchman in attendance, see Pisani, *Prince Napoleon in America*, 103–14.

131. Tad, and Elizabeth Grimsley soon joined him.: Miers reports that Mary, Robert, Willie, and Tad all left Washington for New York on the same train. See Miers, ed., *Lincoln Day by Day*, part III, 60. However, newspaper articles clearly place Robert in New York on August 13 and have Mary arriving on August 15. See *New York Tribune*, August 14, 1861, and *New York Herald*, August 18, 1861, which was reported from Long Branch. Darrin suggests that Robert first met up with Mary in Long Branch rather than New York. See Charles V. Darrin, "Your Truly Attached Friend, Mary Lincoln," *Journal of the Illinois State Historical Society* XLIV, no. 1 (Spring, 1951): 23. Given that the August 18 *Herald* article was reported from Long Branch, this is possible, but not probable, as it seems unlikely that Robert and Mary would have been in New York together but taken separate trains to Long Branch.

131. Mary predicted that the venue would be "perfectly quiet.": Mary Lincoln to Hannah Rathbun Shearer, July 11, 1861, in Turner and Turner, eds., *Mary Todd Lincoln*, 93–95.

131. too busy to make the trip, so he stayed in Washington.: For a summary of Lincoln activities while the family was on vacation, see Miers, ed., *Lincoln Day by Day*, part III, 61–64.

131. who will take charge, of your children also.": Mary Lincoln to Hannah Rathbun Shearer, July 11, 1861, in Turner and Turner, eds., *Mary Todd Lincoln*, 93–95.

132. left for Cambridge to begin his sophomore year at college.: Oliver S. Halstead Jr., to Abraham Lincoln, August 27, 1861, Abraham Lincoln Papers, Library of Congress; Darrin, "Your Truly Attached Friend, Mary Lincoln," 23; Grimsley, "Six Months in the White House," 72; Gary, *Following in Lincoln's Footsteps*, 262.

132. Robert settled in for another year at Harvard.: Robert Todd Lincoln, Autobiographical Sketch.

132. themes, chemistry, elocution, and botany.: Kimball C. Elkins, senior assistant in the Harvard University Archives, to John S. Goff, July 28, 1958, cited in Goff, *Robert Todd Lincoln*, 42, n. 5.

132. "Secret Society," the name of which he never publicly revealed.: Robert Todd Lincoln, Autobiographical Sketch.

132. taxed their ingenuity and patience to make it presentable.": Grimsley, "Six Months in the White House," 47.

133. approving the expenditures, and Lincoln promptly signed them.: Entry of December 16, 1861, *Journal of Benjamin Brown French*, in Donald B. Cole and John

J. McDonough, eds., *Benjamin Brown French: Witness to the Young Republic, A Yankee's Journal, 1828–1870* (Hanover, NH, and London: University Press of New England, 1989), 382; Benjamin Brown French to Pamela French, December 24, 1861, Benjamin Brown French Manuscript Collection, Library of Congress, cited in Randall, *Mary Lincoln*, 264–65.

133. The meeting lasted until 2:00 p.m.: Entry of December 25, 1861, Howard K. Beale, ed., *The Diary of Edward Bates, 1859–1866* (Washington, DC: United States Government Printing Office, 1933), 213.

133. Crackers and Pistols" with Bud and Holly, and then ate a late lunch.: Entry of December 25, 1861, Diary of Horatio Nelson Taft, Manuscript Division, Library of Congress.

133. thus resolving the *Trent* Affair and averting war with Britain.: Entry of December 25, 1861, Pease and Randall, eds., *The Diary of Orville Hickman Browning*, vol. I, 518–19.

134. "We were having *so much bliss*.": Mary Lincoln to Hannah Rathbun Shearer, November 20, 1864, in Turner and Turner, eds., *Mary Todd Lincoln*, 188–89.

135. in his office dictating correspondence related to the war.: John G. Nicolay to Edward Bates, January 2 and 3, 1862, John G. Nicolay Papers, Library of Congress, cited in Miers, ed., *Lincoln Day by Day*, part III, 87; and *Washington Evening Star*, January 1, 1862; Basler, ed., *Collected Works of Abraham Lincoln*, vol. V, 86–88.

135. with the Lincoln boys all the evening and had a rare time.": *Washington Evening Star*, January 8, 1862; Entry of January 7, 1862, Diary of Horatio Nelson Taft, Library of Congress.

135. who was recovering from an illness.: Entry of January 8, 1862, Diary of Horatio Nelson Taft, Library of Congress.

136. Our boys could not go on Sunday," he wrote tersely.: Entry of January 8, 1862, Diary of Horatio Nelson Taft, Library of Congress.

136. Mary stayed in her bedroom nursing a mild illness.: E. M. Shields to Edwin M. Stanton, February 1, 1862, Salmon P. Chase Papers, Library of Congress; Diary Entry of January 27, 1862, Samuel P. Heintzelman Papers, Library of Congress, cited in Miers, ed., *Lincoln Day by Day*, part III, 92; and Robert V. Bruce, *Lincoln and the Tools of War* (Indianapolis, IN: The Bobbs-Merrill Co., 1956), 169–70.

136. the Lincolns decided to proceed with the ball.: Elizabeth Keckley, *Behind the Scenes, or Thirty Years a Slave, and Four Years in the White House* (New York: G.W. Carleton & Co., 1868), 95–98, 100.

137. Mrs. Keckley has met with success.": John E. Washington, *They Knew Lincoln* (New York: E.P. Dutton & Co., 1942), 225; Keckley, *Behind the Scenes*, 88. See generally, Jennifer E. Fleischner, *Mrs. Lincoln and Mrs. Keckley: The Remarkable Story of the Friendship Between a First Lady and a Former Slave* (New York: Broadway Books, 2004).

137. By morning, Willie's condition had worsened further.: Keckley, *Behind the Scenes*, 100–02; John G. Nicolay to Edward Bates, February 2 and 11, 1862, John G. Nicolay Papers, Library of Congress, cited in Miers, ed., *Lincoln Day by Day*, part III, 93; *Washington Evening Star*, February 6, 1862.

137. suffering from either typhoid fever or bilious fever.: *New York Tribune*, February 12, 1862; *Washington Evening Star,* February 10 and 13, 1862; and John G. Nicolay to Edward Bates, February 11 and 21, 1862, John G. Nicolay Papers, Library of Congress, cited in Miers, ed., *Lincoln Day by Day*, part III, 94; Stoddard, *Inside the White House in War Times*, 120.

137. "in consequence of the continued illness in the family.": *Washington Evening Star,* 14 February 1862.

138. We'll know more in the morning.": Stoddard, *Inside the White House in War Times*, 111–19. The exact date that Lincoln and Stoddard visited McClellan is unknown. Randall suggested that the meeting occurred sometime before the ball on February 5. Randall, *Mary Lincoln*, 283. This is probably not correct. McClellan later wrote that, after Lincoln and he exchanged detailed correspondence over war strategy on February 3, "many verbal conferences ensued." George B. McClellan, *Report on the Organization and Campaigns of the Army of the Potomac* (Freeport, New York: Books for Libraries Press, 1970), 107. Thus, it is highly probable that the meeting occurred after the ball on February 5. Also, Stoddard implied that days rather than weeks passed between the meeting and Willie's death on February 20. Stoddard, *Inside the White House*, 119–20. Thus, the meeting almost certainly occurred after February 5 and a few days before February 20.

139. and "carried him tenderly to bed.": Bayne, *Tad Lincoln's Father*, 82. See also, Nicolay, *Lincoln's Secretary*, 132–33.

139. as the sun set over Washington, Willie Lincoln died.: *New York Herald*, February 17, 1862; Entry of February 18, 1862, Beale, ed., *Diary of Edward Bates*, 233; *New York Herald*, February 20, 1862; Bayne, *Tad Lincoln's Father*, 82. See also, Charles Sumner to Francis W. Bird, February 19, 1862, in Beverly Wilson Palmer, ed., *The Selected Letters of Charles Sumner*, vol. 2 (Boston: Northeastern University Press, 1990), 101.

139. It is hard, hard to have him die.'": Keckley, *Behind the Scenes*, 102–03; Notebook, February 1862, John G. Nicolay Papers, Library of Congress, cited in Miers, ed., *Lincoln Day by Day*, part III, 96, and Nicolay, *Lincoln's Secretary,* 132–33.

140. and caused strangers to speak of him as a fine little fellow.": Bayne, *Tad Lincoln's Father*, 3; Mary Lincoln to Francis Bicknell Carpenter, December 8, 1865, in Turner and Turner, eds., *Mary Todd Lincoln*, 297–300; Grimsley, "Six Months in the White House," 48; William Florville to Abraham Lincoln, December 27, 1863, in Harold Holzer, ed., *Dear Mr. Lincoln: Letters to the President* (New York: Addison-Wesley Publishing Company, 1993), 320–21; Howard Glyndon, "The Truth About Mrs. Lincoln," *The Independent* XXXIV (August 10, 1882): 4–5.

140. drawn to the frontier life that defined Thomas's very existence.: Entry of February 20, 1862, Beale, ed., *Diary of Edward Bates*, 235.

141. Willie, who would never speak to him any more.": Entries of February 20, 21, 22 and 23, 1862, Pease and Randall, eds., *The Diary of Orville Hickman Browning*, vol. I, 530–31; Sandburg, *Abraham Lincoln: The War Years*, vol. III (New York: Charles Scribner's Sons, 1942), 277; Randall, *Mary Lincoln*, 285; Boyden, *Echoes from Hospital and White House*, 54–55.

141. Mr. Lincoln feels his loss very deeply.": *Harper's Weekly*, March 8, 1862.

141. expressing the sincere & deep sympathy I feel for you.": McClellan to Lincoln, February 22, 1862, Abraham Lincoln Papers, Library of Congress.

141. scheduled the funeral for February 24.: Memorandum, February 20, 1862, in Michael Burlingame, ed., *With Lincoln in the White House: Letters, Memoranda, and Other Writings of John G. Nicolay*, 1860–1865 (Carbondale, IL: Southern Illinois University Press, 2000), 71; Entry of March 2, 1862, Cole and McDonough, eds., *Journal of Benjamin Brown French*, 389; *Washington Evening Star*, February 22, 1862.

142. and alone sat quietly with the boy.: Entry of February 21, 1862, Beale, ed., *Diary of Edward Bates*, 235; *Washington Evening Star*, February 21, 1862. The *New York Herald* reported that Willie was dressed in a brown suit. *New York Herald*, February 24, 1862. Charles Edward Lester, who viewed the body, reported that Willie was dressed in a soldier's uniform. Charles Edward Lester, *The Light and Dark of the Rebellion* (Philadelphia: George W. Childs, 1863), 142–44.

142. Bud and Holly never saw Tad or his parents again.: Bayne, *Tad Lincoln's Father*, 82.

143. sat with his father during the "solemn affair.": Entry of February 2, 1862, Beale, ed., *Diary of Edward Bates*, 236; Keckley, *Behind the Scenes*, 105; Entry of February 24, 1862, Pease and Randall, eds., *The Diary of Orville Hickman Browning*, 531; Entry of March 2, 1862, Cole and McDonough, eds., *Journal of Benjamin Brown French*, 389.

143. entwine himself round the hearts of those who knew him best.: Funeral Address delivered by Rev. Dr. Phineas D. Gurley, on the occasion of the death of William Wallace Lincoln, February 24, 1862, Lincoln Collection, Abraham Lincoln Presidential Library.

144. so imposing." The procession stretched for a half mile.: Boyden, *Echoes from Hospital and White House*, 56–57; *Washington National Intelligencer*, February 24, 1862.

144. Willie's casket was placed in the vault.: Entry of March 2, 1862, in Donald B. Cole and John J. McDonough, eds., *Journal of Benjamin Brown French: Witness to the Young Republic*, 389.

144. "The beauty and fragrance robs death and the grave of half its gloom.": Recollection of Mary Hill Miner, N. W. Miner Papers, Abraham Lincoln Presidential Library.

145. and divine guidance I must work my destiny as best I can.": Noyes W. Miner, "Personal Recollections of Abraham Lincoln," N. W. Miner Papers, Abraham Lincoln Presidential Library.

145. He wills to do it.": Lincoln to Mrs. Horace Mann, April 5, 1864, Basler, ed., *Collected Works of Abraham Lincoln*, vol. VII, 287.

145. If Mr. Lincoln was not a Christian, he was acting like one." Noyes W. Miner, "Personal Recollections of Abraham Lincoln," N. W. Miner Papers, Abraham Lincoln Presidential Library.

146. to draw his thoughts away from his bereavement.": *New York Examiner*, March 3, 1862.

146. "and he was dressed just as if he was alive and well.": Entry of February 25, 1862, Beale, ed., *Diary of Edward Bates*, 237; Francis B. Carpenter, *The Inner Life of Abraham Lincoln: Six Months at the White House* (New York: Hurd and Houghton, 1868), 116–17; Recollection of Mary Hill Miner, N. W. Miner Papers, Abraham Lincoln Presidential Library.

147. Mary has confined herself to her room.": Elizabeth Parker Todd Edwards to Julia Edwards, March 2, 1862, Elizabeth Parker Todd Edwards Papers, Abraham Lincoln Presidential Library.

147. table where the boy could watch every pen stroke.": Nicolay, *Lincoln's Secretary*, 133.

147. he eventually shook off the illness and regained his health.: Randall, *Lincoln's Sons*, 103–04; Basler, ed., *Collected Works of Abraham Lincoln*, 154.

147. "saying he could not play with them again.": Elizabeth Parker Todd Edwards to Julia Edwards, April 9, 1862, Elizabeth Parker Todd Edwards Papers, Abraham Lincoln Presidential Library.

147. between them grew stronger after [Willie's] death.": Nicolay, *Lincoln's Secretary*, 133.

148. I would have given the boy who went away," Lincoln once told a White House visitor.: Edna M. Colman, *Seventy-Five Years of White House Gossip: From Washington to Lincoln* (Garden City, NJ: Doubleday, Page & Company, 1925), 292.

148. Lincoln found the entire episode exceedingly humorous.: Carpenter, *The Inner Life of Abraham Lincoln*, 300; Noah Brooks, "A Boy in the White House," *St. Nicholas* X (November 1882 to May 1883): 61–62; John P. Usher, *President Lincoln's Cabinet* (Omaha, NE: Nelson H. Loomis, 1925), 22; Emanuel Hertz, "Ties that Tugged at Lincoln's Heart: His Relations With His Son Tad, the Boy Who Played at Being Colonel, Cheered His Days in the White House," *New York Times Magazine* (June 21, 1931): 10. See also, Matthew Pinsker, *Lincoln's Sanctuary: Abraham Lincoln and the Soldiers' Home* (Oxford: Oxford University Press, 2003), 151.

148. and some important papers that he was holding.: Wayne Whipple, *Tad Lincoln: A True Story* (New York: George Sully & Company, 1926), 24–29.

148. 'Come, Tad; Buell is abusing you.'": David Homer Bates, *Lincoln in the Telegraph Office: Recollections of the United States Military Telegraph Corps During the Civil War* (New York: The Century Co., 1907), 212–13.

149. what they would do to that boy, if they had half a chance.": Fisher-Browne, *The Every-Day Life of Abraham Lincoln*, 640; Brooks, "A Boy in the White House," 59; Boyden, *Echoes from Hospital and White House*, 86; Hay, "Life in the White House in the Time of Lincoln," *Century Magazine* XLI (November 1890 to April 1891): 35; Nicolay, *Lincoln's Secretary*, 134.

149. "He is very much pleased with them.": Lincoln to Michael Crock, April 2, 1862, Basler, ed., *Collected Works of Abraham Lincoln*, vol. V, 177; Bayne, *Tad Lincoln's Father*, 49.

150. to "tell dear Tad, poor 'Nanny Goat,' is lost.": Lincoln to Mary Lincoln, August 8, 1863, Basler, ed., *Collected Works of Abraham Lincoln*, vol. VI, 371–72.

150. Tell Tad the goats and father are very well especially the goats.": Lincoln to Mary Lincoln, April 28, 1864, Basler, ed., *Collected Works of Abraham Lincoln*, vol. VII, 320.

150. Tad, seizing the precious bit of paper, fled to set him at liberty.": Brooks, *Washington in Lincoln's Time*, 217; Fisher-Browne, *The Every-Day Life of Abraham Lincoln*, 642–43.

150. and petted by him through the whole meal.": Boyden, *Echoes from Hospital and White House*, 82.

150. now that Tad and Willy were when they left for Washington.": William Florville to Lincoln, December 27, 1863, in Holzer, ed., *Dear Mr. Lincoln: Letters to the President*, 320–21.

150. "He has grown & improved more than any one you ever saw.": Mary Lincoln to Julia Ann Sprigg, May 29, 1862, in Turner and Turner, eds., *Mary Todd Lincoln*, 127–28.

150. several hundred feet, above, our present situation.": Mary Lincoln to Julia Ann Sprigg, May 29, 1862, in Turner and Turner, eds., *Mary Todd Lincoln*, 127–28.

151. horseback ride to and from his White House office in about thirty minutes.: Pinsker, *Lincoln's Sanctuary*, 2–3.

151. "[W]hen we are in sorrow, quiet is very necessary to us": Mary Lincoln to Julia Ann Sprigg, May 29, 1862, in Turner and Turner, eds., *Mary Todd Lincoln*, 127–28.

151. Robert, who had just completed his final exams.: Wayne C. Temple, "Mary Todd Lincoln's Travels," *Journal of the Illinois State Historical Society* LII (Spring 1959): 185–86; Miers, ed., *Lincoln Day by Day*, part III, 120–26; John A. Dahlgren Diary, John G. Nicolay Papers, Library of Congress, cited in Miers, ed., *Lincoln Day by Day*, part III, 126.

151. Lincoln during this time was drafting the Emancipation Proclamation.: Gideon Welles, *Diary of Gideon Welles, Secretary of the Navy Under Lincoln and Johnson*, vol. I (New York: Houghton Mifflin, 1911), 70–71; Entry of July 15, 1862, Pease and Randall, eds., *The Diary of Orville Hickman Browning*, vol. I, 559–60.

152. Yet I know, a great sin, is committed when we feel this.": Mary Lincoln to Mrs. Charles Eames, July 26, 1862, in Turner and Turner, eds., *Mary Todd Lincoln*, 130–31.

152. Robert returned to Cambridge to begin his junior year.: *New York Herald*, August 20, 1862; Temple, "Mary Todd Lincoln's Travels," 187.

152. chemistry, declamations, themes, and rhetoric.: Kimball C. Elkins, senior assistant in the Harvard University Archives, to John S. Goff, July 28, 1958, cited in Goff, *Robert Todd Lincoln*, 42, n. 5.

153. a little woman like Mrs. Stratton you would look just like her.'": Keckley, *Behind the Scenes*, 122–24; Alice Curtis Desmond, "General Tom Thumb's Widow: Autobiography of the Countess M. Lavinia Magri," *New York Historical Society Quarterly* XXXVIII, no. 3 (July 1954): 311–315.

153. Your mother very slightly hurt by her fall.": Lincoln to Robert Lincoln, July 3, 1863, Basler, ed., *Collected Works of Abraham Lincoln*, vol. VI, 314.

153. bluntly saying only, "Come to Washington.": Lincoln to Robert Lincoln, July 11, 1863, Basler, ed., *Collected Works of Abraham Lincoln*, vol. VI, 323.

153. "Why do I hear no more of you?": Lincoln to Robert Lincoln, July 14, 1863, Basler, ed., *Collected Works of Abraham Lincoln*, vol. VI, 327.

153. John Wilkes Booth, also a famous actor, who would later assassinate Robert's father.: Robert Todd Lincoln to Richard Watson Gilder, February 6, 1909, Abraham Lincoln Presidential Library, cited in Goff, *Robert Todd Lincoln*, 71. There is some uncertainty as to exactly when this event occurred, so it may not necessarily have happened on the trip noted above. Compare Helm, *The True Story of Mary, Wife of Lincoln*, 251–52, with Eleanor Ruggles, *Prince of Players, Edwin Booth* (New York: W.W. Norton

& Company, 1953), 171. For an account of this episode that tries to separate fact from fiction, see, Jason Emerson, "How Booth Saved Lincoln's Life." *American History* 44, no. 1 (April 2005): 44–49.

154. I could have whipped them myself.": Carl Sandburg, *Abraham Lincoln: The War Years*, vol. II (New York: Charles Scribner's Sons, 1942), 354. For additional recollections of Lincoln's reaction to Lee's escape, see Nicolay, *Lincoln's Secretary*, 171; and Clara Hay, ed., *Letters of John Hay and Extracts from His Diary*, vol. I (Washington, DC: United States Government Printing Office, 1908), 86.

154. at the second Battle of Bull Run. Porter was later court-martialed.: Testimony of Robert Todd Lincoln before the United States Senate, Committee of the Whole, regarding consideration of The Bill (S. 1844) for the relief of Fitz John Porter, in John Alexander Logan, *Fitz-John Porter: Speech of Hon. John Alexander Logan, of Illinois, in the Senate of the United States* (Washington, DC, 1883), 10.

154. before traveling around New Hampshire and Vermont.: Sandburg, *Abraham Lincoln: The War Years*, vol. II, 294. Lincoln to Mary Lincoln, July 28, 1863, Basler, ed., *Collected Works of Abraham Lincoln*, vol. VI, 353; Temple, "Mary Todd Lincoln's Travels," 189.

154. forensics, philosophy, and political economy.: Kimball C. Elkins, senior assistant in the Harvard University Archives, to John S. Goff, July 28, 1958, cited in Goff, *Robert Todd Lincoln*, 42, n. 5.

154. leaving Tad in the care of Mary and a nurse.: Jay Monaghan, *Diplomat in Carpet Slippers: Abraham Lincoln Deals With Foreign Affairs* (Indianapolis, IN: Bobbs-Merrill, 1945), 340.

155. scarlet fever that develops from a strep infection.: Miers, ed., *Lincoln Day by Day*, part III, 220–25.

155. Tad's conditions, and Lincoln faithfully complied.: Lincoln to Mary Lincoln, December 4, 5, 6, and 7, 1863, Basler, ed., *Collected Works of Abraham Lincoln*, vol. VII, 34–35. For Mary's inquires to Lincoln during that period, see Mary Lincoln to Lincoln, December 4 and 6, 1863, and Mary Lincoln to Edward McManus, December 8, 1863, in Turner and Turner, eds., *Mary Todd Lincoln*, 159–60.

155. Answer by telegraph at once." No response by Robert survives.: Lincoln to Robert T. Lincoln, January 11, 1864, Basler, ed., *Collected Works of Abraham Lincoln*, vol. VII, 121.

155. on general matters—at least he never did so.": Robert Todd Lincoln to William Herndon, October 1, 1866, Wilson and Davis, eds., *Herndon's Informants*, 364.

155. If you think it would help you make us a visit.": Lincoln to Robert T. Lincoln, October 11, 1864, Basler, ed., *Collected*, vol. VIII, 44.

155. high opinion of him." Welles soon arranged the appointment.: Lincoln to Gideon Welles, October 27, 1862, Basler, ed., *Collected Works of Abraham Lincoln*, vol. V, 480.

156. bounty received," and then forwarded the letter to the military authorities.: Endorsement of Lincoln, cited in Basler, ed., *Collected Works of Abraham Lincoln*, vol. VIII, 571. One biographer says that Lincoln once responded with a stern rebuke to a letter from Robert recommending a postmastership appointment: "If you do not attend to your studies and let matters such as you write about alone, I will take you away from college." That biographer also states that Robert carried the letter with him and showed it to those who requested his help in getting appointment in order to politely turn them away. H. S. Huidekoper, *Personal Notes and Reminiscences of Lincoln* (Philadelphia: Bicking Print, 1896), 5. However, such letter has never been found, and Robert's biographer, noting other instances in which Lincoln entertained Robert's recommendations, casts doubt on the plausibility of the story. See Goff, *Robert Todd Lincoln*, 48–49.

156. beaten Lincoln for the Republican vice-presidential nomination in 1856.: *Daily Ohio Statesman*, January 4, 1865.

156. Robert achieved more career success than most of his peers.: Goff, *Robert Todd Lincoln*, 45, 56–57.

156. who had inquired about Lincoln's plans.: Robert T. Lincoln to H. P. Sprague, July 18, 1864, Abraham Lincoln Presidential Library, cited in Goff, *Robert Todd Lincoln*, 57.

156. previous year, gave the commencement address.: *New York Herald*, July 21, 1864.

156. responding to General Grant's request for 300,000 more troops.: Lincoln to Ulysses S. Grant, January 20, 1864, Basler, ed., *Collected Works of Abraham Lincoln*, vol. VII, 452.

156. Robert, of course, was not one of them.: Randall, *Lincoln's Sons*, 111.

156. Are the sons of the rail-splitter, porcelain, and these other common clay?": *The Crisis* (Columbus, OH), December 16, 1864.

156. serve his country with more intelligent purpose than an ignoramus.": Helm, *The True Story of Mary, Wife of Lincoln*, 229–30.

156. about Robert going into the Army," Mary's half-sister, Emilie Todd Helm, wrote in her diary.: Keckley, *Behind the Scenes*, 121; Helm, *The True Story of Mary, Wife of Lincoln*, 227.

157. than the sons of other people are to their mothers.": Keckley, *Behind the Scenes*, 121.

158. will immediately enter the army as a private.": *Chicago Journal*, July 15, 1864.

158. advice I had from my father as to my career.": Sandburg, *Abraham Lincoln: The War Years*, vol. III, 417.

158. He said he thought I was right.": Robert T. Lincoln to Winfield M. Thompson, March 2, 1915, quoted in Louis A. Warren, ed., "The Captain Lincoln Episode,: *Lincoln Lore* no. 1410 (April 16, 1956).

158. an issue to use against him in the 1864 presidential election.: Goff, *Robert Todd Lincoln*, 62.

159. issued a request for an additional 500,000 volunteers.: Miers, ed., *Lincoln Day by Day*, part III, 273–74.

159. and in the end the people stood with the president.: Jessie Ames Marshall, ed., *Private and Official Correspondence of Gen. Benjamin F. Butler*, vol. 5 (Norwood, MA: Plimpton Press, 1917), 35. See also, Memorandum, August 23, 1864, Basler, ed., *Collected Works of Abraham Lincoln*, vol. VII, 514.

159. Tad quickly replied: "Oh, no; he isn't of age yet.": Correspondence by Noah Brady, May 17, 1865, reported in the *Sacramento Daily Union*, June 14, 1865, in Michael Burlingame, ed., *Lincoln Observed: Civil War Dispatches of Noah Brooks* (Baltimore, MD: Johns Hopkins University Press, 1998), 198–99.

160. including his attempt to suspend the writ of habeas corpus.: Samuel F. Batchelder, "Old Times at the Law School," *Atlantic Monthly* XC (November, 1902): 651; Mark De Wolfe Howe, *Justice Oliver Wendell Holmes: The Shaping Years, 1841–1870* (Cambridge, MA: The Belknap Press of Harvard University Press, 1957), 186.

160. you shall not be encumbered as you can be yourself.: Lincoln to Ulysses S. Grant, January 19, 1865, Basler, ed., *Collected Works of Abraham Lincoln*, vol. VIII, 223.

161. and I would still say give the rank of Capt.: Ulysses S. Grant to Lincoln, January 21, 1865, Basler, ed., *Collected Works of Abraham Lincoln*, vol. VIII, 223–24.

162. when I will have the honor to report to you in person.": Robert T. Lincoln to Ulysses S. Grant, January 22, 1865, quoted in John Y. Simon, ed., *The Papers of Ulysses S. Grant*, vol. 13 (Carbondale: Southern Illinois University Press, 1967), 282.

162. sent a letter to the Army accepting the appointment.: Basler, ed., *Collected Works of Abraham Lincoln*, vol. VIII, 224; Horace Porter, *Campaigning With Grant* (New York: The Century Company, 1897), 388; Robert T. Lincoln to Maj. S. F. Chalfin, February 20, 1865, National Archives, Washington, DC, cited in Goff, *Robert Todd Lincoln*, 65.

162. horse was ordered to be delivered to the White House stables.": Recollection of John M. Bullock, in Wilson, ed., *Lincoln Among His Friends*, 358.

162. "Capt. Lincoln reported on the 22nd and was assigned to duty at my headquarters.": Lincoln to Ulysses S. Grant, February 24, 1865, Basler, ed., *Collected Works of Abraham Lincoln*, vol. VIII, 314; Ulysses S. Grant to Lincoln, February 25, 1865, Basler, ed., *Collected Works of Abraham Lincoln*, 314.

162. general subsequently gave Robert leave to attend the inauguration festivities.: The author found neither correspondence from Grant rejecting Robert's request for a delay in reporting nor correspondence or other writings from Robert indicating why he decided to report early. In any case, Robert attended both the swearing-in ceremony on March 4 and the inaugural ball on March 6, where he wore his captain's uniform. Grant also sent two other captains from his staff to represent the Army at the swearing-in ceremony. *Washington Evening Star*, March 4, 1865; and *New York Times*, March 8, 1865.

164. if they were sure they were not intruding," Robert said respectfully.: Julia Dent Grant, *The Personal Memoirs of Julia Dent Grant*, ed. John Y. Simon (New York: G.P. Putnam's Sons, 1975), 141–42.

164. and Mary to join the general at the front.: Lincoln to Ulysses S. Grant, March 20, 1865, Basler, ed., *Collected Works of Abraham Lincoln*, vol. VIII, 367.

165. occasionally join the family for meals on the ship.: Miers, ed., *Lincoln Day by Day*, part III, 322–23.

165. good judge of the time when operations should commence.": David D. Porter, *Incidents and Anecdotes of the Civil War* (New York: D. Appleton and Company, 1886), 281.

165. as also were the flashes of the guns upon the clouds.": Lincoln to Edwin M. Stanton, March 30, 1865, Basler, ed., *Collected Works of Abraham Lincoln*, vol. VIII, 377.

165. all I have heard from him since you left.": Lincoln to Mary Lincoln, April 2, 1865, Basler, ed., *Collected Works of Abraham Lincoln*, vol. VIII, 381.

165. and your party at the time you name": Lincoln to Mary Lincoln, April 2, 1865, Basler, ed., *Collected Works of Abraham Lincoln*, vol. VIII, 384.

165. start to him [in Petersburg] in a few minutes.": Lincoln to Edwin M. Stanton, April 3, 1863, *The War of the Rebellion: A Compilation of the Official Records of the Union and Confederate Armies*, Series I, vol. 46 (Washington, DC: United States Government Printing Office, 1894), 508.

166. is the political head of a nation in the same condition?": Edwin M. Stanton to Lincoln, April 3, 1863, *The War of the Rebellion*, 509; T.S. Bowers to Edwin M. Stanton, April 3, 1863, *The War of the Rebellion*, 509.

166. I will keep *my* part of the bargain.'": Carpenter, *The Inner Life of Abraham Lincoln*, 93–94.

166. Robert was waiting for him at Hancock Station in Petersburg.: Robert T. Lincoln to Lincoln, April 3, 1865, Robert Todd Lincoln Papers, Library of Congress; Ulysses S. Grant to T. S. Bowers, April 3, 1863, *The War of the Rebellion*, 509.

167. "but it never seemed to strike him as wanting in any way.": Porter, *Incidents and Anecdotes of the Civil War*, 290.

167. which Lincoln promptly bought for him.: Lincoln to Edwin M. Stanton, April 3, 1863, *The War of the Rebellion*, 509. Porter, *Incidents and Anecdotes of the Civil War*, 288–91. For Grant's description of their meeting, see Ulysses S. Grant, *Personal Memoirs of U.S. Grant*, vol. II (New York: Charles L. Webster & Company, 1886), 459–61.

167. and now the nightmare is gone. I want to see Richmond.": Porter, *Incidents and Anecdotes of the Civil War*, 294. For a summary description of the fall of Richmond, see Dallas D. Irvine, "The Fall of Richmond: Evacuation and Occupation," *The Journal of the American Military Institute* 3, no. 2 (Summer 1939): 66–79. Back at the telegraph office at the War Department, when the wire to Stanton informing him of the fall of Richmond was read aloud, "the whole department was in an uproar; men rushed into each other's arms with cries and tears like long separated brothers or lovers; an hour was required to reduce even the clerks to order, and many did not return to their desks the next day." Albert Gallatin Riddle, *Recollections of War Times: Reminiscences of Men in and Events in Washington, 1860–1865* (New York: G.P. Putnam's Sons, 1895), 328–29, n. 1.

167. I will take care of myself.": Lincoln to Edwin M. Stanton, April 3, 1863, *The War of the Rebellion*, 509.

167. He is well and in good spirits.": Lincoln to Mary Lincoln, April 3, 1865, Basler, ed., *Collected Works of Abraham Lincoln, Supplement*, 285.

167. harbors and inlets, and altogether she suited me.": Porter, *Incidents and Anecdotes of the Civil War*, 284, 294.

168. followed the *Malvern* aboard the *River Queen*.: Bates, *Lincoln in the Telegraph Office*, 353–54.

168. care that had been taken to clear the river.": Porter, *Incidents and Anecdotes of the Civil War*, 294.

168. old pair of trousers. But it is well to be humble.": Porter, *Incidents and Anecdotes of the Civil War*, 294–95.

169. the nearest good landing site he could find.: Porter, *Incidents and Anecdotes of the Civil War*, 295.

169. I am but God's humble instrument.": Porter, *Incidents and Anecdotes of the Civil War*, 295.

170. who were even then seeking an opportunity to slay him.": Porter, *Incidents and Anecdotes of the Civil War*, 296–98; Gustavua A. Myers, "Abraham Lincoln in Richmond," *The Virginia Magazine of History and Biography* (October 1933): 319–26.

170. that liberty which you seem to prize so highly.": Porter, *Incidents and Anecdotes of the Civil War*, 298.

170. walking the streets caused some to disregard that order.: "From Richmond," *New York Times*, April 8, 1865.

170. He continued to hold Tad's hand as the boy nestled closely to his father.: Porter, *Incidents and Anecdotes of the Civil War*, 298; Thomas Thatcher Graves, "The Occupation," in *Battles and Leaders of the Civil War* , vol. 4 (New York: The Century Co., 1884, 1888), 727.

170. looked out "with eager, peering faces.": Porter, *Incidents and Anecdotes of the Civil War*, 299–300.

171. or merely peeped through the window blinds.: R.J.M. Blackett, ed., *Thomas Morris Chester, Black Civil War Correspondent: His Dispatches from the Virginia Front* (Baton Rouge, LA: Louisiana State University Press, 1989), 295–96.

171. I suppose, were ashamed of it.: Entry of April 6, 1865, Judith W. McGuire, *Diary of a Southern Refugee During the War by a Lady in Virginia* (New York: E.J. Hale & Son, 1867), 350.

171. a doubt there would have been a large addition to the numbers present.: "From Richmond," *New York Times*, April 8, 1865.

172. through the hardships of war, but yet of stately bearing.": Charles C. Coffin, "The President's Entry into Richmond," in E. Littell, *Littell's Living Age* 3, vol. XXIX (Boston: Littell, Son, & Company, 1865), 138.

172. through the crowd and onto the sidewalk.: Porter, *Incidents and Anecdotes of the Civil War*, 301.

172. Lincoln's party to "walk along uninterruptedly.": Porter, *Incidents and Anecdotes of the Civil War*, 302.

173. the heat he, too, had to endure during the long walk.: Porter, *Incidents and Anecdotes of the Civil War*, 302; Myers, "Abraham Lincoln in Richmond," 319–21; Blackett, ed., *Thomas Morris Chester*, 295.

173. which Lincoln politely declined but the others accepted.: John S. Barnes, "With Lincoln From Washington to Richmond in 1865," *Appleton's Magazine* IX, nos. 5 and 6 (May and June 1907): 515–24; Graves, "The Occupation," in *Battles and Leaders of the Civil War*, 728.

173. a tired man whose nerves had carried him beyond his strength.": Barnes, "With Lincoln From Washington to Richmond in 1865": 749; *New York Herald*, April 9, 1865. While none of those reporting this scene specifically mention Tad's presence, it is likely that Tad was indeed there. Up to that point the boy had clung tightly to his father, and it seems doubtful that Lincoln would have separated from him so soon after entering the house. Nevertheless, it is possible that Tad had been placed under the supervision of one of the lower-ranking military officers while Lincoln toured the house. See Harry Kollatz Jr., "Lincoln in Richmond," *Richmondmagazine.com* (April 2009).

173. Oh, how gladly I would have seen it burn!": Entry of April 6, 1865, McGuire, *Diary of a Southern Refugee*, 350.

174. and the three men ended their meeting.: John A. Campbell, *Recollections of the Evacuation of Richmond, April 2d, 1865* (Baltimore, MD: John Murphy & Co., 1880), 8; John A. Campbell to Horace Greeley, April 26, 1865, Campbell Family Papers #15. Southern Historical Collection, Wilson Library, University of North Carolina at Chapel Hill; Michael R. Ridderbusch, ed., "The Lincoln Reminiscence Manuscript in the Francis Harrison Pierpont Papers," *West Virginia History* 1, no. 1 (Spring 2007): 86.

174. "I have been requested not to mention their names.": "From Richmond," *New York Times*, April 8, 1865.

175. Lincoln kissed the baby and said goodbye.: David D. Ryan, *Four Days in 1865: The Fall of Richmond* (Richmond, VA: Cadmus Marketing, 1993), 123–25; Rembert W. Patrick, *The Fall of Richmond* (Baton Rouge, LA: Louisiana State University Press, 1960), 134; Larry Tagg, *The Generals of Gettysburg: The Leaders of America's Greatest Battle* (Cambridge, MA: Da Capo Press, 2003), 236. The recollections of Mrs. Pickett (LaSalle Corbell Pickett) regarding this incident are contained in "General Pickett: Mrs. Pickett Tells the Story of Her Husband's Career," *New York Times*, September 23, 1899, and LaSalle Corbell Pickett, *Pickett and His Men* (Philadelphia: J.B. Lippincott & Company, 1913), 37–40. Michael Shaara used some of Mrs. Pickett's writings in his best-selling book *The Killer Angels* (New York: Ballantine Books, 1975), and those writings were then read in Ken Burns's 1990 television documentary *The Civil War*. Since that time, however, some scholars have argued that Mrs. Pickett fabricated letters and exaggerated or made up recollections used in her book, and that she plagiarized several passages in her writings from other sources. While there is no direct evidence that Lincoln's visit to her home in Richmond was made up or exaggerated, the accuracy of her story about this incident can certainly be fairly questioned. See David I. Holmes, Lesley J. Gordon, and Christine Wilson, "A Widow and Her Soldier: Stylometry and the American Civil War," *Literary and Linguistic Computing* 16, no. 4 (2001): 403–420; and Gary W. Gallagher, "A Widow and Her Soldier: LaSalle Corbell Pickett as the Author of George E. Pickett's Civil War Letters," *The Virginia Magazine of History and Biography* 94, no. 3 (1986): 329–44.

175. I'd let 'em up easy. Let 'em up easy.": Ryan, *Four Days in 1865*, 123–25; Godfrey Weitzel, *Richmond Occupied*, Official Publication No. 16 (Richmond, VA: Richmond Civil War Centennial Commission, 1865), 56, cited in Ryan, *Four Days in 1865*, 125, n. 11.

177. being the son of the Chief Executive of the nation.": Porter, *Campaigning With Grant*, 388–89.

177. Grant introduced the president's son to General Lee.: Robert Todd Lincoln to Judd Stewart, June 1, 1918, Judd Stewart Collection, Huntington Library, San Marino, CA.

178. tell whether you will make a lawyer or not.": Keckley, *Behind the Scenes*, 137–38.

178. we have both, been very miserable.": Mary Lincoln to Francis B. Carpenter, November 15, 1865, in Turner and Turner, eds., *Mary Todd Lincoln*, 283–85.

178. to travel some, perhaps to Europe and California.: Arnold, *The Life of Abraham Lincoln*, 429–30; Mary Todd Lincoln interview, September 1866, Wilson and Davis, eds., *Herndon's Informants*, 359.

179. Robert remained at the White House, studying Spanish with John Hay.: Mary Lincoln to J. B. Gould, April 22, 1880, in Turner and Turner, eds., *Mary Todd Lincoln*, 697; Tyler Dennett, *John Hay: From Poetry to Politics* (New York: Dodd, Mead & Company, 1933), 36; Barnes, "With Lincoln From Washington to Richmond in 1865": 518.

179. , and then the two friends rushed to the theater.: Thomas F. Pendel, *Thirty-Six Years in the White House* (Washington, DC: The Neale Publishing Company, 1902), 42–43. Robert's own memory of how he first heard the news of the shooting was fuzzy. For a discussion of the various accounts of who actually informed Robert of the shooting of Lincoln, including Robert's own recollections, see Emerson, *Giant in the Shadows: The Life of Robert T. Lincoln*, 101–02.

179. "It's my father! My father! I'm Robert Lincoln.": Jim Bishop, *The Day Lincoln Was Shot* (New York: Harper & Brothers, 1955), 225.

179. and leaning on the shoulder of Senator Sumner.": Recollections of Charles Sabin Taft, in Wilson, ed., *Lincoln Among His Friends*, 396; Entry of April 15, 1865, Welles, *Diary of Gideon Welles*, vol. II, 288.

180. hardly able to realize the truth," bore the additional burden of trying to comfort Mary.: Robert T. Lincoln to Edwin M. Stanton, December 24, 1869, quoted in Benjamin P. Thomas and Harold M. Hyman, *Stanton: The Life and Times of Lincoln's Secretary of War* (New York: Alfred A. Knopf, 1962), 638.

180. Lincoln "would speak to him because he loved him so.": John P. Usher to Mrs. Usher, April 16, 1865, John P. Usher Papers, Kansas State Historical Society. A short time later, Mary changed her mind, saying, "O do not send for him, his violent grief would disturb the House." Entry of April 30, 1865, Diary of Horatio Nelson Taft, Manuscript Division, Library of Congress.

180. laid down next to Tad until the broken-hearted boy fell asleep.: Pendel, *Thirty-Six Years in the White House*, 44.

180. just strength enough left to drag myself off the field.": Entry of April 30, 1865, Diary of Horatio Nelson Taft, Manuscript Division, Library of Congress.

181. "nor give the poor boy a satisfactory answer.": Entry of April 15, 1865, Welles, *Diary of Gideon Welles*, vol. II, 290.

181. Don't cry, Mamma, or I will cry too.": Keckley, *Behind the Scenes*, 192, 196.

181. until a larger family tomb was completed in 1874.: Pease and Randall, eds., *The Diary of Orville Hickman Browning*, vol. II, 20; and King, *Lincoln's Manager, David Davis*, 227.

181. a severe cold that eventually caused his lungs to fill with fluid.: Recent forensic analysis suggests that Tad may have actually suffered from medullary thyroid cancer. John Sotos, *The Physical Lincoln: Finding the Genetic Cause of Abraham Lincoln's Height, Homeliness, Pseudo-depression, and Imminent Cancer Death* (Mt. Vernon, VA: Mt. Vernon Book Systems, 2008).

182. which made Robert a very wealthy man.: Robert never returned to Harvard. He took some law classes at the University of Chicago, but received the bulk of his legal training after joining a Chicago law firm. Goff, *Robert Todd Lincoln*, 91–105, 125–58, 192–208, 222–26.

182. attend the play he may have thwarted the assassination.: Stevens, *A Reporter's Lincoln*, 110.

182. McKinley died there a few days later.: Robert T. Lincoln to Norman Williams, July 28, 1881, Robert T. Lincoln Papers, Library of Congress, cited in Goff, *Robert Todd Lincoln*, 119–20; Goff, *Robert Todd Lincoln*, 234.

183. Mary died in 1882, having survived her husband by seventeen years.: Randall, *Mary Lincoln*, 430–34; Oswald Garrison to Isaac Markens, March 26, 1927, Lincoln Collection, Brown University Library.

186. produce a three-volume study called *Lincoln the President*.: James G. Randall, "Has the Lincoln Theme Been Exhausted?" *The American Historical Review* 41, no. 2 (January 1936): 270–94; James G. Randall, *Lincoln the President*, 3 vols. (New York: Dodd, Mead & Company, 1945–1952).

189. not only for Lincoln scholars but for all historians.: Wilson and Davis, eds., *Herndon's Informants*, xx–xxiv.

Bibliography

Unpublished Manuscripts and Papers and Published Primary Sources

Barton, William E., William E. Barton Papers, University of Chicago.

Basler, Roy P., ed., *Collected Works of Abraham Lincoln*. 8 vol. New Brunswick, NJ: Rutgers University Press, 1952–55.

Beale, Howard K., ed. *The Diary of Edward Bates, 1859–1866*. Washington, DC: United States Government Printing Office, 1933.

Black, Elizabeth Gundaker Dale. Elizabeth Gundaker Dale Black Papers. Abraham Lincoln Presidential Library, Springfield, IL.

Blackett, R.J.M., ed. Thomas Morris Chester, Black Civil War Correspondent: *His Dispatches from the Virginia Front*. Baton Rouge, LA: Louisiana State University Press, 1989.

Browne Family Papers. Schlesinger Library, Radcliffe College, Cambridge, MA.

Burlingame, Michael, ed. *With Lincoln in the White House: Letters, Memoranda, and Other Writings of John G. Nicolay, 1860–1865*. Carbondale, IL: Southern Illinois University Press, 2000.

———. *An Oral History of Abraham Lincoln, John G. Nicolay's Interviews and Essays*. Carbondale, IL: Southern Illinois University Press, 1996.

Butterfield, L. H., ed. *Diary and Autobiography of John Adams*. 4 vol. Cambridge, MA: Harvard University Press, 1961.

———. *Adams Family Correspondence*. 4 vol. Cambridge, Massachusetts: The Belknap Press, 1963.

Campbell Family Papers #15. Southern Historical Collection, Wilson Library, University of North Carolina at Chapel Hill.

Carter, Thomas Butler. Thomas Butler Carter Papers. Midwest Manuscript Collection, Newberry Library, Chicago, IL.

Catalogue of the Officers and Students of Illinois State University, 1858–59, Archives of the University of Illinois, Springfield, IL.

Chase, Salmon P. Salmon P. Chase Papers. Library of Congress, Washington, DC.

Cole, Donald B., and John J. McDonough, eds. *Benjamin Brown French: Witness to the Young Republic, A Yankee's Journal, 1828–1870*. Hanover, NH: University Press of New England, 1989.

Conkling, James C. James C. Conkling Papers. Abraham Lincoln Presidential Library, Springfield, IL.

Davis, David. David Davis Papers. Chicago History Museum, Chicago, IL.

Davis, George T. M. *Autobiography of the Late Col. Geo. T.M. Davis, Captain and Aide-de-Camp Scott's Army of Invasion (Mexico)*. New York: Jenkins & McCowan, 1891.

Edwards, Elizabeth Parker Todd. Elizabeth Parker Todd Edwards Papers. Abraham Lincoln Presidential Library, Springfield, IL.

Emerson, Ralph Waldo. *The Complete Works of Ralph Waldo Emerson*, 12 vol. Boston: Houghton Mifflin Company, 1903.

Ewing, Thomas. Thomas Ewing Papers. Library of Congress, Washington, DC.

French, Benjamin Brown. Benjamin Brown French Manuscript Collection. Library of Congress, Washington, DC.

Graebel, Richard Paul. Richard Paul Graebel Papers. Abraham Lincoln Presidential Library, Springfield, IL.

Grant, Julia Dent. *The Personal Memoirs of Julia Dent Grant*, ed. John Y. Simon. New York: G. P. Putnam's Sons, 1975.

Grant, Ulysses S. *Personal Memoirs of U.S. Grant*. 2 vol. New York: Charles L. Webster & Company, 1886.

Grimsley, Elizabeth Todd. Elizabeth Todd Grimsley Papers. Abraham Lincoln Presidential Library, Springfield, IL.

Gurley, Phineas D. Funeral Address delivered on the occasion of the death of William Wallace Lincoln, Lincoln Collection, Abraham Lincoln Presidential Library, Springfield, IL.

Hatch, O. M. O. M. Hatch Manuscript Collection. Abraham Lincoln Presidential Library, Springfield, IL.

Hay, Clara, ed. *Letters of John Hay and Extracts from His Diary*. 3 vol. Washington, DC: United States Government Printing Office, 1908.

Heintzelman Samuel P. Samuel P. Heintzelman Papers. Library of Congress, Washington, DC.

Lincoln, Abraham. Abraham Lincoln Papers. Library of Congress, Washington, DC.

Lincoln, Abraham, Lincoln Collection, Brown University Library, Providence, RI.

Lincoln Home Chronology Drawings, Abraham Lincoln Cottage 1848–50, Lincoln Home National Historic Site, United States Department of Interior, National Park Service.

Lincoln Reminiscences, Abraham Lincoln Centennial Association, Abraham Lincoln Presidential Library, Springfield, IL.

Lincoln, Robert Todd. Robert Todd Lincoln, Autobiographical Sketch. Harvard University Archives, Cambridge, MA.

———. Robert Todd Lincoln Papers, Library of Congress.

Logan, John Alexander. Fitz-John Porter: Speech of Hon. John Alexander Logan, of Illinois, in the Senate of the United States. Washington, DC, 1883.

Marshall, Jessie Ames, ed. *Private and Official Correspondence of Gen. Benjamin F. Butler*. 5 vol. Norwood, MA: Plimpton Press, 1917.

McClellan, George B. *Report on the Organization and Campaigns of the Army of the Potomac*. Freeport, NY: Books for Libraries Press, 1970.

McGuire, Judith W. *Diary of a Southern Refugee During the War by a Lady in Virginia.* New York: E.J. Hale & Son, 1867.

Mearns, David C. ed. *The Lincoln Papers.* 2 vol. Garden City, NY: Doubleday & Company, 1948.

Miner, N. W. N. W. Miner Papers. Abraham Lincoln Presidential Library, Springfield, IL.

Moore, John W. John Moore Collection. Huntington Library, San Marino, CA.

Nicolay, John G. John G. Nicolay Papers. Library of Congress, Washington, DC.

Pease, Theodore Calvin and James G. Randall, eds. *The Diary of Orville Hickman Browning.* 2 vols. Springfield, IL: Illinois State Historical Society, 1925.

Proceedings of the First Three Republican National Conventions, 1856, 1860 and 1864. Minneapolis, MN: Charles W. Johnson, 1893.

Randall, James G. James G. Randall Papers, Library of Congress, Washington, DC.

Report of the Commissioner of Patents, for the Year 1849, part 1, Arts and Manufactures. Washington, DC: Office of Printers to House of Representatives, 1850.

Scott, Winfield. *Memoirs of Lieutenant General Scott.* 2 vol. New York: Freeport Press, 1864, reprinted 1970.

Simon, John Y., ed., *The Papers of Ulysses S. Grant.* 31 vol. Carbondale, IL: Southern Illinois University Press, 1967-.

Stanton, Edwin M., F. Lauriston Bullard and James Buchanan. *The Diary of a Public Man and a Page of Political Correspondence: Stanton to Buchanan.* Foreword by Carl Sandburg. New Brunswick, NJe: Rutgers University Press, 1946.

Stewart, Judd. Judd Stewart Collection, Huntington Library, San Marino, CA.

Taft, Horatio Nelson. Diary of Horatio Nelson Taft. Manuscript Division, Library of Congress, Washington, DC.

Tarbell, Ida M. Ida Tarbell Lincoln Collection. Allegheny College Library, Meadville, PA.

Turner, Justin G., and Linda Levitt Turner, eds. *Mary Todd Lincoln: Her Life and Letters.* New York: Alfred A. Knopf, 1972.

United States Census Office. *Eighth Census of the United States, 1860.* Washington, DC: United States Government Printing Office, 1864.

———. Mortality Statistics of the Seventh Census of the United States, 1850. Washington, DC, 1855.

Usher, John P. John P. Usher Papers, Kansas State Historical Society.

Van Cleave, J.R.B. J.R.B. Van Cleave Manuscript Collection, Abraham Lincoln Presidential Library, Springfield, IL.

The War of the Rebellion: A Compilation of the Official Records of the Union and Confederate Armies, Series I. 70 vol. Washington, DC: United States Government Printing Office, 1880–1901.

Welles, Gideon. Diary of Gideon Welles, Secretary of the Navy Under Lincoln and Johnson, 3 vol. New York: Houghton Mifflin, 1911.

White, Horace. Horace White Papers, Abraham Lincoln Presidential Library, Springfield, IL.

Wilson, Douglas L. and Rodney O. Davis, eds. *Herndon's Informants: Letters, Interviews, and Statements About Abraham Lincoln.* Chicago: University of Illinois Press, 1998.

SECONDARY SOURCES

Addison, Joseph. "Thoughts on Westminster Abbey." *Spectator* 26, March 30, 1711.

Anderson, Mrs. K.T. "Some Reminiscences of Pioneer Rock Island Women." *Transactions of the Illinois State Historical Society* (May 23–24, 1912), 63–76.

Angle, Paul M., ed. *Herndon's Lincoln: The History and Personal Recollections of Abraham Lincoln as Originally Written by William H. Herndon and Jesse W. Weik*. Cleveland: The World Publishing Company, 1942.

——. A Portrait of Abraham Lincoln in Letters by His Oldest Son. Chicago: Chicago Historical Society, 1968.

Ariés, Phillipe. *Centuries of Childhood: A Social History of Family Life*. Translated by Robert Baldick. New York: Vintage, 1962.

——. *Western Attitudes Toward Death: From the Middle Ages to the Present*. Baltimore: Johns Hopkins University Press, 1974.

Arnold, Isaac N. *The Life of Abraham Lincoln*. Chicago: Jansen, McClurg, & Co., 1885.

Ayers, Philip W. "Lincoln as a Neighbor." *The American Review of Reviews* (January–June 1918): 183–85.

Bailhache, Preston H. "Recollections of a Springfield Doctor." *Journal of the Illinois State Historical Society* (Spring 1954): 57–63.

Baker, C. T. "How Abe Saved the Farm." *Grandview Monitor* [Indiana], August 26, 1920. Reprinted October 14, 1926.

——. "The Lincoln Family in Spencer County." Unpublished manuscript dated 1928, a copy of which is located in the Southwestern Indiana Historical Society Annals, 977.23, So728a, vol. 3 and 4, pages 10–21, in the Indiana Room at Central Library of the Evansville-Vanderburgh Public Library.

Baker, Jean H. *The Lincoln Marriage: Beyond the Battle of Quotations*. Gettysburg College: Robert Fortenbaugh Memorial Lecture, 1999.

——. *Not Much of Me: Abraham Lincoln as a Typical American*. Fort Wayne, IN: Louis A. Warren Lincoln Library and Museum, 1988.

——. *Mary Todd Lincoln: A Biography*. New York: W.W. Norton Company, 1987.

Barnes, John S. "With Lincoln From Washington to Richmond in 1865." *Appleton's Magazine* IX, nos. 5 and 6, May and June 1907, 515–24, 742–51.

Barton, William E. *The Life of Abraham Lincoln*. 2 vols. Indianapolis, IN: The Bobbs Merrill Company, 1925.

——. *The Lineage of Lincoln*. Indianapolis, IN: The Bobbs-Merrill Company, 1929.

——. *The Soul of Abraham Lincoln*. New York: George H. Doran Company, 1920.

Batchelder, Samuel F. "Old Times at the Law School." *Atlantic Monthly* XC , November 1902, 643–55.

Bates, David Homer. *Lincoln in the Telegraph Office: Recollections of the United States Military Telegraph Corps During the Civil War*. New York: The Century Co., 1907.

Bayne, Julia Taft. *Tad Lincoln's Father*. Lincoln, NE: University of Nebraska Press, 2001.

Bledstein, Burton J. *The Culture of Professionalism: The Middle Class and the Development of Higher Education in America*. New York: W.W. Norton & Company, Inc., 1976.

Beveridge, Albert J. *Abraham Lincoln 1809–1858*. 2 vols. Boston: Houghton Mifflin Company, 1928.

———. *Lincoln*. London: Victor Gollancz Ltd., 1928.

Bishop, Jim. *The Day Lincoln Was Shot*. New York: Harper & Brothers, 1955.

Blumin, Stuart M. *The Emergence of the Middle Class: Social Experience in the American City, 1760–1900*. New York: Cambridge University Press, 1989.

Boime, Albert. *Unveiling of the National Icons: A Place for Patriotic Iconoclasm in a Nationalist Era*. Cambridge, UK: Cambridge University Press, 1997.

Bonham, Jeriah. *Fifty Years' Recollections: With Observations and Reflections on Historical Events*. Peoria, IL: J.W. Franks & Sons, 1883.

Boyden, Anna L. *Echoes from Hospital and White House: A Record of Mrs. Rebecca R. Pomroy's Experience in War Times*. Boston: D. Lathrop and Company, 1884.

Boydston, Jeanne. *Home and Work: Housework, Wages, and the Ideology of Labor in the Early Republic*. New York: Oxford University Press, 1990.

Brooks, Noah. *Washington in Lincoln's Time*. New York: Century Co., 1895.

———. "A Boy in the White House." *St. Nicholas* X. November 1882 to May 1883, 61–62.

———. "Personal Reminiscences of Lincoln." *Scribner's Monthly* XV, no. 4. February 1878, 561–69.

Bruce, Robert V. *Lincoln and the Tools of War*. Indianapolis, IN: The Bobbs-Merrill Co., 1956.

Bryan, George S. *The Great American Myth*. New York: Carrick & Evans, Inc., 1940.

Burlingame, Michael. *The Inner World of Abraham Lincoln*. Urbana, IL: University of Illinois Press, 1994.

———. *Lincoln Observed: Civil War Dispatches of Noah Brooks*. Baltimore, MD: Johns Hopkins University Press, 1998.

———. *The Real Lincoln*. Lincoln, NE: University of Nebraska Press, 2002.

Busey, Samuel C. *Personal Reminiscences and Recollections of Forty-Six Years' Membership in the Medical Society of the District of Columbia and Residence in this City, with Biographical Sketches of Many of the Deceased Members*. Philadelphia: Dornan, 1895.

Calhoun, Arthur W. *A Social History of American Family Life From Colonial Times to the Present*. New York: Barnes & Noble, Inc., 1960.

Campbell, John A. *Recollections of the Evacuation of Richmond, April 2d, 1865*. Baltimore, MD: John Murphy & Co., 1880.

Capps, Elizabeth A. "My Early Recollections of Abraham Lincoln," Manuscript Files, Lincoln Collection, Abraham Lincoln Presidential Library, Springfield, IL.

Carpenter, Francis B. *The Inner Life of Abraham Lincoln: Six Months at the White House*. New York: Hurd and Houghton, 1868.

Carroll, Daniel. "Abraham Lincoln and the Minister of France, 1860–1863." *Lincoln Herald* 70, no. 3, Fall 1968, 142–53.

Clark, Allen C. *Abraham Lincoln in the National Capital*. Washington, DC: W. F. Roberts Co., 1925.

Coffin, Charles C. "The President's Entry into Richmond," in E. Littell, *Littell's Living Age* 3, Vol. XXIX. Boston: Littell, Son & Company, 1865.

Colman, Edna M. *Seventy-Five Years of White House Gossip: From Washington to Lincoln.* Garden City, NJ: Doubleday, Page & Company, 1925.

Concklin, Edward F. *The Lincoln Memorial.* Washington, DC: United States Government Printing Office, 1927.

Conzen, Kathleen Neils. "A Saga of Families." In *The Oxford History of the American West*, ed. Clyde A. Milner II, Carol A. O'Connor, and Martha A. Sandweiss. New York: Oxford University Press, 1994.

Cowan, Benjamin Rush. *Abraham Lincoln: An Appreciation by One Who Knew Him.* Cincinnati, OH: The Robert Clarke Co., 1909.

Crosbie, Laurence M. *The Phillips Exeter Academy: A History.* Norwood, MA: The Plimpton Press, 1924.

Cunningham, Frank H. *Familiar Sketches of the Phillips Exeter Academy and Surroundings.* Boston: James R. Osgood and Company, 1883.

Darrin, Charles V. "Your Truly Attached Friend, Mary Lincoln." *Journal of the Illinois State Historical Society* XLIV, no. 1 (Spring 1951): 7–25.

———. "Robert Todd Lincoln and a Family Friendship," *Journal of the Illinois State Historical Society* XLIV, no. 3 (Spring 1951): 210–17.

Dennett, Tyler. *John Hay: From Poetry to Politics.* New York: Dodd, Mead & Company, 1933.

Desmond, Alice Curtis. "General Tom Thumb's Widow: Autobiography of the Countess M. Lavinia Magri." *The New York Historical Society Quarterly* XXXVIII, no. 3 (July 1954): 311–315.

Donald, David Herbert. *Lincoln.* London: Jonathan Cape, 1995.

———. *Lincoln at Home: Two Glimpses of Abraham Lincoln's Family Life.* New York: Simon & Schuster, 1999.

Dyba, Thomas J. and George L. Painter. *Seventeen Years at Eighth and Jackson: The Lincoln Family in Their Springfield Home.* Chicago: IBC Publications, 1985.

Dye, Nancy Schrom and Daniel Blake Smith, "Mother Love and Infant Death, 1750–1820." *The Journal of American History* 73, no. 2 (September 1986): 329–46.

Eisenhower, John S. D. *Agent of Destiny: The Life and Times of General Winfield Scott.* New York: The Free Press, 1997.

Emerson, Jason. *Giant in the Shadows: The Life of Robert T. Lincoln.* Carbondale and Edwardsville: Southern Illinois University Press, 2012.

———. "How Booth Saved Lincoln's Life." *American History* 44, no. 1 (April 2005): 44–49.

———. "'Of Such is the Kingdom of Heaven,' The Mystery of Little Eddie." *Journal of the Illinois State Historical Society* (Autumn 1999): 207–21.

Epstein, Daniel Mark. *The Lincolns: Portrait of a Marriage.* New York: Ballantine Books, 2008.

Evans, W. A. *Mrs. Abraham Lincoln: A Study of Her Personality and Her Influence on Lincoln.* New York: Alfred A. Knopf, 1932.

Evjen, Harry. "Illinois State University, 1852–1868." *Journal of the Illinois State Historical Society* XXXI, no. 1 (March 1938): 58–62.

Ewing, Thomas. "Lincoln and the General Land Office, 1849." *Journal of the Illinois State Historical Society* XXV, no. 3 (October 1932): 139–53.

Fehrenbacher, Don E. *Prelude to Greatness: Lincoln in the 1850s.* Stanford, CA: Stanford University Press, 1962.

Fisher-Browne, Francis. *The Every-Day Life of Abraham Lincoln.* Minneapolis, MN: Northwestern Publishing Co., 1886.

Fiske, A. Longfellow. "A Neighbor of Lincoln." *Commonweal* (March 2, 1932): 494.

Fleischner, Jennifer E. *Mrs. Lincoln and Mrs. Keckley: The Remarkable Story of the Friendship Between a First Lady and a Former Slave.* New York: Broadway Books, 2004.

Forgie, George B. *Patricide in the House Divided: A Psychological Interpretation of Lincoln and His Age.* New York: W.W. Norton & Company, 1979.

Frank, Stephen M. *Life With Father: Parenthood and Masculinity in the Nineteenth Century American North.* Baltimore: The Johns Hopkins University Press, 1998.

Fuller, Frank. *A Day With the Lincoln Family,* booklet, Abraham Lincoln Presidential Library.

Gallagher, Gary W. "A Widow and Her Soldier: La Salle Corbell Pickett as the Author of George E. Pickett's Civil War Letters." *The Virginia Magazine of History and Biography* 94, no. 3 (July 1986): 329–44.

Gary, Ralph. *Following in Lincoln's Footsteps.* New York: Carroll & Graf Publishers, 2001.

Gibson, William Harris. "My Recollections of Abraham Lincoln." *Woman's Home Companion* 30 (November 1903): 9–11.

Glyndon, Howard. "The Truth About Mrs. Lincoln." *The Independent* XXXIV, 10 August 1882: 4–5.

Goff, John S. *Robert Todd Lincoln: A Man in His Own Right.* Norman, OK: University of Oklahoma Press, 1969.

Goltz, Carlos W. *Incidents in the Life of Mary Todd Lincoln: Containing an Unpublished Letter.* Sioux City, IA: Press of Deitch & Lamar Company, 1928.

Graff, Harvey J. *Conflicting Paths: Growing Up in America.* Cambridge, MA: Harvard University Press, 1995.

Graves, Thomas Thatcher. "The Occupation." In *Battles and Leaders of the Civil War,* vol. 4. New York: The Century Co., 1884, 1888.

Grey, Ethel. *Sunset Gleams from the City of the Mounds.* New York: John F. Trow, 1952.

Gridley, Eleanor. *The Story of Abraham Lincoln.* Chicago: M.A. Donohue, 1900.

Grimsley, Elizabeth Todd. "Six Months in the White House." *Journal of the Illinois State Historical Society* XIX (October 1926–January 1927): 43–73.

Griswold, Robert L. *Fatherhood in America: A History.* New York: Basic Books, 1993.

Hale, Edward Everett, *James Russell Lowell and His Friends.* Boston: Houghton, Mifflin and Company, 1899, 200.

Hamilton, Charles and Lloyd Ostendorf. *Lincoln in Photographs: An Album of Every Known Pose.* Dayton, OH: Morningside, 1985.

Havlik, Robert J. "Abraham Lincoln and the Reverend Dr. James Smith: Lincoln's Presbyterian Experience of Springfield." *Journal of the Illinois State Historical Society* (Autumn 1999): 222–37.

Hay, John. "Life in the White House in the Time of Lincoln." *Century Magazine* XLI (November 1890 to April 1891), 33–37.

Helm, Katherine. *The True Story of Mary, Wife of Lincoln, Containing the Recollections of Mary's Sister Emilie (Mrs. Ben Hardin Helm), Extracts from Her War-Time Diary, Numerous Letters and Other Documents Now First Published.* New York: Harper, 1928.

Herndon, William H. and Jesse William Weik. *Herndon's Lincoln: The True Story of a Great Life.* 3 vol. New York: Belford, Clarke & Company, 1889.

Hertz, Emanuel. "Ties that Tugged at Lincoln's Heart: His Relations With His Son Tad, the Boy Who Played at Being Colonel, Cheered His Days in the White House." *New York Times Magazine* (June 21, 1931), 10.

Hickox, Volrey. "Lincoln at Home," *Illinois State Journal* (October 15, 1874).

Hill, Frederick Trevor. *Lincoln the Lawyer.* New York: The Century Co., 1906.

———. "Lincoln the Lawyer," *The Century Magazine* LXXI (March 1906): 745–61.

Hill, John Wesley. *Abraham Lincoln: Man of God.* New York: G.P. Putnam's Sons, 1920.

Hoffert, Sylvia D. "'A Very Peculiar Sorrow': Attitudes Toward Infant Death in the Urban Northeast, 1800–1860." *American Quarterly* 39, no. 4 (Winter 1987): 601–16.

Holmes, David I., Lesley J. Gordon, and Christine Wilson, "A Widow and Her Soldier: Stylometry and the American Civil War." *Literary and Linguistic Computing* 16, no. 4 (2001): 403–420.

Holzer, Harold, ed. *Dear Mr. Lincoln: Letters to the President.* New York: Addison-Wesley Publishing Company, 1993.

———. *Father Lincoln: Lincoln and His Sons.* Honesdale, PA: Calkins Creek, 2011.

———. *Lincoln President-Elect.* New York: Simon & Schuster (2008).

Houser, M. L. *Lincoln's Education and Other Essays.* New York: Bookman Associates, 1957.

Howe, Mark De Wolfe. *Justice Oliver Wendell Holmes: The Shaping Years, 1841–1870.* Cambridge, MA: The Belknap Press of Harvard University Press, 1957.

Huidekoper, H. S. *Personal Notes and Reminiscences of Lincoln.* Philadelphia: Bicking Print, 1896.

Hunt, Frazier. "The Little Girl Who Sat on Lincoln's Lap." *Good Housekeeping* (February 1921).

Irvine, Dallas D. "The Fall of Richmond: Evacuation and Occupation." *The Journal of the American Military Institute* 3, no. 2 (Summer 1939): 66–79.

Johansen, Shawn. *Family Men: Middle-Class Fatherhood in Early Industrializing America.* New York: Routledge, 2001.

Jones, Edgar DeWitt. *Lincoln and the Preachers.* New York: Harper & Brothers Publishers, 1948.

Kaine, John Langdon. "Lincoln as a Boy Knew Him." *The Century Illustrated Magazine* LXXXV (November 1912 to April 1913), 555–59.

Keckley, Elizabeth. *Behind the Scenes, or Thirty Years a Slave, and Four Years in the White House.* New York: G. W. Carleton & Co., 1868.

King, Willard L. *Lincoln's Manager, David Davis*. Cambridge: Harvard University Press, 1960.

Kollatz, Jr., Harry. "Lincoln in Richmond," Richmondmagazine.com (April 2009).

Lamb, Brian, and Susan Swain, eds. *Abraham Lincoln—Great American Historians on our Sixteenth President*. New York: Public Affairs, 2010.

Lamon, Ward Hill. *Recollections of Abraham Lincoln, 1847–1865*. Dorothy Lamon Teillard, ed. Chicago: A.C. McClurg and Company, 1895.

LaRossa, Ralph. *The Modernization of Fatherhood: A Social and Political History*. Chicago: The University of Chicago Press, 1997.

Larson, Magali Sarfatti. *The Rise of Professionalism: A Sociological Analysis*. Berkeley: University of California Press, 1977.

Lester, Charles Edward. *The Light and Dark of the Rebellion*. Philadelphia: George W. Childs, 1863.

Lincoln, Waldo. *History of the Lincoln Family: An Account of the Descendants of Samuel Lincoln of Hingham Massachusetts, 1637–1920*. Worcester, MA: Commonwealth Press, 1923.

Lindhal, Carl. "Transition Symbolism on Tombstones," *Western Folklore* 45, no. 3 (July 1986): 165–85.

Longfellow, Samuel, ed. *Life of Henry Wadsworth Longfellow, With Extracts from His Journals and Correspondence*. 2 vol. Boston: Ticknor and Company, 1886.

Marten, James. "Fatherhood in the Confederacy: Southern Soldiers and their Children." *The Journal of Southern History* 63, no. 2 (May 1997): 269–92.

McPherson, Lucy Harmon. *Life and Letters of Oscar Fitzalan Harmon*. Trenton, NJ: MacCrellish & Quigley, 1914.

Mellon, James. *The Face of Lincoln*. New York, Viking Press, 1979.

Menz, Katherine B. *The Lincoln Home: Historic Furnishings Report*, United States Department of Interior, National Park Service, 1983.

Meredith, Roy. *Mr. Lincoln's Camera Man, Matthew B. Brady*. New York: Scribner's, 1946.

Miers, Earl Schenk, ed. *Lincoln Day by Day: A Chronology 1809–1865*. Dayton, OH: Morningside, 1991.

Mintz, Steven and Susan Kellogg, *Domestic Revolution: A Social History of American Family Life*. New York: The Free Press, 1988.

Mitchell, Betty L. "Out of the Glass House: Robert Todd Lincoln's Crucial Decade." *Timeline* 5, no. 1 (February–March 1988): 2–8.

Monaghan, Jay. *Diplomat in Carpet Slippers: Abraham Lincoln Deals With Foreign Affairs*. Indianapolis, IN: Bobbs-Merrill, 1945.

Monkkonen, Eric H. America Becomes Urban: The Development of U.S. Cities & Towns 1780–1980. Berkeley: University of California Press, 1988.

Moore, Ruth. "American Epitaphs and Tombstones." *American Speech* 1, no. 7 (April 1926): 383–90.

Morel, Lucas E. "Lincoln Among the Reformers: Tempering the Temperance Movement." *Journal of the Abraham Lincoln Association* 20, no. 1 (Winter 1999): 1–34.

Morgan, Arthur E. "New Light on Lincoln's Boyhood." *Atlantic Monthly* 125 (February 1920), 208–18.

Morse, Jr., John T. *Abraham Lincoln.* 2 vol. New York: Houghton, Mifflin and Company, 1893.

Myers, Gustavua A. "Abraham Lincoln in Richmond." *The Virginia Magazine of History and Biography* (October 1933), 319–26.

Nicolay, Helen. *Lincoln's Secretary: A Biography of John G. Nicolay.* New York: Longmans, Green and Co., 1949.

Nicolay, John G. and John Hay. *Abraham Lincoln: A History.* 10 vol. New York: The Century Co., 1890.

Norton, Mary Beth. *Liberty's Daughters: The Revolutionary Experience of American Women, 1750–1800.* Boston: Little, Brown & Co., 1980.

Owen, G. Frederick. *Abraham Lincoln: The Man and His Faith.* Wheaton, IL: Tyndale House Publishers, Inc., 1984.

Page, Elwin L. *Abraham Lincoln in New Hampshire.* Boston: Houghton Mifflin Company, 1929.

Palmer, Beverly Wilson, ed. *The Selected Letters of Charles Sumner.* 2 vol. Boston: Northeastern University Press, 1990.

Palmer, John M., ed. *The Bench and Bar of Illinois: Historical and Reminiscent.* 2 vol. Chicago: The Lewis Publishing Company, 1899.

Patrick, Rembert W. *The Fall of Richmond.* Baton Rouge, LA: Louisiana State University Press, 1960.

Pendel, Thomas F. *Thirty-Six Years in the White House.* Washington, DC: The Neale Publishing Company, 1902.

Pickett, LaSalle Corbell. *Pickett and His Men.* Philadelphia: J.B. Lippincott & Company, 1913.

Pinsker, Matthew. *Lincoln's Sanctuary: Abraham Lincoln and the Soldiers' Home.* Oxford: Oxford University Press, 2003.

Pisani, Camille Ferri. *Prince Napoleon in America, 1861: Letters From His Aide-de-Camp.* Translated by Georges J. Joyaux. London: The Galley Press, 1959.

Porter, David D. *Incidents and Anecdotes of the Civil War.* New York: D. Appleton and Company, 1886.

Porter, Horace. *Campaigning With Grant.* New York: The Century Company, 1897.

Pratt, Harry E. *The Personal Finances of Abraham Lincoln.* Springfield, IL: Abraham Lincoln Association, 1943.

———. "Little Eddie Lincoln—'We Miss Him Very Much.'" *Journal of the Illinois State Historical Society* XLVII, no. 2 (Summer 1954): 300–05.

Pugh, David G. *Sons of Liberty: The Masculine Mind in Nineteenth-Century America.* Westport, CT: Greenwood Press, 1983.

Putnam, George Haven. "The Speech that Won the East for Lincoln." *Outlook* 130, (February 8, 1922), 220–23.

Randall, James G. *Lincoln the President.* 3 vol. New York: Dodd, Mead, 1945–55.

———. "Has the Lincoln Theme Been Exhausted?" *The American Historical Review* 41, no. 2 (January 1936): 270–94.

Randall, Ruth Painter. *Mary Lincoln: Biography of a Marriage*. Boston: Little, Brown and Company, 1953.

———. *Lincoln's Sons*. Boston: Little, Brown and Company, 1955.

Reep, Thomas P. *Lincoln at New Salem*. Chicago: Old Salem Lincoln League, 1927.

Ridderbusch, Michael R., ed. "The Lincoln Reminiscence Manuscript in the Francis Harrison Pierpont Papers." *West Virginia History* 1, no. 1 (Spring 2007): 75–92.

Riddle, Albert Gallatin. *Recollections of War Times: Reminiscences of Men in and Events in Washington, 1860–1865*. New York: G.P. Putnam's Sons, 1895.

Roberts, Octavia. *Lincoln in Illinois*. New York: Houghton Mifflin Company, 1918.

———. "We All Knew Abr'ham Lincoln," *Abraham Lincoln Quarterly* (March 1946): 25–28.

Rotundo, E. Anthony. "American Fatherhood: A Historical Perspective." *American Behavioral Scientist* 29, no. 1 (September/October 1985): 7–25.

———. "Learning About Manhood: Gender Ideals and the Middle-Class Family in Nineteenth Century America." In *Manliness and Morality: Middle-Class Masculinity in Britain and America 1800–1940*, ed. J. A. Mangan and James Walvin. New York: St. Martin's Press, 1987.

———. "Boy Culture: Middle-Class Boyhood in Nineteenth-Century America." In *Meanings for Manhood: Constructions of Masculinity in Victorian America*, ed. Mark C. Carnes and Clyde Griffen. Chicago: The University of Chicago Press, 1990.

Ruggles, Eleanor. *Prince of Players, Edwin Booth*. New York: W.W. Norton & Company, 1953.

Ryan, David D. *Four Days in 1865: The Fall of Richmond*. Richmond, VA: Cadmus Marketing, 1993.

Sandage, Scott A. "A Marble House Divided: The Lincoln Memorial, the Civil Rights Movement, and the Politics of Memory, 1939–1963." *The Journal of American History* 80, no. 1 (June 1993): 135–67.

Sandburg, Carl. *Abraham Lincoln: The Prairie Years*. 2 vol. New York: Charles Scribner's Sons, 1942.

———. *Abraham Lincoln: The War Years*. 4 vol. New York: Charles Scribner's Sons, 1942.

Sandburg, Carl and Paul M. Angle. *Mary Lincoln: Wife and Widow*. New York: Harcourt, Brace & Co., 1932.

Saum, Lewis O. "Death in the Popular Mind of Pre-Civil War America." *American Quarterly* 26 (December 1974): 477–95.

Scripps, John Locke. *The Life of Abraham Lincoln*. Peoria, IL: Edward J. Jacob, 1860, reprinted.

Shaara, Michael. *The Killer Angels*. New York: Ballantine Books, 1975.

Shenk, Joshua Wolf. *Lincoln's Melancholy: How Depression Challenged a President and Fueled His Creativity*. New York: Houghton Mifflin Company, 2005.

Shorter, Edward. *The Making of the Modern Family*. New York: Basic Books, 1975.

Shutes, Milton. "Mortality of the Five Lincoln Boys." *Lincoln Herald* 57 (Spring 1955), 3–11.

Sigelschiffer, Saul. *The American Conscience: The Drama of the Lincoln-Douglas Debates*. New York: Horizon Press, 1973.

Simon, John Y. *House Divided: Lincoln and His Father*. Fort Wayne, IN: Louis A. Warren Lincoln Library and Museum, 1987.

Slater, Peter G. "'From the Cradle to the Coffin': Parental Bereavement and the Shadow of Infant Damnation in Puritan Society." In *Growing Up in America: Children in Historical Perspective*, ed. N. Ray Hiner and Joseph N. Hawes. Urbana, IL: University of Illinois Press, 1985.

Soltow, Lee. *Men and Wealth in the United States 1850–1870*. New Haven, CT: Yale University Press, 1975.

Sotos, John. *The Physical Lincoln: Finding the Genetic Cause of Abraham Lincoln's Height, Homeliness, Pseudo-depression, and Imminent Cancer Death*. Mt. Vernon, VA: Mt. Vernon Book Systems, 2008.

Sparks, Edwin E., ed. *The Lincoln-Douglas Debates of 1858*. Springfield, IL: Illinois State Historical Library, 1908.

Spears, Zarel C., and Robert S. Barton. *Berry and Lincoln, Frontier Merchants: The Store that Winked Out*. New York: Stratford House, 1947.

Speed, Joshua Fry. *Reminiscences of Abraham Lincoln and Notes of a Visit to California*. Louisville, KY: John P. Morton and Company, 1884.

Stannard, David E. *The Puritan Way of Death: A Study in Religion, Culture, and Social Change*. New York: Oxford University Press, 1977.

Starr, Jr., John W. *Lincoln and the Railroads*. New York: Dodd, Mead & Company, 1927.

——. "Abraham Lincoln's Religion in His Eldest Son's Estimation," privately printed manuscript, 1926, William E. Barton Papers, University of Chicago.

Steiner, Mark E. *An Honest Calling: The Law Practice of Abraham Lincoln*. DeKalb, IL: Northern Illinois University Press, 2008.

Steiner, Franklin. *Religious Beliefs of Our Presidents: From Washington to F.D.R.* Amherst, NY: Prometheus Books, 1995.

Sterling, James T. "How Lincoln 'Lost' His Inaugural Address." Address Before Michigan Commandery of Military Order of the Loyal Legion, November 3, 1898. Reprinted in *Lincoln Herald* XLV, February 1944, 23–25.

Stevens, Walter B. *A Reporter's Lincoln*. Michael Burlingame, ed. St. Louis, MO: Missouri Historical Society, 1916; Lincoln, NE: University of Nebraska Press, 1998.

Stoddard, William O. *Inside the White House in War Times*. New York: C.L. Webster & Co., 1890.

Suitor, J. Jill. "Husbands' Participation in Childbirth: A Nineteenth Century Phenomenon." *Journal of Family History* 6 (Fall 1981): 278–93.

Sunley, Robert. "Early Nineteenth Century American Literature on Child Rearing." In Margaret Mead and Martha Wolfenstein, eds. *Childhood in Contemporary Cultures*. Chicago: University of Chicago Press, 1955.

Swett, Leonard. "Mr. Lincoln's Story of His Own Life." In *Reminiscences of Abraham Lincoln by Distinguished Men of His Time*, Allen Thorndike Rice, ed. New York: North American Publishing Company, 1886.

Tagg, Larry. *The Generals of Gettysburg: The Leaders of America's Greatest Battle*. Cambridge, MA: Da Capo Press, 2003.

Tarbell, Ida M. *In the Footsteps of the Lincolns*. New York: Harper & Brothers, 1924.

Temple, Wayne C. *Abraham Lincoln: From Skeptic to Prophet*. Mahomet, IL: Mayhaven Publishing, 1995.

———. *Lincoln's Connections With the Illinois & Michigan Canal, His Return from Congress in '48, and His Invention*. Springfield, IL: Illinois Bell, 1986.

———. "Lincoln Rides the Circuit." *Lincoln Herald* 62 (Winter 1960): 139–43.

———. "Mary Todd Lincoln's Travels." *Journal of the Illinois State Historical Society* LII (Spring 1959): 180–94.

———. "Sketch of 'Tad' Lincoln." *Lincoln Herald* 60, no. 3 (Fall 1958): 79–81. Reprint of John Hay, "Tad Lincoln." *Illinois State Journal* (July 21, 1871).

Thayer, William Roscoe. *The Life and Letters of John Hay*. 2 vol. Boston: Houghton Mifflin Company, 1908.

Thernstrom, Stephen and Peter R. Knights, "Men in Motion: Some Data and Speculations About Urban Population Mobility in Nineteenth Century America." In Tamara K. Hareven, ed., *Anonymous Americans: Explorations in Nineteenth Century Social History*. Englewood Cliffs, NJ: Prentice-Hall, Inc., 1971.

Thomas, Christopher A. *The Lincoln Memorial & American Life*. Princeton: Princeton University Press, 2002.

Thomas, Benjamin P. *Lincoln's New Salem*. New York: Knopf, 1954.

———. "Lincoln the Postmaster." *Bulletin of the Abraham Lincoln Association* 31 (June 1933): 1–9.

Thomas, Benjamin P., and Harold M. Hyman. *Stanton: The Life and Times of Lincoln's Secretary of War*. New York: Alfred A. Knopf, 1962.

Townsend, William H. *Lincoln and His Wife's Home Town*. Indianapolis, IN: The Bobbs-Merrill Company, 1929.

Trueblood, Elton. *Abraham Lincoln: Theologian of American Anguish*. New York: Harper and Row Publishers, 1973.

Usher, John P. *President Lincoln's Cabinet*. Omaha, NE: Nelson H. Loomis, 1925.

Vaughn, John E. "A Handful O' Sorts." *Illinois State Journal* (November 12, 1927).

Villard, Henry. *Lincoln on the Eve of '61: A Journalist's Story*. New York: A.A. Knopf, 1941.

Warren, Louis A. *Lincoln's Parentage and Childhood: A History of the Kentucky Lincolns Supported by Documentary Evidence*. New York: The Century Co., 1926.

———. *Lincoln's Youth: Indiana Years Seven to Twenty One, 1816–1830*. Indianapolis, IN: Indiana Historical Society, 1991.

Warren, Louis A., ed. "The Captain Lincoln Episode." *Lincoln Lore* no. 1410 (April 16, 1956).

Washington, John E. *They Knew Lincoln*. New York: E.P. Dutton & Co., 1942.

Weitzel, Godfrey. *Richmond Occupied*. Official Publication No. 16, Richmond, VA: Richmond Civil War Centennial Commission, 1965.

Wheeler, Joe. *Abraham Lincoln: A Man of Faith and Courage*. New York: Howard Books, 2008.

Wheeler, Samuel P. "Solving a Lincoln Literary Mystery: 'Little Eddie.'" *Journal of the Abraham Lincoln Association* 33, no. 2 (Summer 2012): 34–46.

Whipple, Wayne. *Tad Lincoln: A True Story*. New York: George Sully & Company, 1926.

Whitney, Henry C. *Life of Lincoln: Lincoln the Citizen*. New York: The Baker & Taylor Company, 1908.

———. *Life on the Circuit With Lincoln*. Caldwell, IN: Caxton Printers, 1940.

Wiebe, Robert H. "Lincoln's Fraternal Democracy," in John L. Thomas, ed., *Abraham Lincoln and the American Political Tradition*. Amherst, MA: The University of Massachusetts Press, 1986.

Williams, Myron R. *The Story of Phillips Exeter*. Exeter, New Hampshire: The Phillips Exeter Academy, 1957.

Wilson, Rufus Rockwell, ed. *Intimate Memories of Lincoln*. Elmira, NY: Primavera Press, 1945.

———. Lincoln Among His Friends: A Sheaf of Intimate Memories. Caldwell, ID: Caxton Printers, 1942.

Wilson, Woodrow. *Division and Reunion 1829–1889*. New York: Longmans, Green and Co., 1893.

Winkle, Kenneth J. "Abraham Lincoln: Self-Made Man." *Journal of the Abraham Lincoln Association* 21, no. 2 (Summer 2000), 1–16.

———. *Young Eagle: The Rise of Abraham Lincoln*. Dallas, TX: Taylor Trade Publishing, 2001.

Wolf, Stephanie Grauman. *As Varied as Their Land: The Everyday Lives of Eighteenth-Century Americans*. New York: Harper Perennial, 1993.

Wolf, William J. *The Religion of Abraham Lincoln*. New York: The Seabury Press, 1963.

NEWSPAPERS

Chicago Defender
Chicago Journal
Crisis [New York]
Daily Ohio Statesman
Frank Leslie's Illustrated
Harper's Weekly
Illinois Daily Journal
Illinois State Journal
Illinois State Register
Macon Daily Telegraph [Georgia]
New York Evening Post
New York Examiner
New York Times
New York Tribune
New York Herald
Omaha Daily News
Peoria Press
Philadelphia Inquirer
Richmond Times Dispatch

Sangamo Journal
Semi Weekly Breeze [Taylorville, IL]
The Crisis [Columbus, OH]
Washington Evening Star
Washington National Intelligencer
Washington National Republican
Washington Post
Washington Tribune

INDEX

ABOUT THE AUTHOR

ALAN MANNING IS AN INDEPENDENT HISTORIAN AND TEACHER. HE received a BS in Business Administration from the University of Southern California, an MA in History from the University of West Florida, and a JD from the UCLA School of Law, where he was an editor of the *Law Review*. Manning practiced law for more than twenty-five years at international and regional law firms before taking an early retirement in order to teach American history and to write. He currently teaches as an adjunct in the History Department at the University of West Florida and at Pensacola Catholic High and is a frequent speaker and lecturer on presidential history, a subject for which he has a particular passion. As he researched and wrote this book, Manning's experience of practicing law while raising four daughters gave him a unique insight into Lincoln's life. He lives in Pensacola, Florida, with his wife and children.